religion, culture and society

religion, culture and society

a global approach

Andrew Singleton

Los Angeles | London | New Delhi
Singapore | Washington DC

Los Angeles | London | New Delhi
Singapore | Washington DC

SAGE Publications Ltd
1 Oliver's Yard
55 City Road
London EC1Y 1SP

SAGE Publications Inc.
2455 Teller Road
Thousand Oaks, California 91320

SAGE Publications India Pvt Ltd
B 1/I 1 Mohan Cooperative Industrial Area
Mathura Road
New Delhi 110 044

SAGE Publications Asia-Pacific Pte Ltd
3 Church Street
#10-04 Samsung Hub
Singapore 049483

Editor: Chris Rojek
Editorial assistant: Gemma Shields
Production editor: Katherine Haw
Copyeditor: Rose James
Proofreader: Rosemary Morlin
Marketing manager: Michael Ainsley
Cover design: Jennifer Crisp
Typeset by: C&M Digitals (P) Ltd, Chennai, India

Library of Congress Control Number: 2013946898

British Library Cataloguing in Publication data

A catalogue record for this book is available from
the British Library

ISBN 978-1-4462-0290-6
ISBN 978-1-4462-0291-3 (pbk)

table of contents

list of tables

list of figures

about the author

Andrew Singleton, PhD, is a sociologist in the School of Political and Social Inquiry at Monash University, Australia. His research interests in the sociology of religion include secularization, youth religion, personal belief and alternative religions. Singleton has published extensively in these areas both nationally and internationally. He is co-author (with Michael Mason and Ruth Webber) of the book *The Spirit of Generation Y: Young People's Spirituality in a Changing Australia* (Garrett Publishing 2007).

acknowledgements

I gratefully acknowledge the copyright owners for permission to use the following material: Figure 6.1 adapted from the ONS licensed under the Open Government Licence v. 1.0. Table 7.1 was originally published in Barry A. Kosmin and Ariela Keysar (2009) *American Religious Identification Survey (ARIS 2008), Summary Report*. Hartford, CT: Institute for the Study of Secularism in Society and Culture, © 2009 The Institute for the Study of Secularism in Society and Culture. Figure 8.2 is from the Pew Research Center's Forum on Religion and Public Life, *Global Christianity: A Report on the Size and Distribution of the World's Christian Population*, © 2011 Pew Research Center. http://pewforum.org. Figure 10.1 © Ayazad/Fotolia. The epigraphs in Chapter 4 are from Rodney Stark (1999) 'Secularization, R.I.P.', *Sociology of Religion*, 60 (3): 249–273 and Steve Bruce (2001) 'Christianity in Britain, R. I. P.', Sociology of Religion 62, (2): 191–203 respectively, both used with permission from Oxford University Press.

Parts of Chapter 13, including the three tables, were previously published as: Michael Mason, Andrew Singleton and Ruth Webber (2010) 'Developments in spirituality among youth in Australia and other western societies', in Giuseppe Giordan (ed.), *Annual Review of the Sociology of Religion, vol 1: Youth and Religion*, Leiden: Brill. Used with permission from Brill. Special thanks to Michael Mason who created Table 13.1, and who wrote the paragraph which introduces that table. A version of the case study in Chapter 11 was published previously as Andrew Singleton (2012) 'Beyond heaven: young people and the afterlife', *Journal of Contemporary Religion*, 27 (3): 453–68. Used with permission from Taylor and Francis. Some paragraphs in Chapters 1, 6 and 13 were adapted from Andrew Singleton (2011) 'Religion and spirituality', in John Germov and Marilyn Poole (eds.), *Public Sociology*, 2nd edn. Sydney: Allen & Unwin. Used with permission from Allen & Unwin.

I'd like to thank the team at Sage Publications who helped bring this book to fruition. Chris Rojek invited the proposal and offered very helpful suggestions and guidance as I developed the contents of the book. Chris also suggested the title of the book. Jai Seaman, Martine Jonsrud and Gemma Shields answered all my queries with good grace and efficiency and assisted me greatly as I prepared the manuscript. Thanks also to production editor Katherine Haw and copyeditor Rose James for attending to the finer points of the manuscript.

I conducted some of my research on Spiritualism, Theosophy and afterlife belief at the Donner Institute for Research in Religious and Cultural History, Turku, Finland. They have a wonderful library, situated in a beautiful location on the River Aura and it was a delight to work there. Special thanks to the Donner staff and academics, including Björn Dahla, Ruth Illman and Joakim Alander.

I wrote several chapters while living in Goroka, Eastern Highlands Province, Papua New Guinea. I'd like to thank several people there, including scholars from the Melanesian Institute: Nick Schwarz, who suggested several books to read and Franco Zocca and Jack Urame who kindly answered my many questions about religion in Melanesia. Lee Wilson, an anthropologist from Cambridge University, was working in Goroka, and was an excellent source on Islam and a great conversationalist about all things religious. The Reverend Kumoro Vira generously talked to me about the Foursquare Gospel Church in PNG, which I appreciate very much. Also a special word of thanks to the Friday night football crew at Akogere, *bos meri* Christina, Anna Colwell, Gordon, Charlie and Peter. *Tenkyu olgeta*.

Closer to home, I'd like to thank several of my Monash University colleagues, including Arunachalam Dharmalingam, Jo Lindsay, Jude McCulloch and Kirsten McLean for their support of my book-writing enterprise. I'm grateful to the students of my 'Spiritualities, faiths and religions' class on whom I road-tested much of the content of this book and who generated so much stimulating discussion. Several of my graduate students completing dissertations in the sociology of religion have brought books or scholars to my attention, or listened patiently as I've talked about my pet topics. I'm especially indebted to Susan Carland and Rachmad Hidayet for their work on different aspects of Islam and to Clare Diviny whose work on supernatural TV and teen spirituality brought the *Secret Circle* TV show to my attention. I wish them all the best as they continue their academic careers.

I made my own start in the sociology of religion under the guidance of Gary Bouma at Monash University. I strive to emulate the clarity and directness of Gary's work. I completed two large projects on youth religion with Michael Mason and Ruth Webber from the Australian Catholic University. Both have been terrific colleagues, intellectual sparring partners, teachers and friends.

I am appreciative of those who read and commented on different chapters, including Seumas Spark, Julian Millie, Kirsten McLean, Michael Mason and Rachmad Hidayet. The anonymous scholar who reviewed the manuscript for Sage made many excellent suggestions and I am especially grateful to that person for taking the time to read and comment on the manuscript. Helen Spark carefully proofed and edited almost all of the chapters. I remain in awe of her knowledge of grammar and thank her for her outstanding generosity. I had three bursts of writing in the country town of Bealiba, supported each time by my indefatigable mother, Heather Cooper, who entertained the children, brewed coffee and allowed me to sit in St David's church hall so I could type away uninterrupted.

In their acknowledgements many authors apologize to their family for the imposition book writing brings to family life. I'd like to think that producing this book didn't affect my children too much. Then again, we were at a friend's house recently, and at a loss for things to do, one declared, 'Let's play Seventh Day Adventists!' The other two replied with an enthusiastic 'Yes!' That might not have anything to do with me, but either way, I dedicate this book to Tamas, Mairead and Hamish. And to Ceridwen – who always cared when I began a sentence with 'My book …', read and commented insightfully on several chapters, took two of the photos, and understands better than anyone what religion means to me – this book is also dedicated to you.

introduction: religion, culture and society

John Kriosaki is from Port Moresby, Papua New Guinea (PNG) and recently wrote a letter to the country's national newspaper, *The Post Courier*, stating:

> As a Christian ... and spirit filled in the Lord Jesus Christ ... I won't have a problem in the USA because that country has a lot of Christians who give in cash or kind and I am travelling for a special purpose and God will provide for me.

John wrote to the newspaper seeking financial sponsors for a fact-finding mission to the United States. He is hoping to travel there for 'Educational and Spiritual purposes', but doesn't spell out precisely what this entails. While seeking initial funds for airfares and accommodation from fellow Papua New Guineans, he is confident that once in America, his fellow Christians will recognize a brother Christian and extend the hand of friendship to him. Letters with religious themes are common in PNG's national newspaper. Indeed, religion receives plenty of coverage generally. *The Post Courier* even has a weekly section, *Daily Bread*, that provides news about religious matters throughout the country.

Papua New Guinea is a beautiful, mountainous and developing nation of more than six million people located on the southern rim of the Pacific Ocean. Granted independence from Australia in 1975, one of its key industries is coffee, grown in lush plantations. Many Papua New Guineans live in basic conditions and rely on gardens for much of their food and a little extra income. As the publication of a letter like John Kriosaki's suggests, PNG is also a deeply Christian country. The last census of the population revealed that 96 percent of all people identified as Christian.

Part of this book was written while I was living in a town called Goroka, situated in the PNG highlands. I was reminded on an almost daily basis of the prominent place religion has in that country, whether it be the gospel music played at the town's few supermarkets and restaurants, or my daughter's karate lessons being stopped midway through for prayers. I discovered that a popular FM radio station in town was a dedicated Christian channel broadcasting 'fire and brimstone' sermons warning of the dangers of alcohol, drugs and betel-nut chewing. These were not the only signs of a vibrant religious culture: on Saturdays and Sundays hordes of well-dressed families would make their way to the many churches dotted around town, most of which were nothing more than tin sheds or grass huts. Sermons from these churches were broadcast loudly on powerful PA systems and rang out across the neighborhood.

Christianity arrived here via missionaries from Australia, Europe and America. In the PNG highlands first contact with whites occurred in the 1930s, so the spread of Christianity has been very rapid. Now, there are literally thousands of churches dotted throughout the highland provinces, and just as many in the coastal areas. One Sunday morning I climbed to the top of a 6500-foot mountain above the town and there I found a group from a nearby village planning the construction of yet another church. The missionaries are still there too. Some translate the Bible into local languages, while others provide more practical support, such as health services or air transportation. One of the American-based missionary organizations has built a huge compound for their missionaries on the edge of town, complete with an American-themed school, shop and medical service. While the missionaries are still an important presence, nationals now run most of the churches. PNG's story is like that of many countries in what is known as the 'Global South'. Across the past century, Christianity has grown markedly in countries throughout Africa, Latin America, Asia and the Pacific. Places like these, along with the United States, are Christianity's beating heart.

The letter-writer, John Kriosaki, is optimistic that his fellow Christians in the United States will help sustain his travels. He has good reason to be, for the United States is probably the most religious of the world's industrialized countries. More Christians live in the United States than any single other country. Its citizens report consistently high levels of religious affiliation, belief and practice. But the United States is somewhat of an anomaly among the world's most developed countries.

Take Australia, for example, which is the closest industrialized nation to PNG. Although PNG and Australia are separated by a small body of water, they are vastly different when it comes to religion. Australia was once a nation of people who called themselves Christian. Back in the 1950s, the overwhelming majority of people identified with a Christian denomination, and almost half the population attended services of worship monthly or more often. Fifty years later, identification with a Christian denomination has dropped sharply and fewer than a fifth of the population attend services monthly or more often. Research in Canada and Great Britain shows a similar turn away from Christianity. In places such as these books by well-known atheists, like Richard Dawkins, have been best-sellers.

While Christianity appears to be waning throughout countries in the West, religions apart from Christianity seem to be prospering there. In the Australian city where I live, there are numerous Hindu and Buddhist temples, Jewish synagogues and Islamic mosques. At my children's school, pupils can take religious education lessons in either Christianity or Buddhism, while the Muslim children who fast during the holy month of Ramadan are allowed to have restful lunchtimes. While the proportion of Muslims, Hindus and Buddhists living in the West has increased markedly, these religions, like Christianity, are a powerful force in other parts of the globe.

Clearly, the world is a religiously complex place, characterized by decline, growth and increased religious pluralism. How did all of this come about? And what do these changes mean for societies and individuals? This book explores religion around the world from the perspective of the social sciences. It seeks to explain why the world's religious life is what it is, and to consider how this impacts on everyday life. In the pages that follow the social scientific approach is introduced as a valuable way of making sense of these changes – how contemporary religious patterns can be explained and understood through reference to sociocultural factors and social theory, hence the title of the book, *Religion, Culture and Society*.

The book is divided into two parts. The aim of the first part of the book is to familiarize readers with the important terms, methods and theories in the social scientific study of religion. The book does this chronologically, examining the development of the social sciences from the nineteenth century to the mid-twentieth century, before considering contemporary theories and debates. Part I concludes with a chapter on conducting social research on religion.

The second part of the book has an applied focus, and makes use of the various methodological and interpretative tools discussed in Part I in order to critically assess contemporary patterns of religion and spirituality around the world. It starts by addressing the religious situation in the West, examining in particular recent religious change in Great Britain, Western Europe, Canada, Australia and the United States.

Attention is then turned to other important global trends, including the spread of Islam, Buddhism and Hinduism and the emergence of Pentecostalism as the major force in Christianity, particularly in Asia, Africa and Latin America. A chapter on lived religion follows this global survey. This enables the reader to understand how social factors influence everyday, individual religiosity. The book concludes with a consideration of faith in the future, discussing the rise of the 'new atheism' and religion among young people. The abiding emphasis throughout is on explaining recent religious change using the tools of the social sciences.

In each chapter there are case studies to illustrate various issues, points to stimulate further discussion (under the heading 'Points to ponder') along with suggestions for further reading (under the heading 'Next steps …') and documentaries to watch.

The world's religious and spiritual life is not a simple story of revival or decline, but an intriguing mix of both, within and between countries. This book offers a critical introduction to developments in social theory and research on recent religious change. The reader will better understand the complexities of contemporary religious life and the social and cultural forces that are driving religious change around the world.

part one

making sense of religion and religious change: theoretical and methodological approaches

1

what is religion and spirituality?

After reading this chapter you will:

- be able to define religion and spirituality;
- know the seven substantive elements of religion; and
- understand how social scientists study religion.

This book examines religions, spiritualities and faiths in the contemporary world. Due consideration will be given to apparently diverse groups: Christians in Latin America who, during their exuberant services of worship, appear to speak in unknown languages; Buddhists in England who gather each week in someone's house to meditate; teenage witches in Australia celebrating in spring an ancient, European pagan festival. What do these diverse groups have in common? What makes their activities religious? How would a social scientist study them? This chapter examines the fundamental features of religion and spirituality, and introduces the social scientific way of studying religions.

WHAT IS RELIGION?

Recently I was filling my car with fuel when I noticed that the cashier, whose car was parked out front, had a license plate with the word 'F'BAHCE' on it. I was pretty sure I knew what that meant. When I was paying for the fuel, I asked the cashier if he was a supporter of Fenerbahçe, the Turkish football team. He eyed me suspiciously and asked how I knew about this team, living here in Australia, so far away from Turkey. I mentioned that I was a keen student of the world game, and now, in this globalized era, it was easy to follow teams and leagues anywhere in the world. So, I asked him again. Was he a fan of Fenerbahçe? Tears almost welled in his eyes. 'It's my life', he said. This made me wonder: is it his religion?

One of football's most outstanding exponents, Diego Maradona, reputedly once said, 'Football isn't a game, nor a sport, it's a religion.' In like manner, a BBC journalist, Stephen Tomkins (2004) wrote: 'We're increasingly deserting the church in favour of the pitch. Players are gods, the stands are the pews, football is the new religion.' Can football – in all its variations – reasonably be described as a religion? Many football fans will declare happily that football is their religion. Football teams have places of 'worship', devoted followers, heroes with glorious past deeds, creeds and supporting music. For the individual fan, following a team might give life meaning, purpose and fulfillment. But it seems wrong to declare that football is a religion. Isn't religion about the transcendent? Believing that there is some being, power or force that is greater than humans?

Substantive and functional definitions of religion

It is important to distinguish between religious and nonreligious phenomena, behavior and meaning systems, otherwise a scholarly investigation of religion ought to treat the powerful social forces of football and, say, Islam equally. To my mind they are far from the same, and I can't imagine writing a book that covered all the world's religions and football.

So what makes football and Islam different from each other, and why is one a religion and the other not? Here we must look at definitions of religion. Some scholars feel that defining religion is inherently problematic (e.g. Asad 1993). For these scholars, definitions are either too exclusive or too broad, historically limited or culturally specific, a point I expand upon later. Others have attempted definitions of religion, and while there is considerable variation, they tend to fall into one of two camps: **substantive** definitions, which describe the 'substance' of religions, that is, their distinctive properties or attributes; and **functional** definitions, which focus on the 'function' religions perform in the lives of individuals and communities. Both these ways of defining and understanding religion are helpful for those interested in studying it.

Substantive definitions explained

Most substantive definitions emphasize that religion is about humanity's relationship with the supernatural, the transcendent or the otherworldly. For example, Australian sociologist Gary Bouma (1992: 17) defines religion as 'a shared meaning system which grounds its answers to questions of meaning in the postulated existence of a greater environing reality and its related sets of practices and social organization'. This definition draws attention to the fact that religion has a 'beyond-this-world' dimension to it. This sets religion apart from other worldly systems of beliefs, values and practices. Marxism, for example, a well-known political ideal and philosophy, is very much focused on the material world. For Marxists, there is no god. Humanity's problems are caused by social forces and can be resolved through social action.

All religions posit the existence of some kind of transcendence, that is, something greater than the individual *and* beyond the earthly or natural world. Followers of the Abrahamic religions – Judaism, Christianity and Islam – believe in the existence of a single invisible entity, called variously God, Yahweh or Allah. A belief in this entity is an irreducible part of these religions. The Hindu tradition posits the existence of many gods. Some Buddhist traditions do not believe in the existence of a god or gods; indeed Buddhism is often described as 'a philosophy of life'. However, Buddhists believe that when humans die they are reborn, a process that occurs many times over. It is possible to break free of this cycle and pass into a state where consciousness ceases to exist. The belief that one can be reborn is a belief in a different order of existence, one that transcends the 'here and now'. Other Buddhist traditions believe in a complex supernatural world with gods and demons. In contrast, the heroes of football are not gods, but mere mortal men and women. As such, and because it lacks a transcendent or otherworldly dimension, football cannot be counted as a religion.

The transcendent element posited by all religions may or may not exist – a question we can not ultimately answer – but all religions proceed as if this transcendent dimension is real. That said, religion involves more than just a belief in the transcendent; it has several other important elements as well. This will be discussed briefly.

The seven elements of religion

Most readers would be familiar with hip-hop or rap music. For the purists of this musical genre, music is only part of the equation. The culture of hip-hop has five distinct elements: rapping itself, dancing, graffiti, DJing and beat-boxing (drum noises made with mouth). To truly live the hip-hop life, or be immersed in its culture, a person must partake of all of these elements, and do so with other like-minded individuals. So it is with other kinds of social life, such as religion.

In his book *Dimensions of the Sacred: An Anatomy of the World's Beliefs* (1996), renowned scholar Ninian Smart argues that religion has seven elements to it. These are: ritual; mythological; doctrinal; ethical; experiential; social and material. Each of the dimensions are explained below.

Ritual

Religious rituals are deliberate, traditional actions and activities which forge a link between a religious person or religious community and the 'transcendent' (that which is beyond). Performing a religious ritual can assist a person to feel some kind of connection – be it intellectual, emotional or physical – to the transcendent. Every religion has distinct rituals. Well-known examples include prayer, Holy Communion, pilgrimage and meditation. Some religious rituals, like the Catholic Mass, or the Hajj (the pilgrimage to Islam's Holy City of Mecca) are governed by formal rules, while other rituals occur informally and spontaneously, such as the Pentecostal

Christian practice of 'speaking in tongues'. (All of these rituals are discussed later in this book.)

Mythological

Religious myths are the stories and teachings shared among members of a religious group. These stories address topics such as the origins of the universe, ways in which to live, the nature of the universe or a religious group's history. Calling something a 'myth' doesn't mean it is untrue. Rather, calling it a 'myth' signifies that it is a story or teaching that has great social significance. Mostly, religious myths are recorded in sacred or important texts. Latter Day Saints (Mormons), a Christian group, have two sacred texts, the Book of Mormon and the Christian Bible. The Hindu tradition has many important scriptures, including the Bhagavad-Gita. In some religious traditions, myths are shared by word of mouth.

Doctrinal

Religious doctrines are the formal or accepted teachings that govern a religion. Doctrines usually address matters of belief, practice or morality. If you attended a Catholic school you will recall reciting the Nicene Creed during Mass: 'We believe in one God, the Father, the Almighty, maker of heaven and earth, of all that is seen and unseen. We believe in one Lord, Jesus Christ, the only Son of God ...'. This statement of belief was first formulated in the fourth century CE. For Catholics, the sources of doctrine are scripture (the Bible) and tradition (the constant teaching of the Church). The same is true of most religions.

Ethical

Followers of a religion are expected to obey a code of ethics. These are the values and standards of behavior expected of the faithful (or even of all humans). For example, Muslims are required to refrain from consuming alcohol and to eat meat that has been prepared according to stringent guidelines (Halal meat). Many evangelical Christian teenagers in the United States will formally pledge not to have sex before marriage as part of the 'True Love Waits' program. Some Buddhist traditions insist that people should not eat meat. Following a code of ethics enables the believer to draw closer to the transcendent – in this life, or the next.

Experiential

Via rituals and other means, religions facilitate religious experiences, that is, 'direct, subjective experiences of ultimate reality and supernatural agency' (Yamane and Polzer 1994: 2). For Hindus, this might be achieved by walking in a circular fashion around the inside of a temple, a ritual that draws them closer to the particular deity that resides there. Among the snake-handling Pentecostal churches of the American South, a moment of transcendence might be achieved by holding a deadly copper-head snake, an act which, done successfully (i.e. no deadly bite), leads believers to consider themselves 'anointed' by God.

Social

Religion is a profoundly social enterprise – it is not something conceived of and practiced by just one person. One of the earliest sociologists, Frenchman Emile Durkheim, called the collective, shared component of religion the 'Church', not in the Christian sense, but more broadly: 'A society whose members are united by the fact that they think in the same way in regard to the sacred world and its relations with the profane world, and by the fact that they translate these common ideas into common practices' (Durkheim 1912/1995: 42–3). Humans practice religion together, agree on important beliefs together and have organizations and institutions (like churches or mosques) that assist individuals to encounter the transcendent.

Material

All religions have a material dimension: sacred spaces, objects and places, whether it be a temple, a place in a forest or a statue. In some religions, temples, places or statues

Figure 1.1 Example of a place of worship (I): a traditional Australian 'bush' church
Source: The author

Figure 1.2 Example of a place of worship (II): statue of Mazu the Heavenly Queen, a Chinese folk religion deity

Source: The author

are of utmost importance, as deities are thought to reside there. For other religions, buildings are simply a place to gather and worship. Figures 1.1 and 1.2 show two very different kinds of worship places in contemporary Australia.

These seven elements, along with the posited existence of the transcendent, represent the *substance* of any religion. People who partake in these dimensions are those we describe as **religious** (although the strength of this commitment can vary); the involvement and meaning it has for them in their everyday life is their **religiosity**. Drawing attention to the substantive features of religion is useful because it sensitizes us to some of things the social scientific study of religion typically examines: religious belief, ritual, experience, ethics and social organization.

Functional definitions explained

Functional definitions are helpful too, pointing to the various functions that religion performs for individuals, religious communities and the larger society. The prominent anthropologist of religion, Clifford Geertz (1966), offered this definition:

[Religion is] … (1) a system of symbols which acts to (2) establish powerful, pervasive, and long-lasting moods and motivations in men [sic] by (3) formulating conceptions of a general order of existence and (4) clothing these conceptions with such an aura of factuality that (5) the moods and motivations seem uniquely realistic. (Geertz 1966: 3)

Here, religion is something that establishes 'long-lasting moods and motivations' among people by relating aspects of everyday life to something transcendent. At the individual level studies have shown that religious faith can contribute to, and promote, wellbeing, personal security and social connectedness (for examples see Kinnvall 2004; McClain-Jacobson et al. 2004). Religion can also motivate people to be altruistic and civically minded (for examples see Smith and Denton 2005; Mason et al. 2007).

Religion has a broader impact beyond influencing individual lives. I noted above that a key element of religion is ritual. Durkheim (1912/1995) argued that 'collective effervescence' is generated in the midst of large religious ceremonies or during religious rituals. The experience of collective effervescence can unite members of the same religion and reinforce group solidarity and collective identity. One notable example of a massed religious ritual that has this effect is the yearly Muslim pilgrimage to Mecca, known as the Hajj.

Doctrines and beliefs can also function to consolidate and strengthen the identity of a religious community. For example, many religions have clearly defined concepts of 'good' and 'evil'. Pentecostals, a modern Christian movement, believe that the forces of good and evil are engaged in a real spiritual war, fought in an unseen, spiritual realm populated by angels and demons, God and the devil. This spiritual war may manifest itself in the material world through demon possession or personal misfortune. Prayer from faithful believers can influence activity in both the spiritual and material realms. Pentecostals also believe that God has won this war for all time, even though small battles still rage. Because of this sense of victory many Pentecostal Christians believe that their worldview is right and that those who share their worldview – their community – are truly God's people (see Singleton 2001a). This is just one example of how belief strengthens community.

Arguably, football can perform these different functions for both individuals and communities. Following one's team each week can provide meaning, purpose and act as a comfort in times of trouble. If a team beats its fierce rivals in a closely fought match – be it Real Madrid vs. Barcelona or the Alabama Crimson Tide vs. the Auburn Tigers – the experience of the match and the ecstasy of victory might engender among supporters a profound sense of 'collective effervescence' that solidifies the belief that theirs is the greatest of clubs. But this is not religion: religions link the world of the everyday with some 'truly transcendent being, force or principle' (Bouma 1992: 15). Football doesn't forge a link with some greater transcendent reality; it simply makes the everyday more worthwhile for those who love it.

To summarize what we have learned about religion: religions posit the existence of some kind of transcendence, and each religion has many elements to it; myths about the world, guidelines for living, rituals for the faithful to follow, and specific experiences of transcendence. These elements also perform certain functions in the life of individuals and for larger communities, whether that be a motivation for altruistic action, or consolidating group identity. Importantly, religions link the world of the everyday with a transcendent reality.

These elements and functions can be found, more or less, in anything collectively understood to be a religion, whether it be Wicca (contemporary witchcraft), Scientology (a religion founded in the twentieth century by science fiction writer L. Ron Hubbard) or Mandaeism, a religion founded in what is now modern Iraq. Mandaeans follow the teachings of John the Baptist and see Jesus and Muhammad (central figures in Christianity and Islam respectively) as 'false prophets'.

The foregoing discussion has presented a social scientific understanding of what constitutes a religion. As noted above, such efforts are not without controversy. Anthropologist Talal Asad (1993: 29) argues that what has come to be defined as religion is 'not merely an arbitrary collection of elements and processes' of the kind identified in the previous section. Rather, definitions of religion are essentially the product of Western thought, arising largely from 'Christian attempts to achieve a coherence in doctrines and practices, rules and regulations' (Asad 1993: 29). Hinduism and Buddhism, for example, came to be seen as religions largely because of Western systems of classification, first applied in the nineteenth century, and not because Hindus and Buddhists thought what they doing was 'religion' (see Fitzgerald 1990; Faure 2009). For such reasons, Asad (1993: 29) argues: 'there cannot be a universal definition of religion, not only because its constituent elements and relationships are historically specific, but because that definition is itself the historical product of discursive processes.'

So where to from here? Definitions of religions and their constituent elements are best used as heuristic tools, and for imposing a border around an area of inquiry. Different 'religions' do not accord equal weight or importance to the various dimensions described above, and each religion has its own distinctive cultural and historical trajectory which shapes the lives and experiences of those who follow, in whatever fashion, that religion.

Having defined religion it is valuable to understand its relationship to an increasingly popular word: spirituality.

WHAT IS SPIRITUALITY?

Spirituality is a term that is being used more frequently in Western societies, and often as an alternative to religion. In the past twenty years, works by some of the most important contemporary scholars of religion have appeared that treat spirituality as both a part of religion, and something beyond religion. Examples include the American books *After Heaven: Spirituality in America Since the 1950s* by Robert Wuthnow (1998), *Spiritual Marketplace: Baby Boomers and the Remaking of American Religion* by Wade Clark Roof (1999) and *Spiritual But Not Religious* (2001) by Robert Fuller. Australian and European examples include Gary Bouma's (2006) *Australian Soul: Religion and Spirituality in the 21st Century* and Paul Heelas and Linda Woodhead's (2005) *The Spiritual Revolution: Why Religion is Giving Way to Spirituality*.

Recent research suggests that many people believe that religion and spirituality refer to different things (Marler and Hadaway 2002). A national study of US teens found that 8 percent thought it was 'very true' that they were 'spiritual but not religious' and 46 percent thought this was 'somewhat true' of themselves (Smith and Denton 2005: 77). What we see here is the widespread idea – among both scholars and the general public – that religion and spirituality can be different things.

So what is 'spirituality'? Well, in the first instance, it is *part* of religion. It was noted above that religion is something experienced by the individual. A person participating in a religious ritual, such as a communal prayer, liturgical dancing, meditation or chanting, may well have an experience of transcendence. This might be a moment of ecstasy, an experience of God or the gods as real, or a mystical vision. This 'personal, interior dimension' of religion (Singleton et al. 2004: 250) is traditionally described as spirituality. Spirituality has long been understood as the personal, affective element of religion.

As noted above, spirituality is now thought of as something that can exist outside of organized religion. For the purposes of this book, and summarizing what I think is common to many contemporary understandings, I suggest that **spirituality** is any enduring, meaningful experience or consciousness of something greater than the self. This something 'greater than the self' might be some ethical ideal, a supernatural concept (like karma or reincarnation), supernatural beings (the spirits of the deceased) or it might be something more nebulous, like a sense of 'oneness with all living things'. Sociologist Robert Wuthnow proposes a similar definition. He argues that 'spirituality can be defined as a state of being related to a divine, supernatural or transcendent order of reality or, alternatively, as a sense or awareness of a suprareality [sic] that goes beyond life as ordinarily experienced' (Wuthnow 2001: 307).

Clearly, people believe they can be spiritual without the aid of religion. This kind of spirituality might be achieved through the regular practice of yoga, tai-chi, astrological consultation or tarot-card reading, or a strong commitment to beliefs such as reincarnation. However, religious people also maintain that spirituality is an irreducible element of religion too; religious experiences, rituals and practices cultivate for the individual an enduring sense of transcendence.

Thus far, I have defined religion and spirituality, and discussed elements of both. I now look very briefly at the many different *kinds* of religion found all around the world. Specific detail about different religious traditions is provided later in the book.

THE WORLD'S RELIGIONS: BIG, SMALL, OLD AND NEW

A remarkably large proportion of the world is religious – estimates suggest almost nine out of ten people around the world affiliate with a religion (Johnson and Ross 2009: 6). Several religions claim the majority of the world's adherents: Islam, Christianity, Hinduism, Judaism, Sikhism and Buddhism. These are the **major world religions**. They have ancient histories and long-established creeds and practices. All have ancient texts or oral traditions which provide guidance for their followers. Each of these religions has a global reach: while originating in one place long ago, substantial groups of followers can be found everywhere.

The religions of Islam, Christianity and Buddhism comprise people from different cultural and ethnic backgrounds. The other major religions – Hinduism, Sikhism and Judaism – are mainly **ethno-religions**, where cultural and ethnic identity are closely aligned to religious identity. Hinduism and Sikhism are predominantly found among peoples living in modern India, and people of Indian heritage living elsewhere. The size of these diasporic communities is extremely large: hundreds of thousands live in Britain, the United States and Australia. Judaism is the religion of the Jewish people, who have settled all around the world. Each of these major world religions has regional characteristics and customs, and important divisions when it comes to matters of doctrine.

The world has plenty of other **traditional religions** (old and long-established), but these are smaller, and remain more confined to one location, culture or people. Examples include Asian religions like Shinto and various African, Brazilian, Native American and Aboriginal religions. Here we might count **Chinese religions**, which includes Chinese folk religions and Chinese philosophies of life, such as Taoism and Confucianism (some scholars see Confucianism and Taoism as distinct religions, while others see them as systems of ethics). Chinese folk religion, according to Cheng and Wong (1997: 300) is a 'loose category for traditional syncretic beliefs [e.g. ancestor veneration] with a mixture of elements from Taoism, Buddhism and Confucianism'. The phrase 'Chinese folk religion' refers also to the worship of one of many traditional Chinese gods, such as Mazu, the Heavenly Queen (see Figure 1.2). The migration of people has meant that communities of these traditional religions can be found across the globe, but not in the same numbers as the major world religions (with perhaps the exception of Chinese religions).

Many of the world's new religions – those founded in the last two hundred years – have an international reach, but have far fewer adherents than the major world religions. These are often called **new religious movements**. Examples include Spiritualism, Wicca and Scientology. These are discussed in detail elsewhere in this book. There's one last group worth mentioning: nonreligious people. Estimates suggest that around 12 percent of the world's population is nonreligious, that is, either atheist or agnostic (Johnson and Grim 2013: 10). Chapter 12 discusses in detail the different ways in which people are nonreligious, including atheism, agnosticism and humanism.

Figure 1.3 shows the religious affiliation of the world's population. These are estimates, and as will be discussed later in this book, the importance of the place religion takes in a person's life varies considerably from one person to the next.

None of the world's faiths are monolithic, and each has many doctrinal (agreed or official statements of belief) divisions and branches, along with considerable regional variation in ritual. Scholars have formulated typologies – conceptual maps – for making sense of these divisions. The most well known typology in the sociology of religion is the Christian-focused **church–sect typology**, developed by German Ernest Troeltsch (1931), among others. I won't elaborate upon it here, as it has limited utility for making sense of differences among other religions.

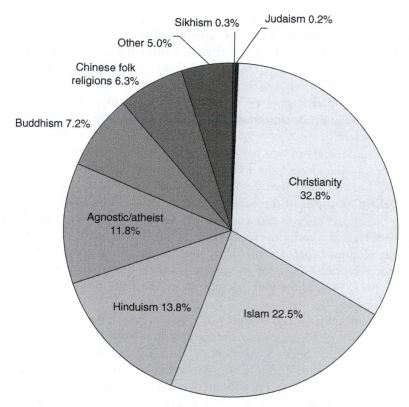

Figure 1.3 Religious affiliation of the world's population

Data Source: Johnson and Grim (2013: 10). Percentages may not add up to 100 because of rounding.

THE SOCIAL SCIENTIFIC STUDY OF RELIGION

This book takes a largely comparative, social-scientific approach to the study of religion. Many academic disciplines study religion. The fields of religious studies and theology are devoted entirely to religion. Sociology, history, psychology, political science, communication studies, human geography and anthropology all have significant sub-branches that consider different aspects of religion. While these disciplines each have a slightly different focus, together they represent the social sciences.

The social sciences use empirical methods to study human activity and look to explain this activity through reference to social and cultural factors, rather than religious or biological factors. I am a sociologist by training, and when I started writing this book I was intending to write about my discipline only. While this remains my abiding emphasis, along the way I make use of insights and studies from across the social sciences. This section describes how the social scientific study of religion proceeds.

The social scientific study of religion is well over one hundred years old. Important nineteenth-century thinkers, like Max Weber and Emile Durkheim, had much to say about religion. Their work and its enduring influence is the subject of the next chapter. Indebted to these early thinkers, contemporary social scientists focus on the *interrelationship* between religion and the social and cultural worlds. Any aspect of religion can be studied, large-scale or small: religious change at a societal level, the functioning of religious organizations or the contours of personal religiosity.

The social scientific study of religion considers the interrelationship between religion, culture and society in two key ways. The first of these examines how social and cultural factors *influence* religion. I consulted several recent issues of a field-leading journal, the *Journal for the Scientific Study of Religion* (JSSR), and as expected, found many excellent examples of this kind of analysis. Jonathan Hill (2011), for example, examines the impact college education has on aspects of religious belief. Using representative survey data and some sophisticated statistical methods, he finds that 'some, but not all, religious beliefs are altered by higher education ... respondents become slightly more skeptical of the super-empirical if they attend and graduate from college' (Hill 2011: 548). Here, Hill examines how the culture of university *influences* personal religiosity.

Sociologists of religion also examine the ways in which society, groups and individuals are *influenced* by religion. Another example from the JSSR illustrates this kind of analysis. Emily Sigalow and colleagues (2012) examine the extent to which religious factors influence decisions about career choice, marriage, place of residence and fertility decision-making. They found that 'particular religious communities differ in their emphasis on the role that religion plays in everyday life. While religion shapes values, beliefs and ideologies and informs cultural and ethical understandings, it seems to motivate decision making in complicated ways' (Sigalow et al. 2012: 318). As these examples illustrate, no matter what aspect of religion is being studied, the social scientist seeks to explain and understand religion through reference to social and cultural factors. Another ingenious example of this way of studying religion is the subject of this chapter's case study.

CASE STUDY

RODNEY STARK ON THE RISE OF CHRISTIANITY

The birth, growth and death of religions are inextricably linked to human activity. The world's major religions have grown and spread across the world through a variety of means, including military expansion, sovereign patronage, large-scale migration of the faithful, missionary activity, evangelism and high birth rates. Later in this book, I consider the modern movement of religions around the world. Understanding the distant past is usually the preserve of historians, archeologists and textual scholars, all using methods specific to their discipline. For the most part, social scientists consider recent religious change, rather than the ancient world.

One exception is the book *The Rise of Christianity: A Sociologist Reconsiders History* (1996) by Rodney Stark.

American sociologist of religion Rodney Stark is one of the leading figures in the discipline, best known for his work on 'rational-choice' theorizing of religion (see Chapter 4). In *The Rise of Christianity*, he deployed his considerable sociological skills to understand the growth of Christianity in its earliest days. Stark explores the question: 'How did a tiny obscure Messianic movement from the edge of the Roman Empire ... become the dominant faith of Western Civilization?' (1996: 3). He uses modern sociological theories in order to answer this question. In his view, many interrelated social factors explain the rise of this religion in the centuries before it was promoted through royal patronage (in the fourth century CE Christianity was installed as the official religion of the Roman Empire by Emperor Constantine).

Christianity began in the Roman Empire. Christianity's rapid rise throughout the Roman Empire was not the result of widespread mass conversion, but steady, exponential growth among interconnected networks of people. To explain this point, Stark draws on contemporary sociological theory. He notes first that converts to new religions usually have a personal relationship with existing members. Second, converts are not usually that committed to another religious tradition: 'New religious movements mainly draw their converts from the ranks of the religiously inactive and disconnected' (1996: 19). Third, the religious groups that attract converts usually have open networks rather than closed ones (i.e. brothers, sisters, friends who can join). Stark sees these factors at play in the rise of Christianity. Crucially, the success of Christianity was aided by the fact that the early Christians had 'open networks' and could recruit easily new members.

Like other contemporary religious studies scholars, Stark believes that the growing Christian religion drew its support not from the disenfranchised and poor living in the country, but from the urban middle-class in cities throughout the Mediterranean empire. Recent sociological research suggests the middle classes are attracted especially to new religious movements and cults. Stark thinks the same was likely true of the urban middle class at the time of Christianity's beginning.

Christianity also prospered because of the role, status and fertility of women in the movement. Throughout the Roman Empire there were more men than women, but Christianity appealed disproportionally to women – it treated them better and gave them higher social status. With more women involved – and because of Christianity's prohibition of abortion and infanticide – more Christian children were born, thus enabling Christianity to continue to grow.

Additional to Christianity's success was the way Christians conducted themselves during the various epidemics that swept the Roman world in the first few centuries of the Common Era (CE). The ethos of the Christians led them to take better care of one another, and thus more survived public health disasters. Stark (1996: 89) argues 'Modern medical experts believe that conscientious nursing *without any medications* could cut the mortality rate by two-thirds or more' (italics in original).

In sum, Stark uses various sociological insights to show how (most likely) Christianity prospered. While some might see this growth as an 'act of God', Stark demonstrates that very human processes were at play.

AND FINALLY ... DOES GOD EXIST?

I can still remember my first class in the sociology of religion. It was completely new to me to start thinking sociologically about religion, for example, discussing why women are more likely than men to be religious. I did wonder where personal belief and commitment came into these discussions. Religious people all around the world certainly don't think of their faith in social-scientific terms. For them it is just faith – something they believe, accept or do. A devout, African-American Christian girl living in Louisiana most likely thinks she is religious because God made it so, and she made a choice to follow Jesus, not because being black, female and living in America's South increases the likelihood that she will be Christian rather than Buddhist (which it does).

So, where does God fit in the social scientific enterprise? First, social scientists do not typically try and provide answers to existential, theological or philosophical questions (e.g. 'Does God exist?'). Such questions are simply not the focus of our inquiry. James McClenon (1994: 2), a sociologist who studies paranormal phenomena, argues that social scientific research examines and makes conclusions that are pertinent to the *social* domain, not the religious, theological or philosophical. We answer questions about the social and cultural aspects of religious life, like 'Why are women more likely than men to believe in God?', and ground our answers in the cultural and social domains. In any case, it is possible to discuss people's beliefs, what these mean to them and why they believe without needing to resolve whether such beliefs are true or not.

As for personal opinions, the idea is that we 'check our beliefs at the door'. The social scientific study of religion is not about promoting any theological point of view. As much as possible, personal commitments shouldn't be allowed to influence the conclusions that are made. In this book, I do not comment on the 'truth claims' of any religion. I consider, for example, the atheism of Richard Dawkins and the beliefs of Muslims, without passing comment on the veracity of their beliefs.

This chapter has defined religion and spirituality and examined the social scientific approach to the study of religion. The next chapter considers the first steps in the development of this mode of analysis.

Points to ponder

Think of a religious ritual. How does this forge a link between the practitioner and the transcendent? How would you define spirituality? Would you describe yourself as spiritual, but not religious? If so, how do you express this?

Next steps ...

For a nuanced discussion of the complexities of defining religion, see James Beckford's book *Social Theory and Religion* (2003) and Talal Asad's *Genealogies of Religion: Discipline and*

Reasons of Power in Christianity and Islam (1993). Do the differences between religions matter? Scholar Stephen Prothero, in his provocative and thoughtful book, *God is Not One: The Eight Rival Religions That Run the World and Why Their Differences Matter* (2010), argues they do. Those interested in the emerging social scientific study of spirituality should consult Flanagan and Jupp's edited collection *The Sociology of Spirituality* (2007).

Documentaries

A wonderful introduction to the wide world of faiths is the 2009 BBC TV series, *Around the World in 80 Faiths*, hosted by Anglican vicar Peter Owen-Jones. Available on DVD.

Web

A reliable source of information about the world's religions is the website: www.religionfacts.com Also highly recommended is the BBC religion website: http://www.bbc.co.uk/religion. The World Christian Database http://www.worldchristian database.org provides reliable statistical information on the world's religions.

2

modern times: classical approaches in the social scientific study of religion

After reading this chapter you will:

- be able to describe the elements of modernization;

- be familiar with how Marx, Durkheim and Weber explained the relationship between religion and modernity; and

- understand how the emerging modern world shaped religious sensibilities.

In 1866 an American woman, Mary Baker Eddy, slipped on an icy footpath and severely injured herself. She was wary of conventional medicine, and had a general interest in alternative forms of treatment (Hall 2007: 83). While convalescing in bed, Eddy read in the Bible a story about Jesus performing a miraculous healing, following which she immediately became well (Hall 2007: 83). Keen to make sense of her own miracle, Eddy began to study the accounts of miraculous healing in the Bible. She became convinced that Jesus was an extraordinary healer and that his method of healing had until now not been properly understood. Eddy concluded that humans are spiritual beings and that suffering, sickness included, is not an actual material state, but an illusion. Sickness can be overcome if people can shed themselves of this illusion.

Mary Baker Eddy published these findings in her 1875 book, *Science and Health with Key to Scriptures*. She soon attracted followers, and after facing hostility from the mainstream churches founded her own church, known as the Church of Christ, Scientist. Her followers called themselves Christian Scientists. There are now about 850,000 Christian Scientists around the world (Johnson 2007). Christian Scientists believe that their religion is a healing system. It is a science 'because it's based upon a set of spiritual principles – laws relating to the nature of God and His creation – that can be applied with expected, consistent results' (Christian Science, nd). Rituals in this church are enacted to enable people to free themselves from the illusion of materiality and to allow them to overcome various illnesses.

This interest in science, and the possibility that a religion could be a verifiable, observable, process, 'applied with consistent results', reflects the age in which this religion emerged – the modern era. This was a time when scientific modes of thinking were becoming ascendant, and shaping religious sensibilities. It is interesting to note this religion was founded by a woman: the modern era was a time when important gains were made in women's rights, particularly the right to vote. This era also gave rise to the modern social sciences.

This chapter examines the work of Karl Marx, Emile Durkheim and Max Weber, all of whom are counted as founders of the modern social sciences. These scholars contributed to the development of sociological modes of studying religion, part of which involved theorizing about the relationship between religion and social change. What follows is not intended as an exhaustive survey of their work. Rather, it highlights their contribution to the development of the contemporary social scientific study of religion. The times in which they wrote exerted a considerable influence on their thinking, so it is important to start by gaining some understanding of their era.

HISTORICAL CONTEXT: THE MODERN ERA

Mary Baker Eddy founded her religion at the height of the modern era – a time of profound social, economic and religious change. Most scholars date the modern period as starting in the late 1700s. By the late nineteenth century, life in Western societies had been transformed by rapidly expanding capitalism, urbanization and industrialization. The changes were radical, far-reaching, and touched every aspect of life, religion included.

The origins of modernity can be traced to the Industrial Revolution. Most observers agree that the Industrial Revolution began in the mid- to late 1700s and reached its apogee in the late nineteenth century. In short, technological advances in the production of goods led to the establishment of factories. These factories produced a greater array of goods more efficiently than traditional hand-crafted methods, and for lower cost. New modes of transport, particularly steam-powered rail and shipping, allowed for the faster movement of goods and people between locations. Urbanization began on a mass scale as people moved from the countryside to labor in the city factories. Agriculture focused less on subsistence and more on large-scale production, in order to supply foodstuffs for city dwellers. By the nineteenth century, a new elite had emerged – wealthy industrialists, who had made fortunes from the burgeoning capitalism of the towns and factories.

The nineteenth century also saw many advances in the fields of science and medicine, aided by the new technologies available to scientists and doctors. Roy Porter's epic history of medicine, *The Greatest Benefit to Mankind* (1997), documents the rise of scientific medicine in this century. Notable advances were made in the field of preventable diseases, pharmacology, bacteriology and surgery. Public health, chronically bad in the big cities, began to improve as vaccines for epidemic diseases like cholera, typhoid and diphtheria were developed. Medical advances extended life expectancy and improved quality of life.

Modernization took place across the Western world, but with particular vigor in Britain and the United States. The latter part of the nineteenth century in the United States, in the aftermath of the Civil War, is known as the Gilded Age, and refers to the widespread industrialization that took place. Modern life as we know it was well and truly underway.

Modernity is now understood to be more than an epoch in the West's recent history – it also refers to a process of social change. According to economist David Landes in his highly regarded work *The Unbound Prometheus* (1972), industrialization is at the heart of the complex process known as modernization, a 'combination of changes – in the mode of production and government, in the social and institutional order, in the corpus of knowledge and in attitudes and values' (1972: 6). These changes, according to Landes (1972: 6), entailed not just **industrialization** and **urbanization**, but also **bureaucratization** (the highly organized administration of daily life by the government and other institutions) and the implementation of **universal education** (state-sponsored education). Other commentators note it included social **differentiation** (the development of specific social institutions that undertook various tasks previously performed by organized religion, notably in education or health care), the rise of the **scientific worldview** (life can be explained through reference to natural or material causes), **rationalism** (there is a rational explanation, which can be adduced by reason, for all phenomena), **individualism** (the individual is a recognized and valued unit in society) and **pluralism** (a multiplicity of ideas, worldviews and institutions) (see, for example Wilson 1966; Tschannen 1991; Bruce 2011). Another important aspect of modernization was the rise of **secularism**, the belief that aspects of social life, like education, should not be encumbered by religion.

Modernity and Christianity

Without doubt, these aspects of modern life presented new challenges for orthodox Christianity, which had supplied society with the prevailing worldview in pre-industrial Europe and America (see Chadwick 1975; McLeod 2000; McLeod and Ustorf 2003; Taylor 2007). Pre-industrial European and American societies were defined by what McLeod (2003: 11) calls 'Christendom', in which Christianity 'is the common language, shared by the devout, the lukewarm and the skeptical, through which a wide range of social needs could be met, and which provided generally accepted concepts and symbols'. McLeod (2003: 20) points to the Enlightenment, the French Revolution and the Industrial Revolution as all playing roles in diminishing Christendom's central place in Western society.

For example, in the nineteenth century, supporters of secularism argued vociferously for the separation of church and state affairs, and enjoyed considerable success. In Victoria, Australia, an Education Act was passed in parliament in 1872 that meant that government-run schools could offer only secular instruction, excluding 'religious matters from the school day' (Grundy 1972: 3). Beyerlein (2003: 160) notes in the 1870s, the American National Education Association opposed the teaching of 'Common Christianity' in public schools. In present-day America, religion can be dealt with in public schools only from a secular perspective.

Academic advances in history and literature led to more progressive, non-literal readings of the Christian Bible, where attention was paid not just to the meaning of passages, but the circumstances in which the text was produced. Scholars questioned the accepted authorship of various books in the Bible, the veracity of biblical stories and many other orthodox teachings. This led to widespread, contextualized interpretation of the Bible and challenged the notion that it was the divinely inspired word of God. In turn, more liberal variations of Christianity grew.

The authority and teachings of the traditional churches were increasingly challenged by the discoveries of science and the rise of rationalist thought. Cambridge scholar Henry Sidgwick wrote in 1867: 'I feel convinced that English religious society is going through a great crisis now and it will probably become impossible soon to conceal from anybody the extent to which rationalist views are held, and the extent of their deviation from traditional [Christian] opinions' (cited in Blum 2006: 41). This tension is best epitomized by the publication in 1859 of Charles Darwin's influential work, *On the Origin of the Species*, in which Darwin proposed his theory of evolution, in which species, including humans, evolve across time through a process of natural selection. Many leading church figures of the age were resistant to such theories, preferring instead 'a biblically inspired world view in which human beings were separate from and superior to the rest of the animal world' (Dixon 2008: 74). According to scholar Thomas Dixon (2008: 74), once Darwin's book was published the secular element in the British scientific establishment grew ever stronger.

Another challenge to religious orthodoxy came from new religious movements, like the Christian Scientists. Many people maintained an interest in the spiritual dimension of life, but felt less bound by the institutional strictures of traditional Christianity. Alternative spiritual movements such as Theosophy and Spiritualism emerged (see this chapter's case study). In sum, developments in the modern age presented many new challenges to traditional religious orthodoxy.

MODERNITY'S RELIGION: SPIRITUALISM

The nineteenth century witnessed widespread and rapid social change; large-scale industrialization, growing urban centres, and life-saving scientific and medical breakthroughs (see Blum 2006; Weisberg 2004). Traditional religious orthodoxies were challenged by the rise of the scientific worldview, increasing individualism, and the development of secular and political philosophies (Singleton 2013: 37). In such a world, everyday folk, especially the educated, had greater intellectual freedom and opportunities to explore spiritual and religious alternatives such as Christian Science (discussed at the start of this chapter), or Eastern religions, like Hinduism and Buddhism (see Chapter 9). It was in this context that a new religious movement was born – Spiritualism – one that truly embodied the spirit of the modern age.

Spiritualists were devoted to contacting the dead, those who had 'passed over' to another plane of existence – heaven – or as the Spiritualists preferred to call it, the Summerland. While it was a diffuse movement, Spiritualists shared in common the idea that life after death is an empirical fact, the deceased do not lose their personalities after death, and specific dead people can be readily contacted by the living (Singleton 2013: 36). It was a wildly popular movement.

Spiritualism emerged first in Hydesdale, New York in 1848, and quickly spread to Great Britain, France, Australia, and Brazil, among other countries. Its exceptional popularity in the late nineteenth century, along with its social progressiveness, has been well documented (Singleton 2013: 37). Spiritualism was popular because it responded to the sensibilities of the age. According to Braude (1990, in Nartonis 2010: 362) 'Unsettled by secular developments, freed from traditional norms, and individually empowered, many Americans were attracted to Spiritualism's "radical individualism"'. It was a popular social movement in the United States until the early 1900s and in Britain until after the First World War, and still claims a modest number of committed followers in the present day.

There is widespread agreement among scholars the movement began with the Fox sisters from upstate New York, who were able to evoke mysterious knocking sounds from the spirit world. Other mediums began conducting their own séances, and soon an entire Spiritualist repertoire of otherworldly phenomena emerged: raps and knocking, table tipping, ectoplasm, automatic writing, trances, and apparitions. (Ectoplasm is a light material that comes from the orifices of trance mediums. Automatic writing is where the medium enters a trance and channels words from the deceased. She does this by writing the words, without conscious participation.) These phenomena were thought to provide evidence of life after death.

Beginning with paid public displays from the Fox sisters, Spiritualist encounters often took the form of theater. Professional, stage-performing mediums were in abundance. Here the curious and devoted could see for themselves some material manifestations of the dead. The medium might produce ectoplasm, or be the conduit for apparitions to appear, or for levitations to take place. Several mediums attained great fame (look up on Wikipedia Daniel Dunglas Home and Eusapia Palladino). Many professional mediums were exposed as frauds, and despite some high-profile devotees, Spiritualism was always controversial.

Private encounters were more intimate affairs, but the desire to contact the dead was just as intense. Friends and acquaintances might gather together for a séance, the purpose of which was to contact those who had 'passed over' to the next life. This could be achieved via table-tipping, or later, through the use of a Ouija board. Queen Victoria of England, and her husband, Prince Albert, were able to table tip themselves (Gabay 2001: 19). Others developed their mediumistic skills in small groups known as 'home circles' and offered séances to those close to them. In these private séances the medium might fall into a trance, and assume the identity of some intercessor – a 'spirit guide' or 'control' – from the other side, or engage in automatic writing.

Critical to the Spiritualist movement was the idea that Spiritualists could, through their séances, provide empirical *proof* of survival after death (Braude 2001: 4). For many affected by the calamity of the American Civil War, and later the First World War, this proof could offer great comfort in their time of grief. Spiritualists themselves believed that they had the means to prove something that had previously

Figure 2.1 A modern-day Spiritualist church, the religion that speaks to the dead

Source: The author

(Continued)

(Continued)

been a matter of faith – theirs was a religion of science. Spiritualism took very seriously its ability to provide proof, and this remains an abiding feature of the movement. The notion that a religion could be 'scientific' shows how deeply held notions about science and reason had become for those living in the nineteenth century. Additionally, many very famous scientists of the nineteenth century became interested in Spiritualism, trying to explain what it was that they were witnessing. Some mediums were shown to be frauds, but other phenomena proved difficult to explain. Some of these scientific investigators became convinced: here was proof that an afterlife existed (see Blum 2006).

Contact with the dead was more than just about proof: it also served as a detailed source of information about what was on the 'other side' (Singleton 2013: 37). So, what did the Spiritualists find there in the Summerland? Historian David Nartonis (2010: 362) argues the Spiritualists described the afterlife as something entirely familiar: 'a place of ... domestic bliss with a reunited earthly family; a place very much like earth'. Little reference was made to traditional Christian themes: judgment or eternal communion with God, and hell was dispensed with entirely. In its heyday, Spiritualism represented a large-scale, legitimate alternative (they had the 'proof') to those seeking freedom from religious authority in afterlife matters (Singleton 2013: 37).

Some Spiritualist groups became more formalized in the early twentieth century; Spiritualist churches and organizations were founded and Spiritualist ministers were ordained. Some modern Spiritualists see themselves as both Christian and Spiritualist, while others claim theirs is a stand-alone religion.

Spiritualism, with its emphasis on progress, evolution, science, proof and freedom from older forms of religious authority, was very much a religion of modernity.

Want to know more?

Three excellent, readable accounts of Spiritualism and the scientists who followed the movement:

- Blum, Deborah (2006) *Ghost Hunters: William James and the Search for Scientific Proof of Life After Death*. New York: Penguin.

- Gutierrez, Cathy (2009) *Plato's Ghost: Spiritualism in the American Renaissance*. New York: Oxford University Press.

- McGarry, Molly (2008) *Ghosts of Futures Past: Spiritualism and the Cultural Politics of Nineteenth-Century America*. Berkeley, CA: University of California Press.

It was in the midst of an expanding secular, rational, scientifically oriented intellectual milieu that the sociology of religion was born. The major theorists who contributed to the development of the sociological approach – Comte, Simmel, Marx, Durkheim and Weber – were very much products of the modern world. They argued that religion could be studied using neutral, scientific-like means, and that religious phenomena could be explained by social rather than supernatural factors.

These thinkers also saw that religion's place in society was changing, and their analysis considered, among many things, the relationship between religion and the emerging modern world. Many in academia, including the first social scientists, accepted the view that religion's primacy in public and personal life was waning in the modern era (see Wilson 1979; Turner 1991). The remainder of this chapter explores the contribution of three major scholars to the development of the social scientific study of religion. It also gives their assessment of what modernity meant for religion.

KARL MARX: SECULARIZING THE SOCIAL SCIENCES

Key ideas: alienation; historical materialism

Many people are familiar with one part of Karl Marx's reflection on religion – the famous quote: 'Religion is the sigh of the oppressed creature, the heart of a heartless world and the soul of soulless conditions. It is the opium of the people' (Marx 1970: 131). It comes from Marx's essay, *A Contribution to the Critique of Hegel's 'Philosophy of Right'*, first published in 1844 in a journal edited by Marx. Marx was born in 1818 and died in 1883. His work predates that of Weber and Durkheim, and unlike them, Marx did not undertake a sustained analysis of religion in his work. Nonetheless, his views about religion have proved influential.

Marx was German, but moved to London in 1849 where he continued his work, having earlier obtained his doctorate in Germany. He was deeply influenced by the atheistic thought that was common among the European intelligentsia at that time. Marx wrote widely, but was particularly interested in social change and the drivers of social change. He accepted the modern view that society was progressing and that the emergence of capitalism and industrialization were factors in bringing great change.

Marx also believed that societies were stratified, that is, marked by class divisions. In pre-modern societies this division was between those who worked the land, and those who owned the land. In modern times, the division was between those who labored in factories and those who owned the means of production. He believed that capitalism was fundamentally alienating to the workers, upon whose labor capitalism and industrialization were built. Marx argued that this system of inequity persisted because ruling class values predominated over other values. In feudal times, religion had played its part in reinforcing these ruling values. Randall Collins (2007: 20) notes that in 'ancient and medieval societies, churches and monasteries were virtually the only places where thinkers could have careers; even the universities were church institutions. Rulers and aristocrats endowed and supported these institutions and received in return a religious covering for their rule.' Marx believed religion continued to propagate ruling class values in the modern era.

Why didn't this oppression and alienation of the workers lead to revolution? Marx believed that Christianity's promise of an afterlife 'sapped the revolutionary zeal of the down-trodden victims of oppression' (Bouma 1992: 20). At the same time as it was 'duping the workers', religion acted also as source of comfort to them. It was a 'popular reaction to oppression' (Furseth and Repstad 2006: 29). This is what Marx means when he says religion is the 'opium of the people'. The drug opium can have a soporific effect, hence Marx's analogy.

Marx also anticipated the demise of religion. Marx's views about social change became known as **historical materialism**. For him, material processes – industrialization, scientific and technological advances – were the drivers of social change. He was optimistic about change, believing that capitalism was a system destined to collapse. Marx believed religion, as an agent of oppression and source of delusion, would be swept away as society progressed beyond capitalism. It would have no place in materialistic, advanced, socialist societies. Here, the logic of inexorable progress – modernity's logic – influenced how an early social scientist viewed religion.

Irrespective of whether his hypothesis has been proven correct or not, Marx placed the early social sciences firmly in the realm of secular and critical scholarship. This orientation was furthered in the work of Emile Durkheim. And like Marx, he too accepted that religion's days were numbered.

EMILE DURKHEIM: RELIGION IS A SOCIAL PHENOMENON

Key ideas: functionalism, collective effervescence, individualism

Emile Durkheim was born in France in 1858 and died at the relatively young age of 59, in 1917. Durkheim wrote widely on topics such as social solidarity, the objectivity of the social sciences and the objective reality of social life. He strongly advocated for the use of empirical methods in the social sciences – methods which use the same principles as those of the natural sciences.

Like many other scholars of his age, he understood the social significance of religion and made it the subject of sociological analysis. His most important work on religion was *The Elementary Forms of Religious Life* (1912). In this book, he analyzes, from the comfort of his armchair, ethnographic data about the Aboriginal Arunta people in Australia, and uses this to make broader claims about religion's origins, its role in society and the purposes of religious beliefs and rituals. He emphasizes particularly that religion is an inherently social activity; it binds members of society together, and yet is also a product of society. These points will be explored briefly.

Much of Durkheim's work focused on the ways in which societies function; what produces social order, and what leads to social chaos. Religion has a part to play in the production and maintenance of social order. To that end, the *Elementary Forms of Religious Life* examined, among other things, the **function** religion performs in producing social order and social solidarity. Religion, with its rituals and beliefs, achieves these outcomes for a society because it provides socially agreed upon values and norms. Most of his analysis was concerned with what happened in traditional societies, but Durkheim felt such conclusions also applied to modern society.

One way religions achieve social order and solidarity is through the ritualized experience of '**collective effervescence**'. When people gather together for the performance of a religious ritual, the mood is heightened, 'effervescence' is generated – by dint of contact with other like-minded individuals who are gathered together for the same explicit purpose. Those participating 'feel a bond of community and unity … [and] as a result the members feel at the end morally strengthened' (Pickering 1984: 385). Durkheim (1912/1995: 219) puts it this way:

> By concentrating itself almost entirely in certain determined moments, the *collective life* [my emphasis] has been able to attain its greatest intensity and efficacy, and consequently to give men [sic] a more active sentiment of the … existence they lead.

Religious ritual heightens group solidarity. This kind of thinking regards religious feelings, sentiments and beliefs not as something produced by the gods, but through human interaction. The feeling of effervescence is not produced by some supernatural power, rather it is a psychological state induced by being part of the collective. In Durkheim's view, society is quite literally the source of religious experiences; these are generated through collective human interaction. Durkheim viewed all aspects of religion as the product of society, whether this be the concept of God or the gods, the rituals used to worship the gods or religious institutions.

Durkheim on religious change

Durkheim lived in a world that was rapidly changing; old ways were being replaced by new. Durkheim, like his peers, believed religion was in retreat in modernity, and traditional forms of religious expression were in decline. He did not explicitly link the rise of *modernity* with religious decline; the seeds of religious decline, in his estimation, had been sown during the Protestant reformation (see Pickering 1984). Moreover, religion would not disappear completely in the modern age; he surmised something new would fulfill the functions of traditional religion in modern societies. The main alternative would be the 'cult of the individual'.

In the modern era, a new prominence was accorded to the individual rather than the collective. This is often called **individualism**, where people are viewed as 'morally autonomous, rights-bearing and property-owning individuals' (Seligman 1998: xx). European medieval societies were centered around the collective. The villages, where a large percentage of the population lived, were homogenous. Most folk were farmers, laborers or craftsmen and most did not own land. The middle class was small, mostly merchants and traders, and there were no factories for mass production. The 'common good' towards which people worked was the welfare, safety and stability of the entire community. This form of social order was profoundly disrupted by the rise of capitalism, which brought with it a new idea of society, one focused around the individual. According to the early twentieth-century theorist

R. H. Tawney (1926/1998), who wrote extensively on this topic: 'The medieval conception of the social order, which had regarded it as a highly articulated organism of members contributing in their different degrees to a spiritual purpose ... was shattered' (1926/1998: 97–8).

Capitalism and industrialization resulted in property rights, greater wealth for more people, a greater range of occupations, mobility and intellectual freedom. People began to see themselves, and experience life, more as individuals and less as part of the whole. The older social ties were less strong. Tawney (1926/1998: 189) argues: 'Society [in the modern age] is not a community of classes with varying functions, united to each other by mutual obligations arising from their relation to a common end. It is a joint-stock company ... and the liabilities of the shareholders are strictly limited.' The common good was now the individual's own prosperity. Notions we now take for granted – individual freedom, the right to choose, our own uniqueness – are in fact recent phenomena, a product of modernity and the loosening of collective ties.

Durkheim believed that as traditional religion waned, the new prominence of the individual would, instead of religion, be the prevailing ethos of modern society. This is what Durkheim argued in an essay he wrote called *Professional Ethics and Civic Morals* (1957):

> This cult ... has all that is required to take the place of the religious cults of former times. It serves quite as well as they to bring about that communion of minds and wills which is a first condition of any social life. It is just as simple for men to draw together to work for the greatness of man as it is to work to the glory of Zeus or Jehovah or Athena. The whole difference of this religion, as it affects the individual, is that the god of its devotion is closer to his [sic] worshippers. (Durkheim 1957 cited in Fish 2005: 56)

The value and ideals associated with the individual, things such as 'respect for the dignity and rights of individuals [would be] a necessary replacement for these outmoded traditional beliefs in modern Western society' (Fish 2005: 56). As much as he predicted that the cult of the individual would supersede traditional religion, Durkheim was worried that if individualism were left unchecked, it would result in the disintegration of a smooth-functioning society. To that end, he argued individualism needed to be checked through the laws of society. While such an assertion might seem a little excessive to the modern reader, Durkheim was correct in thinking that individualism was an important corollary of modernization, a point explored in later chapters of this book.

Like Marx, Durkheim propagated the accepted orthodoxy among scholars of his age that religion was in decline as modernity progressed, even if he did not assert that modernity itself was the main cause (Pickering 1984: 452). His emphasis on the social dimensions of religion remains an abiding focus in the modern sociology of religion. While Durkheim cogently described how religion is the product of society, it was the work of Max Weber that proved particularly influential in understanding how religion can impact on society.

MAX WEBER: MODERNITY, RELIGIOUS CHANGE AND 'DISENCHANTMENT'

Key ideas: the Protestant ethic; rationalization; disenchantment

Max Weber was born in Germany in 1864 and died relatively young, aged 56, in 1920. He worked in Germany and wrote in German. Consequently, his intellectual impact in the English-speaking world was not fully felt until after his death, when his main works were translated into English. He wrote widely, and his books on religion included *The Protestant Ethic and the Spirit of Capitalism* (1930/2001), *The Religion of India: The Sociology of Hinduism and Buddhism* (1958) and *The Sociology of Religion* (1964) among others. Weber was primarily a theorist, and his work was concerned mainly with analysis and theory building. As will be demonstrated later in this book, many of the terms and concepts Weber coined have enduring utility in the social scientific study of religion. A recurring theme in Weber's work was the notion that religious belief has material, lived consequences for wider society (Bouma 1992: 22). Religion does not simply have an effect or influence in its own sphere. This dynamic is particularly evident in Weber's work on religious change.

Religion as an agent of social change

Why did the Industrial Revolution occur first in Britain, and then other parts of Europe and America? Why not in India or China? Scholars agree that industrial advancement occurred in Europe and America, and not elsewhere, because of many intersecting factors. Biologist Jared Diamond (1997), for example, has delved far back into history to conclude that environmental differences gave rise to the technological know-how that meant industrialization took hold in Europe rather than elsewhere.

People did not build factories because they felt like it or because they could; they built factories to make money. Specifically, it was capitalists who built factories; people who were eager to accumulate wealth. To accumulate wealth requires a certain mindset: an appetite for hard work and an interest in one's own personal gain. It is easy to imagine such a person seeing some technological innovation – like the production line, or the steam engine – as a means to help them achieve their goal to make more money. The old saying goes: 'Necessity is the mother of invention'. Necessity, in this case, was the desire to make more money. Max Weber argued that these entrepreneurial characteristics were fostered by a distinctive set of religious ideas that took hold after the Protestant Reformation (*c.*1500s).

This idea, known as the **Protestant ethic**, is explored in Weber's book *Protestant Ethic and the Spirit of Capitalism* (1930/2001). (Often mistakenly referred to as the

Protestant work ethic.) Weber investigated how religion was related to social changes that precipitated, in part, the rampant capitalism that drove the Industrial Revolution. He wondered why Protestant Christians, more than Catholics, were more active in the rapid expansion of capitalist enterprise. He concluded that aspects of the Protestant faith, particularly the values and beliefs associated with Calvinism, were highly conducive to the conduct of business.

Calvinism, named after founder John Calvin, is a theological and doctrinal approach to living the Christian life. It has particular characteristics that lend itself to entrepreneurship, hard work and enterprise. Calvinists believed people could only attain salvation – eternal life in heaven, rather than hell – if God had ordained it to be so. Those who were morally upright and professionally successful in this life were thought to be the ones predestined for heaven. Proving one's eternal fate involved a commitment to hard work. Making money was not a sign of greed and religious indifference; rather it was an expression of piety and devotion, evidence of the sober, ordered and predestined life.

Such a disposition emerged from a particular theological standpoint. Several Protestant religious movements of the sixteenth and seventeenth centuries, particularly the Puritan, Reformed Baptist and Brownist movements, were deeply influenced by Calvin's teaching. Calvinists rose to prominence among the middle classes, particularly in Britain, and in turn, were instrumental in the development of the capitalist economy that drove, and was driven by, industrialization. Weber's analysis focused on religion as a source of values, ideas and motivations. For him, the dimension of religion that produced and sustained the Protestant ethic was belief in certain Christian values, rather than the ritualistic, experiential or material dimensions (Bouma 1992: 22).

A useful companion to Weber's Protestant ethic thesis is the work of R. H. Tawney, whose *Religion and the Rise of Capitalism* (1926/1998) appeared shortly before Weber's work was translated into English. Tawney had read Weber's work in German, and acknowledged Weber's seminal contribution to the idea that religion and capitalism made easy bedfellows. Tawney saw the rise of capitalism as aided by certain ideas and beliefs, not the Protestant ethic, but the rise of individualism, which provided the legitimacy for capitalism to expand. Capitalism can only prosper if people care first and foremost for themselves. Where Weber concentrated his investigation on the effect of Calvinist doctrine and the Puritan spirit on individual motivation (Seligman 1998: xxix), Tawney argued Puritanism *justified* capitalism's rampant individualism. He argues (1926/1998: 226):

> "The capitalist spirit" is as old as history, and was not, as has sometimes been said, the offspring of Puritanism. But it found in certain aspects of later Puritanism a tonic which braced its energies and fortified its already vigorous temper.

Common to both arguments is the central thesis that widespread, collective religious belief can be an instrumental factor in effecting social change. Weber argued also that modernization would have important consequences for religion.

Modernization and disenchantment

Weber believed burgeoning capitalism and modernity would result in the increased **rationalization** of everyday life. Rationalization is a social process whereby social institutions – and social actors – become increasingly governed by processes of efficiency, organization and bureaucracy. There is little doubt that Weber was extraordinarily prescient in his prediction about the creeping rationalization of life in modernity. He witnessed first-hand the rise of bureaucratization and argued that as modernity continued, so too would rationalization. (Think about it next time you are filling in a form, or see that the best car-parking spaces at your university are reserved for the accountants and managers rather than the professors.)

An example of this rationalization enduring is in the sphere of menial labor. When I left school my first job was at a major burger chain. I started at the same time every day and began each shift by punching my time card into the time clock. I would make the hamburgers in the correct order, have a half-hour break for lunch and then clock off at exactly 5 p.m. Failing to adhere to the correct rules of production would result in criticism and perhaps dismissal. The process of making hamburgers had been ordered and made efficient to maximize the profit for the store owners and allow them to make best use of their employees. Each burger had set ingredients, set amounts and was made to a prescribed order. Free-spirited, impulsive creating of burgers was prohibited. Sensual elements like personal taste and desire were denied. On occasions, when the manager wasn't watching, a co-worker and I made our own self-directed burgers – extra cheese, meat patty straight off the broiler, extra dollop of sauce. These were crispy and fresh. We were caught once and roundly reprimanded. Precision, order and efficiency – rationalization – were the fundamental goals of this system.

Weber felt that this widespread rationalization would lead to what he termed '**disenchantment**'. Pre-modern societies, in Weber's view, were 'enchanted', and explanations about the world made reference to the supernatural. Creeping rationalization would lead to disenchantment – materialist explanations about how things work would come to dominate. Science and knowledge derived from science would continue to dominate as modernity continued apace. Weber (2005: 322) wrote:

> Hence, it [disenchantment] means that principally there are no mysterious incalculable powers that come into play, but rather that one can, in principle, master all things by calculation. This means, however, that the world is disenchanted. One need no longer have recourse to magical means in order to master or implore the spirits, as did the savage, for whom such mysterious powers existed. Technical means and calculations perform the service.

Weber did not advocate the disenchantment of the world as being a good thing. Rather, he saw it as an inevitability, an outcome of modernity's progress. Religion would become less important as societies modernized.

CONCLUSION

It is hard to escape the times in which one works. Marx, Durkheim and Weber were not religious themselves and worked in an intellectual milieu in which religious explanations or deference played little part. Importantly, these early theorists established and demonstrated modes of analysis that take seriously the social dimension of religion: religion shapes and is shaped by culture and society. It can bind societies together, while also acting as an agent of social change. Modern social scientists share this orientation and their work is animated by it.

These earlier social scientists also worked in an era of great socio-economic transformation and could clearly see around them that aspects of traditional religion were being challenged by scientific and other intellectual developments. The start of this chapter discussed some of the tangible ways this was occurring. Marx, Durkheim and Weber also shared the common intellectual sentiment of the age that as societies become more modern – individualized, pluralized, bureaucratic and materialistic – so traditional religion will become increasingly marginalized in both public and private life. This link between modernity and religious decline is an idea that was consolidated and extended by a generation of sociologists who rose to fame in the 1960s, and whose work is the subject of the next chapter.

Points to ponder

Have you ever participated in a religious ritual? What effect did this have on you? Those around you? What evidence can you find of rationalization in everyday life? What evidence can you see of the individualization of modern life?

Next steps …

Read the original work of Weber, Marx and Durkheim for yourself. Copies are everywhere, e-copies included, especially via university libraries. Weber, in particular, still makes good reading. Good books that unpack the work of the early theorists include Bryan Turner's *Religion and Modern Society* (2011), Anthony Carroll's *Protestant Modernity: Weber, Secularisation, and Protestantism* (2007) and W. S. F. Pickering's *Durkheim's Sociology of Religion* (1984). Other influential works of the age that are worth a look include William James' *Varieties of Religious Experience* (1902/1985) which developed the psychological study of religion, and featured chapters on religious experience and conversion.

Documentaries

A film on Spiritualism, *No One Dies in Lily Dale*, produced by HBO cable network. This film examines the lives of people in historic Lily Dale, New York, a hub of present-day Spiritualism, and the world's oldest Spiritualist community. Order online or ask your librarian to get a copy.

Web

I always find the *Encyclopedia of Religion and Society* (1998) edited by William Swatos Jr., really helpful, and this is especially the case with the work of the early social scientists. This book is available on the web: http://hirr.hartsem.edu/ency/index.htm.

3

twentieth-century challenges, twentieth-century thinkers

After reading this chapter you will:

- be familiar with the theoretical contributions of Peter Berger, Thomas Luckmann and Bryan Wilson in understanding religious change;

- understand useful theoretical concepts such as the 'sacred canopy' and 'invisible religion'; and

- be able to articulate the central principles of 'classical' secularization theory.

The front cover of the April 8, 1966 issue of *Time* magazine posed the provocative question: 'Is God Dead?' With bold red letters on a black background, it is one of the most famous (and misunderstood) magazine covers of all time. The accompanying article is an interesting artifact of the times. The article was not a master statement about the rise of atheism, but an exploration of the ideas propounded by the 'death of God' theological movement, comprising scholars` such as Harvey Cox, Gabriel Vahanian and Thomas Altizer, among others. (Vahanian's 1961 book was called *The Death of God: The Culture of Our Post-Christian Era*.)

The *Time* piece explored the ideas central to the 'death of God' movement. Written from an American perspective, it made the observation that while religious affiliation and attendance remained relatively robust in America, God had become unknowable and elusive to the average person. The author of the piece, *Time*'s religion editor, John T. Elson, observed that 'all too many pews are filled on Sunday with practical atheists – disguised nonbelievers who behave during the rest of the week as if God did not exist'. 'Particularly among the young', he continued, 'there is an acute feeling that the churches on Sunday are preaching the existence of a God who is nowhere visible in their daily lives' (1966: 41). The 'death of God' scholars wrestled with the question of how to make faith relevant in a 'post-faith', godless world.

What, in Elson's opinion, caused this 'death of God'? He pointed to some of the factors associated with modernization. In particular, the scientific worldview represented a persistent problem for faith: 'the prestige of science is so great that its standards have seeped in other areas of life ... knowledge has become that which can be known by scientific study – and what cannot be known that way somehow seems uninteresting, unreal' (Elson 1966: 42). The popular coverage of this topic points to a widely shared sentiment of the 1960s – that Western societies were struggling to find a place for the supernatural.

Many church leaders, theologians and media pundits believed in the late 1960s that 'church' religion's demise was occurring rapidly. The 1950s are considered by many scholars as a buoyant – or steady – time for the churches in Europe, Australia and the United States (see Hilliard 1997; McLeod 2007; Brown 2009; Putnam and Campbell 2010). Think of the wild success of Billy Graham's evangelism crusades, which drew massive crowds. Yet by the swinging, carefree and liberated mid-1960s, this luster had gone, and there was broad pessimism about religion: it was felt that the church had lost much of its influence in public life, and fewer people had a meaningful personal faith.

Around this time, some scholars argued that the social scientific study of religion had also taken a turn for the worse. While the social science disciplines writ large were flourishing by the 1960s, many critics felt that the sociology of religion had become a rather moribund affair. German scholar Thomas Luckmann (1967: 18) wrote that 'the sociology of religion consists mainly of descriptions of the decline of ecclesiastic institutions – from a parochial viewpoint at that'. He felt that the discipline had 'badly neglected its theoretically most significant task: to analyze the changing social ... basis of religion in modern society' (Luckmann 1967: 18).

This situation changed from the mid to late 1960s with the emergence of what was described as the 'new sociology of religion' (Lemert 1975: 107). Many important theoretical developments occurred in the sociology of religion during this time, found principally, but not exclusively, in the work of Peter Berger, Thomas Luckmann and Bryan Wilson. Other notables include Robert Bellah and David Martin. As Charles Lemert (1975: 95) observed: 'Seldom in the recent history of sociology has there been so concerted an effort to transform the theoretical and empirical substance of a major field of specialization.'

Scholars working in the field of religion largely shared the view expressed in *Time* magazine. The consensus was that the process of secularization was occurring with considerable rapidity. In 1965 Harvard professor of religion Harvey Cox published a book entitled *The Secular City* and offered an important elaboration of the process known as secularization. He suggested that secularization was 'the loosing of the world from religious and quasi-religious understandings of itself, the dispelling of all closed worldviews, the breaking of all supernatural myths and sacred symbols' (1965: 2). Few opposed the view that secularization, driven by modernity, was inevitable. Even influential American sociologist Rodney Stark, later a staunch opponent of secularization theory, admitted this was 'the mood of the time, a mood I shared' (Stark 1999: 251). Indeed, in his 1963 paper which examined the impact of scientific study on religious belief, he concluded:

> A present trend in American society is making the scientific scholar into a cultural hero – the presiding genius of progress. If this results in men [sic] of science having greater influence on our culture and value system, as surely it must, and if by becoming a scientist a man is likely to be detached from traditional religious orientations, then we must suspect that future American society will either become increasingly irreligious, or that religion will be extensively modified. (Stark 1963: 14)

The work of the theorists examined in this chapter is embedded in this milieu. Berger, Luckmann and Wilson are often seen as proponents of a secularization theory that links progress and modernization with religious decline. (As we will see, this is a view many contemporary scholars do not accept.) This characterization, however, obscures the complexity and scope of their work. Certainly, they addressed the question of secularization, but their work is about much more than that. New terms, concepts and theoretical frameworks were introduced that energized the social scientific study of religion. They drew heavily on the work of Weber and Durkheim, and in this sense, represented a reinvigoration of the classical tradition. What they had to say is still very useful for modern social scientists, including their thoughts about religion and social change. To that end, this chapter delves into their work, beginning with Peter Berger.

PETER BERGER: RELIGION IS A 'SACRED CANOPY'

Key ideas: sacred canopy; plausibility structures; pluralism

Peter Berger was born in Austria in 1929 and emigrated to the United States as a teenager, where he later completed his university studies. He eventually became a professor of sociology at Boston University. Berger has written mainly about religion, but is perhaps most famously known for his influential treatise on the sociology of knowledge, *The Social Construction of Reality* (1966), which he co-authored with Thomas Luckmann. This work is well-known beyond the sociology of religion. His books on religion are numerous.

Two books Berger published in the 1960s encapsulated his approach to the sociology of religion: *The Sacred Canopy* (1967) and *A Rumor of Angels* (1969). Both are still widely available, and not difficult to read. Neither is particularly lengthy. Berger's contribution to the field is immense, offering both an analysis of the interaction between religion and society as well as a meta-analysis of what encroaching secularization might mean for contemporary society. Berger's influences include Weber, Durkheim and contemporaries such as Thomas Luckmann (see below). His ability to read German, and his use of various continental theorists in addition to Weber and Durkheim, enabled him to bring together European and American sensibilities in his work. As will be seen, Berger has modified his position on secularization considerably across the course of his career – to the joy of some and the chagrin of others (see Woodhead et al. 2006).

Berger's most comprehensive statement about religion is found in *The Sacred Canopy: Elements of a Sociological Theory of Religion*, and it is this work that is the subject of this chapter. This book has two parts: I. Systematic Elements, and 2. Historical Elements. Part I is a theoretical proposal about the role and function of religion in society: religion's role in 'human world-building'. This analysis is offered as a meta-theory about religion. It is in this part of the book Berger famously introduced the idea that religion is a 'sacred canopy'. The second part of the book applies his theories to make sense of religious change. (Unless noted otherwise, all references in this section are to *The Sacred Canopy*.)

Religion: a 'sacred canopy'

In order to understand Berger's theoretical account of religion, it is first necessary to understand what it means to talk about the 'social construction of reality'. Berger begins with the premise that humans and their social world exist together in a dialectical relationship: 'society is the product of man [sic] and man is the product of society' (3). This idea is articulated most fully in *The Social Construction of Reality* (Berger and Luckmann 1966), but is reprised in *The Sacred Canopy*. The very stuff of society – social institutions such as the law, education, family, along with language, rules and values – is not only the product of collective human inventiveness but also the very thing that shapes human experience. This 'dialectical' process of constructing and being constructed by society proceeds in a particular way: externalization, objectivation and internalization (*The Sacred Canopy*, pp. 4–16).

The example of the modern family can illustrate how this process works. Most readers of this book would have grown up living in a close-knit family arrangement – living with an adult or adults and siblings. People are not alone in this arrangement, but part of a broader social institution called the 'nuclear family'. This is the *externalization* or lived reality of human life: the 'outpouring of human being in the world' (4). The institution of the family has myriad expectations, roles, rules and obligations for all those who participate in it. Humans collectively have worked out what it means to live in a nuclear family. Some of this happens formally, such as when governments legislate about parents' duty of care to their children or women's right to work. Some of it is informal, such as parents deciding how chores are to be done in the family. But it acts as a powerful structure governing family life. It is an external reality. This is the *objectivation* of experience: 'a facticity external' to people (4). The entire *meaning and experience* of family is a collective human product.

Even as humans create this society ('social construction'), it also subconsciously influences them, and thus society is experienced as an 'everyday' or 'normal' *reality* rather than a constructed phenomenon. This is the *internalization* of society. For example, when a father is making a child's breakfast he does not think to himself, 'I am preparing this meal because the government has legislated that I look after my children until the age of 18', or 'I am serving my child a fibrous, low-fat breakfast because of a societal-wide anxiety about obesity'. Instead, he thinks, 'It's breakfast time, got to get some food on the table'. It is through this threefold process that social reality is constructed and then comes to influence humans, structuring their experiences. This 'dialectic' is very important in Berger's theorizing. But how does this idea that society is a social construction relate to religion?

We live in a world of our own making – religion included – but religion also helps us make sense of this world. For example, people usually live in what Berger calls the 'everyday' world, focusing on day-to-day matters and accomplishments, rather than spending time thinking about more complicated existential questions. A person stuck in a traffic jam is most likely thinking about being stuck. They probably do not ponder the meaning of life.

The world of the everyday can of course be breached. Berger notes that one example of this is in dreaming: 'in the world of dreams the everyday is definitely left behind' (42). Sometimes these dreams, particularly nightmares, are remembered in daytime consciousness. Other events or experiences can 'rupture' the everyday world and provoke deeper questioning or thought. Many people report powerful experiences in nature; sitting silently atop a mountain, or finding deep tranquility in a walk through a forest. Berger describes such departures from the everyday as 'marginal situations'. Arguably the most marginal situation of all is the specter of death: one's own or the death of others. Berger notes, 'Death radically puts in question the taken-for-granted, "business-as-usual" attitude in which one exists in everyday life' (43).

Imagine if a person sets off with a friend for a day at university, driving in a car. Everything will appear normal, and assume a taken-for-granted status. If an accident occurs and the passenger dies, the driver's world would be turned upside down. Berger asks: how do people make sense of this world of experience that lurks beyond the everyday? He also wonders how these two 'different spheres of reality' (the everyday and marginal situations) cohere 'in the ongoing experience of everyone' (43).

For Berger, the primary way in which life is made meaningful, and properly integrated, is through 'symbolic universes'. A symbolic universe is a kind of grand, totalizing worldview: 'These are bodies of theoretical tradition that integrate different provinces of meaning and encompass the institutional order in a symbolic reality' (Berger and Luckmann 1966 : 127). Wuthnow (1986: 127) provides examples of various symbolic universes: 'personal philosophies of life, scientific world-views, secular philosophies such as Marxism or nihilism, or commonsensical ideas about luck and fate'. These symbolic universes make sense of the various strands of life: the marginal situations and the everyday world. They also legitimate the social order.

Religion is unique among the various symbolic universes because it links the 'here-and-now' with the transcendent. According to Berger, it locates 'human phenomena within a cosmic frame of reference' (35). The socially constructed world, described by Berger as 'precarious and transitory' is thus 'given the semblance of ultimate security and permanence' (36). It is in this way that religion is a *sacred canopy*: a mode of giving meaning to the social world by locating it in the sacred. In Chapter 1 of this book, I noted that definitions of religion tend to be either functional (what religion does) or substantive (what religion is). In Berger's schema, religion can be understood as something that performs a critical function for humans (making sense of the world) and yet religion is substantially different to other symbolic universes because of its special link to the sacred.

As noted above, Berger argues that the social world is a human construction, but one that influences humans, so that in practice it is experienced as a *reality*, not as the product of social processes. Religion too is a human construction: 'the *same* human activity that produces society also produces religion' (47). In making this argument, Berger is not suggesting that the gods are a human invention (he is neutral on this point); rather, the rituals, organization and theologies of religion are the human-devised ways we socially enact the 'existence' of the gods.

Importantly, the relationship between society and religion is not unidirectional (society produces religious change) but dialectical (if religion changes, so will society, and vice-versa). Berger puts it this way:

> religious legitimations arise from human activity, but once crystallized into complexes of meaning that become part of a religious tradition they can attain a measure of autonomy against this activity ... they may *act back upon* actions in everyday life, transforming the latter, sometimes radically. (41)

Here we see the utility of Berger's approach: society and religion are linked together in a dynamic, interdependent relationship.

Two further points are crucial to Berger's work. He does not see the 'social construction of reality' – religion included – as a static process, but one of *evolution and change*: 'culture must continuously be produced and reproduced by man [sic]. Its structures are, therefore, inherently precarious and predestined to change' (6). Berger believed that in the past, Christianity was Western society's sacred canopy. In Western society in the 1960s, there was no longer a unified vision of the sacred, an idea he explores in Part II of *The Sacred Canopy*.

Religion in modernity

Like most of his peers, Berger accepted that secularization was continuing apace in the twentieth century, observing that 'a high degree of secularization is a cultural

concomitant of modern industrial societies' (1969: 18). The trajectories identified by the earlier sociologists, particularly Weber, were not abating. According to
Berger, secularization has two elements: the objective and the subjective. Objective
secularization refers to the declining influence of 'religious institutions and symbols' in many aspects of culture and society. Berger cites the example of religion's
diminishing influence in education. He also notes that science has become more
prominent 'as an autonomous, thoroughly secular perspective on the world' (107).
The other dimension to secularization is subjective and this is the secularization
of consciousness: 'this means that the modern West has produced an increasing
number of individuals who look upon the world and their own lives without the
benefit of religious interpretations' (108).

Berger is rather vague on the topic of *why* secularization occurs, noting that ideas,
like scientific rationalism, or social processes, such as urbanization and pluralism,
have been posited by others as explanations (1969: 18). In *The Sacred Canopy*, Berger
notes that the seeds of secularization can in fact be found in Christianity itself, particularly the more rationally oriented Protestant belief system that emerged after
the Reformation (128). Earlier scholars, such as Weber, Durkheim and Tawney, also
pointed to Protestantism's rationality and worldliness as precipitating Christianity's
decline.

Berger is also concerned with the implications of secularization. Berger observes
that 'pluralism' is very much a corollary of secularization. In a secularized society, one
single, religious worldview does not dominate. Rather, there are competing worldviews, some of which are highly organized (nationalistic movements, or ideologies
like Marxism), others are more diffuse, such as individualism (137). Because of this
pluralism, people have greater choice, and no longer feel any obligation to follow any
particular way of life. Religious institutions can no longer take for granted a wide
following, and religion 'must be "sold" to a clientele that is no longer constrained to
"buy"' (138). Religions must therefore engage in marketing their wares. Other sociologists, such as Rodney Stark, argue that such competition actually strengthens religious commitments (see Chapter 4). Berger's arguments about the commercialization
of religion have been elaborated on in greater depth by scholars such as Mara Einstein,
in her recent book *Brands of Faith: Marketing Religion in a Commercial Age* (2008).

The other shift that occurred as a consequence of secularization is what Berger
describes as the 'location' of religion in contemporary society. Because religion is
increasingly marginalized in the public sphere, the concerns of religion instead
become focused on the private sphere of life: 'the … family and neighborhood as
well as the psychological "needs" of the private individual' (147). Sociologist Steve
Bruce, reviewing Berger's work, agrees with such an assessment and cites scholar
Wade Clark Roof: 'the religious stance today is more internal than external, more
individual than institutional, more experiential than cerebral, more private than public' (Roof 1996: 153 in Bruce 2006: 90).

After the publication of *The Sacred Canopy* Berger played down some of his conclusions about the magnitude and scope of secularization, particularly its link with

modernity. In his later work he suggests that secularization is not a universal given but a historical process limited to specific regions, such as parts of Europe, and even there conclusions about secularization must be tempered (see Berger 2006; Berger et al. 2008). That said, he does not resile from his conclusions about the implications of pluralism, or substantive ideas about the social construction of religions. I believe he was correct in identifying religion's increasing concern with the minutiae of personal life, a theme explored by his long-time collaborator, Thomas Luckmann.

THOMAS LUCKMANN: 'THE INVISIBLE RELIGION'

Key ideas: symbolic universes; invisible religion; individualism

Thomas Luckmann made his name initially by collaborating with Peter Berger on *The Social Construction of Reality* (1966). He also made an impressive and prescient contribution to the sociology of religion in the 1960s. As with Berger, his analysis has continuing relevance for sociologists of religion today. Although he is often cast as being one of the major proponents of traditional secularization theory, Luckmann is not specifically interested in the *causes* of secularization per se, and actually spends very little time on the topic. He is more interested in documenting what he sees as an important religious development occurring in Western societies – the rise of a 'private', invisible religion.

Luckmann was born in Slovenia in 1927 and studied for his undergraduate degrees in Austria. He then completed his graduate studies in New York before taking up a position at the University of Constance in Germany. His major contribution to the sociology of religion came via his 1967 book *The Invisible Religion* (previously published in German in 1963 under the title *Das Problem der Religion in der Modern Gesellschaft*). His work is embedded in the subjectivist tradition of sociology (focusing on how the individual knows and experiences social life), as expressed most comprehensively in *The Social Construction of Reality*. (Unless noted otherwise, all references in this section are to *The Invisible Religion*.)

As was noted above, Berger's *Sacred Canopy* was part theoretical treatise, part explanation of the modern condition. *The Invisible Religion* proceeds along similar lines. Initially, Luckmann is particularly interested in the *function* religion performs for individuals. Individuals make life meaningful and coherent through various meaning systems and worldviews – those 'symbolic universes' described in the previous section.

People's symbolic universes (the worldviews we use to make sense of the world) can all be thought of, after a fashion, as being 'religious' because they *transcend* the subjective stream of consciousness (78) and help us order reality. Understood in this functional way, a form of 'religion' is 'present in nonspecific forms in all societies and all "normal" (socialized) individuals' (78). In this manner, Luckmann's work can be viewed in the Durkheimian tradition of sociology.

Some kinds of 'religion' are more developed than others. According to Luckmann, 'the familiar forms of religion known to us as tribal religion, ancestor cult, church, sect, and so forth are *specific historical institutionalizations* of symbolic universes' (43) (my italics). These developed symbolic universes become a form of religion characterized by *institutional specialization*: they have clearly articulated doctrines, social organization and full-time specialists (66). In the past, these 'familiar forms of religion' provided the predominant symbolic universes in Western societies (akin to Berger's sacred canopy). Now, in the modern era, these institutionalized, specific forms of religion are being superseded by *new*, individually focused forms of religion. An analysis of these new social forms is Luckmann's most intriguing contribution to the sociology of religion.

In pre-modern times, it was straightforward for religion to be people's major symbolic universe because society was more uniform and structured and an institutionalized version of the 'sacred cosmos' could be readily imposed on the population. In modernity, society is characterized by an ever-increasing number of specialized institutions that regulate different aspects of life – be they educational, political or economic. The church becomes an 'institution among other institutions' (94), what Luckmann refers to as *institutional segmentation*. As individuals go about their daily lives, they will encounter the language, logic and worldview of these various institutions, few of which are now centered around religious themes.

Where can 'official' religion find a place, if other institutions dominate public life? Official religion becomes relegated to addressing concerns in the private sphere; public life is dominated by other institutions and their more worldly themes. In a modern person's private life, the themes of self-realization, autonomy and personal development have become pressing concerns (Mason et al. 2007: 60). Official religion must speak to these needs, but it also faces competition in an increasingly complex world – one of a number of competing worldviews that seek to address the private needs of individuals (104). Competition for religion in the private sphere comes from self-help literature, popular psychology and popular music (104). And, in a rapidly transforming society, the 'official' religious model cannot hope to meet all the private needs of a diverse, mobile and increasingly complex population.

Where does this change in official religion's status leave individuals? Without a society-wide and accepted official symbolic universe, and with official religion facing stiff competition from other worldviews that address private matters, individuals are left in a position where they must formulate or decide upon their own symbolic universe. Some may choose a more fully realized version, such as Christianity or psychoanalysis, while others choose to fashion their own distinct worldview, drawing on a range of themes. Either way, this is religion in modernity – people choosing and authenticating their own worldview, 'whatever works' for them. In the absence of a model accepted across society, people come to have their own, private formulation about life – an invisible religion. This kind of worldview is invisible, because unlike the official religions of times past, 'it is not expressed in the visible institutional form of a church or religious community' (Mason et al. 2007: 61). In other words, modernity has left us in a place where we construct our own worldviews, drawing on whatever resources we want, and this is our religion. Societal-wide patterns of religious socialization no longer dominate; rather **religious individualism** is modernity's overarching theme. (These ideas are explored later, in Chapters 7, 9 and 11.)

Berger and Luckmann shared many themes in their work. Both sought to understand the changing role of religion in society and what this meant for individuals. Many important trends were identified: increasing individualism, the privatization of religion and increasing competition for religion from other worldviews (pluralism). Although both accepted the inevitability of religious decline in the modern West, neither offered a sustained account of this process. Of greater concern was describing what social change meant for religious expression, and here lies their greatest contribution. Some of their contemporaries, including Bryan Wilson, focused more specifically on the mechanisms of religious decline in modernity.

BRYAN WILSON: 'RELIGION IN SECULAR SOCIETY'

Key ideas: secularization; pluralism; sects

Bryan Wilson is one of Britain's foremost sociologists of religion. Born in 1926, he died in 2004. He worked first at the University of Leeds, and then at Oxford University. Towards the end of his career a book was published in his honor, titled *Secularization, Rationalism, and Sectarianism: Essays in Honour of Bryan R. Wilson* (Barker et al. 1993). The title of the book reflects the main themes in Wilson's work. Notable books of his include *Religion in Secular Society* (1966), *Religion in Sociological Perspective* (1982) and *The Social Dimensions of Sectarianism: Sects and New Religious Movements in Contemporary Society* (1992). The first of these works, *Religion in Secular Society* (1966), established Wilson as a leading proponent of so-called 'old paradigm' secularization theory. Although this book was very different in style and tone from Berger and Luckmann, Wilson shared the view that religious change was a consequence of broader sociostructural changes in society. His views were not universally shared at the time. His British contemporary David Martin wrote in 1965 that the term 'secularization' ought to be removed from the sociological dictionary (Martin 1965; Wilson 1979). (Unless noted otherwise, all references in this section are to *Religion in Secular Society*.)

In *Religion in Secular Society* (1966) Wilson engages in a systematic analysis of the ways in which Western societies have become increasingly secular in the modern era. In doing so he established the parameters of contemporary secularization theory, ideas shared by later scholars such as Steve Bruce (see next chapter). Wilson defines secularization simply: 'the process whereby religious *thinking*, *practice* and *institutions* lose social significance' (my italics) (14). This process occurred principally in the twentieth century, but the seeds of decline were sown in the century before that (10). Secularization does not always proceed uniformly, and it is manifested differently in the United States compared with Britain.

How does secularization manifest itself? In terms of religious practice, it will either decrease, or in the case of the United States, its meaning will change, so that people attend for reasons beyond simply having faith, such as social acceptance. Religious institutions, such as denominations, increasingly adopt the modern rational and bureaucratic modes of operation (see the Case Study on Vatican II).

VATICAN II: A CHURCH ENTERS THE MODERN AGE

The Catholic Church is one of the world's oldest continuing institutions and traces its roots back to St Peter, foremost among Jesus' disciples. Christianity survived Roman persecution in the first four centuries CE and the Catholic Church emerged as its major institution in the first millennium. The Reformation in the early 1500s led to a major schism in Christianity between Catholic and Protestants, yet the Catholic Church continued to prosper. By the start of the 1960s it remained Christianity's biggest denomination. It was at this time the Catholic Church held a series of formal meetings that transformed – and modernized – one of the West's oldest and most powerful institutions.

The meetings are known formally as the Second Vatican Council, or Vatican II. (The first Vatican Council had taken place in 1868.) Vatican II was the initiative of Pope John XXIII, but was led mainly by his successor, Pope Paul VI. Vatican II was a complicated process, and took place over four ten-week periods from 1962–65. More than 2500 people attended, including cardinals, bishops and other religious figures. It was an extraordinary logistical and theological exercise.

There were many catalysts for this council. An excellent and accessible account is offered by Catholic scholar John O'Malley (2008) in his book, *What Happened at Vatican II*. O'Malley documents the various challenges that had been facing the Catholic Church since the nineteenth century. These included the secular philosophies of liberalism and modern approaches to scriptural interpretation and pressure from within the Church for the Liturgy to be recited in local languages, not in the traditional Latin, a language no longer used in daily life. Vatican complicity with the Nazis during the Second World War also had created much soul-searching for the Church, and other modern issues, particularly the invention of the contraceptive pill and communism, meant new challenges for the Church. Vatican II was to be the Church's considered response to the new realities of modern life.

An important goal of Vatican II was 'aggiornamento', the Italian word for 'bringing up to date' (O'Malley 2008: 9). This involved appropriating various modernist assumptions and values (O'Malley 2008: 38). Aggiornamento was clearly manifested in two significant and visible changes flowing from the Council. The first of these was a revision of the Liturgy. In order to foster stronger lay (non-ordained, or non-priestly) participation in the Liturgy, and by extension, the laity's affinity with their church, the Liturgy was to be celebrated in local languages. The other change was to do with the life of Catholic Religious (members of the many Catholic religious orders: nuns, priests and monks). This was embodied in a decree: 'Perfectae Caritatis', the Decree on the Adaptation and Renewal of Religious Life. Catholic

Religious were allowed to dress less formally and be more open to the community around them.

Many theological and social changes resulted from Vatican II, the consequences of which are complex and far-reaching. Vatican II makes a fascinating case study of the ways in which a major religious institution can deliberately engage with the world around it.

Want to know more?

- O'Malley, John (2008) *What Happened at Vatican II*. Cambridge, MA: Belknap Press of Harvard University Press.

- Linden, Ian (2009) *Global Catholicism: Diversity and Change since Vatican II*. London: Hurst.

With respect to religious thinking, Wilson argues that rational sensibilities will prevail over religious superstition. We 'assess the world in empirical and rational terms, and find [ourselves] involved in rational organizations and rationally determined roles which allow small scope for such religious predilections as they might previously entertain' (10).

Wilson begins his work by laying out the statistical evidence of religious decline in England and other parts of Europe. He offers various caveats that govern the use of statistics, but argues that 'the statistics do provide some evidence of significant religious change' (22). Most notably: 'The figures reveal a steady diminution in the proportion of people who go to church in European Countries ... and particularly the Protestant countries' (22). Additionally, he presents a series of tables spanning the late 1850s to the early 1960s, each showing some kind of decline for the Church of England, whether it be membership or baptisms.

Like Berger and Luckmann, and Weber before them, in large part Wilson attributes the start of secularization to post-Reformation changes within Christianity. The Protestant emphasis on values such as 'reason' and 'control' produced a worldview that was more oriented to 'this world' than the spiritual realm. Similarly, the denominalization that emerged after the Reformation also contributed to secularization because it promoted religious choices. So much choice makes it difficult for there to be a defined, agreed-upon religious basis for society, and more secular orientations can compete with religious worldviews (30).

Wilson also outlines other ways in which religion has become marginalized in secular societies. One source of this marginalization comes from the rise of science. Wilson moves beyond the simple assertion that science poses a threat to religious belief. He argues that 'the real danger of science to religion ... was rather in the increased prestige of science and the decline of the intellectual prestige of religion. Since science had the answers, and had positive and tangible fruits, it came increasingly to command respect and approval' (47). Science, not religion, became the trusted source of knowledge in society. The scientific perspective in turn fitted a society that was, because of industrialization, concerned with pragmatic matters like efficiency in industry.

Another source of marginalization of religion emerges from the increasingly complex nature of modern life. In his work, Thomas Luckmann describes a modernizing process he calls 'institutional specialization': the emergence of an increasing range of social institutions that govern different aspects of life. Wilson observes the same 'compartmentalizing of life': the spheres of family life, production, recreation and education have become increasingly distant from one another. When these spheres were more unified, Church religion had a 'general presidency' over various life matters (57). Now, with the increased separation of these facets of life, 'life activities have been secularized' (57) and are subject to governance from institutions that are secular in character.

Like Berger and Luckmann, Wilson observes that the process of secularization is not uniform, but restricted to the industrialized West. The United States is also a special case – it maintains higher levels of practice and belief compared to Europe, and thus any theorization about secularization must be context-specific. In Wilson's opinion, however, the United States is not immune from secularization. He argues that rational, instrumental and capitalist values predominate in American public life (112), more so than anywhere else. Moreover, the high levels of religious attendance and affiliation are not a product of great piety but evidence of the symbolic importance of religion in American culture, where a person can only properly be thought 'American' if they identify with a religion or denomination. The faith posited by many Americans is of the empty, godless kind, as described by the article in *Time* magazine.

CONCLUSION

Following the intellectual tradition established by the earlier sociologists of religion, Berger, Luckmann and Wilson affirmed the sociological precept that religion and society are interlinked, and offered lively accounts of how this dialectical process occurs. Their books should be read as examples of cogent sociological theorization. Each offered useful theoretical tools and sociological insights that remain applicable: symbolic universes, plausibility structures, invisible religion, sacred canopies. Wilson's extensive work on sects, although not discussed in detail in this chapter, also has an enduring utility (see Wilson 1992).

The broader conclusion of most scholars of religion in the 1960s was that Western society was becoming increasingly secular. Berger, Luckmann and Wilson described the religious realities of modernity. While there is dispute about the link between modernization and secularization (see the next chapter), fundamental societal shifts *had* occurred across the nineteenth and twentieth centuries. Historians and other scholars agree that Western society had become less communal and more individualistic; scientific and other rational worldviews had become more prominent; everyday life was governed by an increasing array of specialized institutions organized along bureaucratic lines. All of this impacted on the expression of individual faith and Berger, Luckmann and Wilson sought to understand this impact, reaching conclusions that are still valid and thought-provoking. As we move into the twenty-first century, social change has continued apace. Just as the social context of the 1960s demanded new theoretical and conceptual insights, so too does the present day. These developments in theory are presented in the next chapter.

Points to ponder

What are the symbolic universes that structure your life? How do they integrate the everyday with the marginal situations? Do you agree that we no longer have a shared sacred canopy? Ask an older person, like a parent or grandparent, what religious life was like when they were growing up.

Next steps ...

Read the original work of Berger, Luckmann and Wilson. All make good, straightforward and rewarding reading. Other books explore their legacy: *Peter Berger and the Study of Religions* (Woodhead et al. 2006); *Making Sense of Modern Times: Peter L. Berger and the Vision of Interpretive Sociology* (Hunter and Ainlay 1986) and *Secularization, Rationalism, and Sectarianism: Essays in Honour of Bryan R. Wilson* (Barker et al. 1993). Other scholars who rose to prominence at the same time as the three discussed in this chapter include Robert Bellah (1967) who introduced the influential idea of American 'civil religion', and David Martin (1978), who proposed a historically and culturally nuanced approach to understanding secularization (see next chapter).

Documentaries

An interesting 2009 film about Vatican II, *Challenge, Change, Faith: Catholic Australia and the Second Vatican Council*, is worth watching, and suitable for an international audience. Order online at http://www.challengechangefaith.com/order.html or ask your librarian to get hold of a copy.

4

towards contemporary theorizing: secularization, the 'religious economy' and globalization

After reading this chapter you will:

- be aware of contemporary debates about secularization theory;

- possess a critical understanding of alternative theories of religious change, including the 'religious economies' model; and

- understand the key elements of globalization.

> Let me note Karel Dobbelaere's breathtaking evasion in his article.
>
> Rodney Stark, Secularization R.I.P. (1999: 252)
>
> When church attendance falls below 1 percent, will the supply-siders [e.g. Rodney Stark] finally stop insisting that secularization is a myth?
>
> Steve Bruce, Christianity in Britain, R.I.P. (2001: 202)

For about a century, sociologists of religion had accepted the 'inevitability' of religious decline in the modern west. There were a few dissenters (David Martin, for example, wrote in 1965 that the term secularization ought to be removed from the sociological dictionary), but as we have seen in the previous two chapters, this was the accepted orthodoxy of the discipline, from Weber to Berger. In the 1990s, however, scholarly consensus fell apart, and the sociology of religion became embroiled in something of a civil war. An intellectual battle was fought over how to explain religious change in the nineteenth and twentieth centuries, and to supply a theory that might anticipate religious change in the future. On one side were proponents of 'secularization theory', who argued Christianity's hold on Western societies had been declining for centuries, and, in all likelihood, would continue to decline in the future. Squaring off against secularization theorists were scholars of the 'new paradigm', who argued the evidence of religious decline in Europe had been misinterpreted, and secularization theory could not explain religious change in America. These scholars offered an alternative model for making sense of religious change – 'supply-side' or 'religious economy' theories.

The publication in 1999 of a forceful paper, 'Secularization R.I.P', by American sociologist Rodney Stark looked like it might end the war once and for all. An advocate of the new paradigm, Stark argued secularization was essentially a fiction; there had never been, in his reading, a 'golden age' of religious participation in Europe. Stark (1999: 270) concluded his paper: 'After nearly three centuries of utterly failed prophesies and misrepresentations of both present and past, it seems time to carry the secularization doctrine to the graveyard of failed theories, and there to whisper *"requiescat in pace"* [rest in peace].' This pronouncement, along with Peter Berger's famous 'recantation' of his earlier acceptance of secularization (see Stark 1999; Berger 2006; Bruce 2006), suggested there was no longer a place in the social sciences for a 'grand theory' of religious decline.

However, the hope of a realistic theoretical alternative, particularly, the religious economies model, found little support outside of America. Other scholars suggested that the secularization/religious economies debate was passé, or insufficiently broad enough in scope to account for the range of contemporary developments in the world's religious life. To outsiders, the discipline appeared theoretically enervated and irrevocably divided into factions. Had sociology failed in one of its core tasks – the sociocultural explanation of religious change? The short answer is no. While grand theories of change appear to have had their heyday, more modest, context-specific accounts of religious change have won support.

This chapter acts as a bridge between sociological theories of the past and the explanations of contemporary social science which feature in Part II of this book. It charts the demise – and qualified return – of secularization theories, the emergence of the religious economies model, and the recent focus on religion and globalization. In doing so, it sets the scene for what follows in the remaining chapters of this book. Discussion begins with an overview of the events preceding the 1990s civil war, facts about the war itself, and an examination of its aftermath.

EXPLAINING RELIGIOUS CHANGE IN THE WEST: SECULARIZATION THEORIES VS. THE 'NEW PARADIGM'

Sociologist Christian Smith (2008: 1562) observes, 'the single research debate that emerged to dominate theoretical discourse within the field [sociology of religion] was that between the so-called new paradigm, rational choice, religious economies theory [and] secularization theory'. To understand the parameters of this debate, it is necessary to look at the state of secularization theory from the 1960s to the 1990s.

Classical secularization theory

As discussed in the previous chapter, secularization theories gained critical momentum in the 1960s. Perhaps the most decisive articulation of this theory came from Bryan Wilson (1966). He summarized secularization as 'the process whereby religious thinking, practice and institutions lose social significance' (1966: 14). Others seen as critical to advancing this paradigm are Peter Berger (1967), Talcott Parsons (1966) and Thomas Luckmann (1967). This work was extended in the 1970s and 1980s by scholars such as Richard Fenn (1969) and Karel Dobbelaere (1984). This body of knowledge constitutes what has been termed 'the old paradigm' (Warner 1993), or more helpfully, the 'inherited model' (Wilson 1985). The latter term acknowledges the influence of Durkheim and Weber on the development of later secularization theories.

The sociologists of the 1960s and 1970s did not approach the topic of religious decline uniformly – that much is clear from the previous chapter. Berger and Luckmann spent far less time than Wilson discussing the causes of secularization. Indeed, it is better to refer to the body of knowledge generated about religious change as secularization *theories*. Nonetheless, sociologist Olivier Tschannen (1991: 400) argues there are shared elements of this inherited model. These are: differentiation, rationalization and worldliness. These are all processes that have occurred in Western societies during the modern era. Briefly, **differentiation** refers to the development of specific social institutions that now undertake various tasks previously performed by organized religion, be they education or health care. Societies are more complex and specialized. **Rationalization** means the rise of scientific and rational modes of thinking, which supersede superstitious and irrational (read 'religious') worldviews. **Worldliness** means a personal worldview that is grounded in the here and now rather than the transcendent. Because of these factors, in modern societies across the past two centuries, religion was not merely transformed, it *declined* in its importance to society as a whole and in the lives of individuals in that society.

In the inherited model, secularization is a *historical* view about religious transformations that have taken place in Europe, and to a lesser extent in the United States, after the onset of modernity. That is, differentiation, rationalization and worldliness *have* occurred, displacing religion from its central position in society.

Evidence of secularization includes decreases in church affiliation and attendance (see Wilson 1966). Wilson dates the full effects of secularization as occurring in the twentieth century, but the seeds of decline were sown earlier in the modern period, particularly during the nineteenth century.

Classical secularization theory, was, to a lesser extent, a *prediction* about future trajectories; as societies continue to modernize, secularization will continue because one affects the other. Religion will not disappear, but fewer individuals in a modernized society will be religious. Despite characterizations suggesting otherwise, few of the classical theorists predicted secularization would follow some kind of linear trajectory (Goldstein 2009: 157). Rather, secularization occurs unevenly, tempered by local conditions and characteristics (see Martin 1978 for the best articulation of this idea).

Few scholars disagree with the proposition that societal changes associated with modernity impacted on organized religion: most agree society became increasingly differentiated in the modern era, and that religious authority ceased to dominate all the different spheres of public life. English scholar Robert Warner (2010: 37) notes: 'Quite clearly and undeniably something seismic has happened to the condition of religion in the context of modernization in Western Europe.' Even the most ardent critics of secularization theory, Rodney Stark and Roger Finke (2000: 60), admit public religious authority has declined in Europe and 'that the primary aspects of public life [are no] longer suffused with religious symbols, rhetoric or ritual'. Some of these changes and challenges to religion were documented in Chapter 2: the rise of the scientific worldview, challenges to literal interpretations of scripture and new spiritual and secular movements undermining traditional religious authority. But is modernity *synonymous* with religious decline? Perhaps religion just changes in character as society changes, but does not necessarily become less important for individuals within that society?

Critics of the inherited tradition – mainly proponents of the new paradigm (e.g. Warner 1993; Stark 1999) – disputed the link between modernity and religious decline for several reasons. First, there is the United States. The United States is the exception that confounds the rule: what to do about a country that shows consistently higher levels of religious belief and attendance, in what is arguably the most modernized country on earth? The classical theorists, especially Wilson (1966) and Berger (1967), accommodated the US in their analysis, and made claims about the apparent secularization of US religion, but few critics were persuaded.

Another criticism, expressed most notably by Rodney Stark (1999), in the 'Secularization R.I.P' paper, but shared by others, was that there never was a golden age of high individual religiosity in Europe from which there has been steady decline (see Lechner 1991). Stark (1999: 254) argues; 'there has been *no demonstrable long-term decline in European religious participation!* ... religious participation was very low in northern and Western Europe many centuries before the onset of modernization' (italics in original). Proponents of secularization theory were critical of Stark's data and marshaled contradictory evidence showing declines in individual religiosity, particularly in Britain, dating from 1850s to the 1990s (see Wilson 1966; Bruce 2001; 2002). Either way, most agreed present-day personal religiosity in Europe is low, but according to the critics of secularization, it had always been thus, and for reasons they could explain (see below).

Despite some spirited defense and thoughtful modification of classical secularization theories (e.g. Lechner 1991; Chaves 1994; Yamane 1997; Bruce 2001; 2002), it became the accepted scholarly practice to reject such theories, particularly in America. Classical secularization theory appeared to be history. The challenge for scholars critical of secularization theories was to find a cogent explanation of religious change that could explain Europe's low attendance rates and America's vibrant religious life. Proponents of the new paradigm believed they had the answers.

Dynamics of the religious marketplace: models of the religious economy

Many American scholars were unconvinced that modernity, or processes associated with modernity, was producing a religious decline in their country. They sought explanations that accommodated both stagnant (Europe) *and* vibrant (USA) religious cultures. To do this, they turned to a new style of theorizing that had become popular in their country: the religious economies model that was part of the new paradigm in the sociology of religion.

The new paradigm was announced in the early 1990s in a much-cited article by Stephen Warner (1993). This is an umbrella term referring to the ascendency of 'rational-choice' and 'supply-side' theories of religion in the American sociology of religion. According to Lechner (2007: 82), the core of these approaches is the 'twin ideas that for individuals religion is a rational choice and that in society religion takes the form of an economy'. Thus the focus of theorizing and analysis is on *individual religious behavior* and the dynamics of the *'religious marketplace'*. The language and ideas of this approach are indebted to economics (see Finke and Iannaccone 1993). A general sociological overview of the central tenets of rational choice theories is offered by Rodney Stark and Roger Finke (2000) in their book *Acts of Faith*. This book presents 99 propositions about individual religious behavior and the nature of religious organizations.

In terms of individual religious behavior, Stark and Finke claim 'people make religious choices in the same way that they make other choices, by weighing the costs and benefits' (2000: 85). These benefits include 'certain rewards', including 'otherworldly rewards'; something only religions can offer. This idea of 'rewards' is used by scholars to try to better understand things like religious conversion and 'switching' (moving from one congregation or denomination to another). Empirical applications of rational-choice theory to explain 'religious switching' include those of Sherkat and Wilson (1995) and Loveland (2003). Loveland (2003: 155) argues: 'Rational choice is a powerful theory when applied to religious switching because it constructs the individual as an active agent making choices between religious options.'

The dynamics of the 'religious marketplace' are also used by rational choice theorists to explain differences in the religious vitality of the United States and Western Europe (see Stark and Iannaccone 1994). The basic premise is 'religious regulation and monopolies create lethargic religions ... but that capable religions thrive in pluralistic, competitive environments' (Smith et al. 1998: 73). The United States has always allowed freedom of religion, and there has never been a state religion, or quasi-state religion, as in Western Europe, which has endured a highly regulated religious market. In pluralistic, unregulated American conditions, various religions and denominations flourished. Importantly, rational choice theorists believe that religious pluralism *fosters* religious vitality. This works because 'more and more religious consumers are induced into participation by the variety of religious products that satisfy their needs and wants' (Smith et al. 1998: 73). Stark and Iannaccone (1994: 233) put it this way:

> *To the degree that a religious economy is competitive and pluralistic, overall levels of religious participation will tend to be high. Conversely, to the degree that a religious economy is monopolized by one or two state-supported firms, overall levels of participation will tend to be low.* (italics in original)

A helpful way of explaining the religious economies model is an analogy with fast food. Imagine a small town in Europe. The government passes a law allowing one fast-food restaurant to open. The 'Big Burger' corporation wins the tender and opens a store on the main street. People get excited and start to eat burgers. Big Burger does quite well initially but the market is rather small – catering only to those who eat burgers. Nothing for people who like fried chicken, fish 'n' chips, are vegetarians, or are lovers of different kinds of burgers. In the end, only a small group of people in town buys fast food – loyal Big Burger customers. The rest stay at home and cook dinner. This is a bit like religion in Western Europe. Stark and Finke (2000: 284) put it this way: 'lacking competition, the dominant firm[s] will be too inefficient to sustain vigorous marketing efforts, and the result will be a low-level overall level of religious commitment'.

Imagine a similar-sized town in the United States. Here the local authorities allow any fast-food restaurant to open. Big Burger arrives from Europe, and sets up its store on the corner of the main street. It is rather successful, but there is still no fast-food culture, and its appeal is limited to burger lovers. Then, a company called Kansas Broiled Chicken comes and opens a store right next door. This expands the market, so now chicken lovers can purchase fast food. The interest of other non-fast-food people is piqued. A curious onlooker thinks to themself, 'Maybe I should see what's going on here,' and visits both stores to compare. They're delighted by the choices and decide to buy dinner. Other companies see the market is expanding and also set up stores. Pizza Shack opens a store right next door. The Metro Cold-Cuts company sees all of this and realizes that people who prefer healthier options are not catered for. So they open a sandwich store on the main street, and this further expands the market. There are plenty of options, and a greater range of people can make fast food something they choose on a regular basis. All of this fast food also creates a mindset in which people actively think of such meals as a realistic, daily option. It is all around, and there is plenty of choice. Why cook at home when everything can be bought? A fast-food culture develops, spurred on by competition and choice. Fast food becomes a way of life. This is an effective analogy for religion in America. As Stark and Finke (2000: 284) argue: 'To the degree that religious economies are unregulated and competitive, overall levels of religious commitment will be high.' From the rational-choice perspective, a decline in religious participation is unlikely as long as vigorous religious competition is present. Indeed, religious participation will increase in the long term if there is vibrant religious competition.

Just when the rational choice paradigm seemed to promise so much, it, too, met serious objections. Some critiqued the idea that individuals are indeed 'rational actors' when it comes to religious matters (see Chaves 1995; Hunt 2005). The 'pluralistic religious economy' thesis, the idea that 'having a greater diversity of religious groups will have higher rates of religious participation', was also subject to criticism (Olsen 2008: 95). This concept didn't necessarily work in the case of Europe. Pollack (2008: 13) notes: 'Poland, Ireland, Italy, Romania, and Croatia exhibit the highest indices of religiosity among the European Countries, while at the same time displaying exceptionally low levels of religious pluralism.'

Moreover, the empirical data did not conclusively support the pluralism equals vitality thesis. In an important paper, Voas et al. (2002) discovered a methodological flaw in earlier papers, showing quantitative conclusions used to substantiate claims about pluralism fostering vitality were unreliable. Olsen (2008: 101) notes: 'the best conclusion appears ... that pluralism has no noticeable positive or negative effects on religious participation'. Stark et al. (1995) hoped their theory would have general applicability as an account of religious change, but this didn't appear to be the case, and its uptake among scholars outside of the United States was low. The idea of a religious economy is helpful in explaining in part some aspects of American religious vitality, as will be seen in Chapter 7. However, the scholarly consensus is that it is not effective in explaining the religious trajectory of Europe. It appeared that by the mid-2000s, attempts to sustain grand sociological theories of religious change were increasingly problematic. Where to from here?

Secularization in the nineteenth century: the rise of social history

A recent trend evident in scholarship about secularization has been a deeper, and more sustained, historical investigation of the parameters and causes of religious change in the United States and Europe in the modern era, specifically, the nineteenth century. This scholarship, led by social historians, addresses a weakness of the inherited tradition which, for the most part, did not conduct a sustained analysis of the changes taking place in the nineteenth century.

There is widespread agreement on all sides of the debate that dominant aspects of Christianity were challenged markedly as Western societies modernized, particularly in the nineteenth century. Christian Smith (2003b: 5) argues 'something real at the level of macrosocial change ... has actually happened in history, and we need to account for and understand that change'. As noted elsewhere, this was manifested in the nineteenth century in many different ways, including, for example, the rise of 'free-thought' societies and associations, and secular activists campaigning against religious instruction in public schools, all of which challenged the primacy of Christendom (see Smith 2003a; McLeod 2000, 2003). The word 'secularization' is deployed by social historians to describe these changes insofar as it refers to Christianity's *cultural ascendency being challenged at a discrete moment in history*, rather than as it being an 'inevitable and inexorable accompaniment of "modernization"' (Brown 2003: 37).

Many scholars in this emerging social history field do not see the explanations and tools of traditional secularization theory as offering sufficient, if any, help in making sense of these changes. For these scholars, putative causes such as 'differentiation' or 'rationalization' are too abstract or ill-defined to be of much use (Smith 2003b: 14). Instead, they have conducted specific investigations of secularization in the nineteenth century, identifying first the kinds of changes that took place, and second, positing multiple causes. According to Smith (2003b: vii), such analysis brings 'agency, interests, power, resources, mobilization, strategy, and conflict to the foreground in our understanding of macrosocial secularization'. Readers interested in knowing about aspects of secularization in the nineteenth century should read Hugh McLeod's *Secularisation in Western Europe 1848–1914* (2000), McLeod and Ustorf's edited collection *The Decline of Christendom in Western Europe, 1750–2000* (2003), and Christian Smith's (2003a) edited collection, *The Secular Revolution: Power, Interests, and Conflict in the Secularization of American Public Life*. In these works, secularization in the nineteenth century is real, but its manifestations are many, and its causes are complex and multifaceted. This is not to say aspects of modernization are not at play, but rather that the mechanisms and causes of secularization are not attributed to the general processes associated with modernization. Another sociologist to advocate such an approach is David Martin, whose well-known work *A General Theory of Secularization* (1978) advocated a historical and context-specific examination of religious change.

A detailed, historical approach is most helpful in understanding specific changes in the nineteenth and early twentieth centuries in the United States and elsewhere, if only to counter simplistic conclusions about religious change in that period of time. The truth is that the modern era was religiously very complex: there were evangelical Christian revivals, new religious movements, *and* bitter arguments about religion's place in public life. Classical secularization theorists were not particularly interested in offering a sustained, historical account of religious change in the nineteenth century. From their perspective, that century simply set in motion processes that would culminate in widespread religious decline in the twentieth century.

Making sense of the 1960s and beyond

Much of the wrangling during the secularization theory 'civil war' was about whether the data showed evidence of declining religious affiliation and attendance in Europe, and if so, precisely when this occurred. In recent decades the kinds of data available improved, as did their reliability, and these show a very clear pattern; in Britain, Australia, Canada and even in America, levels of religious affiliation, attendance and belief have dropped since the 1960s, particularly among young people (see Chapters 6 and 7 for the actual data). This finding has produced two responses among scholars.

One response has been the publication of socio-historic works (much like the socio-historical works centered on the nineteenth century) which consider the cultural conditions of the 1960s, and how these impacted on religiosity. These books will be described in greater detail in later chapters, but leading examples discussing Britain include Hugh McLeod's *The Religious Crisis of the 1960s* (2007) and Callum Brown's *The Death of Christian Britain* (2009). In America, Putnam and Campbell's *American Grace: How Religion Divides and Unites US* (2010) is arguably the key text on the impact of religious change in the 1960s. Charles Taylor's monumental and ambitious *A Secular Age* (2007) summarizes trends throughout the West. In such books, as I explain in later chapters, decreases in individual beliefs and practices are largely attributed to a 'cultural revolution' that occurred at the time, and the explanations offered are typically restricted to specific contexts, such as Europe or America.

Another response to the data on religious decline from the 1960s has been the re-invigoration of classical secularization theory. Addressing the perceived inadequacies of rational-choice theories, and armed with fresh evidence, several scholars have returned to and updated the inherited model. Foremost among these is Steve Bruce and his book *Secularization: In Defence of an Unfashionable Theory* (2011), an update of his most significant work on the topic, *God is Dead* (2002) (others include Voas 2008). Bruce would in all likelihood resist the idea that we are witnessing a 'comeback' for secularization theory – his commitment and belief in the theory have been unwavering.

Like *God is Dead* (2002), *Secularization: In Defence of An Unfashionable Theory* (2011) has two major aims. It is a re-affirmation of modernity's secularizing impact on religion – as expressed in 'classical' secularization theory – and a riposte to the critics of the theory.

The evidence to substantiate these propositions is presented in the book, and as with social historians Brown (2009) and McLeod (2007), he draws on the latest data showing major decline from the 1960s, most notably in Britain. The impact of secularization is seen as biting most decisively from the 1960s. However, unlike Brown and McLeod, Bruce sees this as the culmination of processes that unfolded across a much longer time frame, and as a direct result of aspects of modernization, e.g. differentiation, individualism, among other factors (see also Voas 2008; Bruce and Glendinning 2010). I will explain this more in Chapter 6.

In updating the inherited tradition, Bruce adds several important qualifications to the theory to tackle some of the more pointed criticisms of the inherited tradition. He notes (2011: 3–4): 'The secularization paradigm is an attempt to explain common features of the recent past of modern industrial liberal democracies ... it is an exercise in historical explanation and has no application to the future.' Other nuances in Bruce's arguments should be noted. Bruce argues in both his books that secularization can be retarded or delayed. This occurs in situations where religion *finds work to do other than relating individuals to the supernatural*' (2002: 30, italics in original). For example, if religion is mobilized to defend one's culture against another in any given society, religion will persist. Religious revival is also possible: in situations where there are strong cultural transitions, such as large-scale waves of migration, religion remains a potent force in 'easing the transition between homeland and the new identity' (2002: 34). In sum, Bruce is proposing that secularization is a tendency associated with modernization, which may or may not be countered by forces opposing secularization (Mason et al., 2007: 57).

A roadmap for making sense of religious change

Which of the different, recent theories is correct about apparent *recent* religious decline in the West? Revitalized secularization theory? Social histories of the 1960s? In Chapters 6 and 7 I look in-depth at the data and explore the relative merits of different kinds of explanation.

That said, this kind of decline is one of many religious changes occurring in the West. Other trends include the growth of conservative forms of religion, the persistence of certain kinds of supernatural belief, the growth of religions other than Christianity and the resurgence of religious discourse in politics (all of which are discussed later in this book). In the later iterations of secularization theory, these trends tend to be given short shrift, described as 'retarding factors'. Not all scholars view such trends this way, regarding them as factors creating religious rejuvenation in certain segments of society. From this perspective, secularization is but one of a number of religious trends occurring in Western societies, and these all need to be taken seriously. No one theory can explain such patterns of religious revival. Rather, myriad social factors are at work and all deserve significant treatment. Societies can be secularizing and experiencing religious revival at the same time.

Discussion thus far has been very Western-centric, focusing on theories of religious change in the West. This reflects the fact that sociology's ambit has traditionally been making sense of religious change in modernized societies. Anthropologists of religion, along with sociologists in the developing world, have long studied religious change elsewhere. In recent years, sociologists in the West have also studied patterns of religious change around the globe. Even the most committed secularization theorists concede the secularization paradigm is not suitable to describe religious change outside the West. Steve Bruce (2011: 194) suggests: 'the secularization paradigm offers little clue as to what is now occurring in the rest of the world'. Patterns include the worldwide resurgence of Islam, Buddhism and Hinduism and the blooming of Christianity in Asia, the Pacific and Africa. Helpfully, as will be seen, scholars have supplied various social explanations of these changes.

Scholars too are recognizing that religious change occurs in a global context, across rather than just within borders. For example, the rise of Pentecostal and evangelical churches in the United States impacts on churches throughout the Global South; growing churches in parts of the Global South send missionaries to proselytize in Germany, Britain and Australia; conservative forms of Islam are nurtured in Saudi Arabia and influence many international Muslims making the pilgrimage to Mecca. Here, the globalization paradigm can be useful in making sense of the interconnectedness of recent religious change.

GLOBALIZATION AND RELIGION: THE OLD AND THE NEW

Secularization was the defining motif of the sociology of religion in the 1960s through to the early 1990s. Since then, the discipline's focus has shifted towards understanding what globalization means for religious change. Definitions of globalization abound, each emphasizing the growing 'interconnectedness' of people around the globe. Steger (2009: 15), for example, notes: 'Globalization refers to the expansion and intensification of social relations and consciousness across world-time and world-space.'

Forms of globalization, especially religious globalization, have been around in one form or another for centuries, or even millennia (see Robertson 2003; Steger 2009). (Insofar as religion moved around the 'world' of the ancients.) Religious ideas, beliefs and practices, for example, have long been shared between cultures. Religions have long engaged in missionary activity. The world's largest religion, Christianity, began its first significant phase of growth when a Roman citizen, Saul of Tarsus, spread Christian teaching around the Mediterranean and into Rome. When people have migrated they have taken their religious practices with them, and there established new religious communities. This is why Jewish communities are found throughout Europe, America, Australia and even parts of Africa. What is unique about the present era is the speed, size and scope of these processes of cultural exchange.

Contemporary globalization involves the deepening of economic, cultural and physical ties between many countries, along with the development of a global consciousness. In short, traditional geographic borders have become less constraining than in any other epoch. Specific elements of globalization include:

- *Global capital and global markets.* Countries and their economies become interdependent through new economic arrangements, and no longer have a simple trading relationship. Major Western companies no longer produce goods in the countries where they have their head offices: it is cheaper to produce goods in developing nations. As manufacturing moves offshore, developed nations have economies centered around service and technology rather than manufacturing. Manufactured goods and foodstuffs are increasingly imported from developing nations. Moreover, companies view their market in global terms rather than national terms.

- *Global communication.* Perhaps the aspect of globalization that has the greatest cultural impact, global forms of communication include the Internet, and worldwide newsagencies like Al Jazeera, CNN, BBC and Reuters. These forms of information exchange have enabled the spread of information to occur more rapidly and democratically than in the past. Social networking on the Internet has also quickened the pace of transnational communication, while allowing greater consumer control over media content.

- *Mobility.* Faster and more economic forms of transport have enabled people to have increased exposure to other cultures.

- *Migration.* Aided and abetted by the improvement in transport and communication (Meyer et al. 2011: 240), the migrant experience is different from that of the pre-globalization era. Migration is faster, more people can move, and from a wider range of countries, than in previous eras of great migration (e.g. nineteenth century). At present 3 percent of the world's population live in a country other than that of their birth (King et al. 2010: 13). Recent migration is characterized by greater diversity. According to King et al. (2010: 61) 'over the past 20 or so years human mobility ... has diversified ... today's migrants are more socially and demographically varied, and exhibit an increasing heterogeneity of forms of mobility and reasons for moving'. It is also easier for migrants to maintain contacts with their country of departure, and move back and forth between the two.

What does contemporary globalization – as a set of social processes – mean for religion? There is no general social theory, like secularization theory, summarizing how globalization impacts on religion. Rather, it is something of a 'paradigm or perspective through which processes and their outcomes are analyzed' (Meyer et al. 2011: 244). Simply put, aspects of globalization – rapid transport, better and faster modes of communication, widespread and diverse migration, the development of global consciousness – have transformed aspects of religion.

Examples of such change abound. Pentecostalism and Mormonism, two of the world's largest new religious movements, have spread much further afield than did earlier Christian revival movements, such as the nineteenth-century evangelical revival that swept through America and Britain.

Elsewhere, the religious tapestry of Britain, Canada, Western Europe, the United States and Australia has been transformed in the last few decades by migration from Buddhist, Muslim and Hindu countries in the Global South. In the early 1950s, far fewer migrants came from these places.

Also significant is the development of a global religious consciousness. In the 1960s, a young Muslim living in Syria would not have had much idea about what a Danish cartoonist thought of her religion. By 2005, this was no longer the case and people all around the Muslim world protested vigorously about blasphemous cartoons published in the Danish newspaper *Jyllands-Posten*. Using the Internet, Muslims could see these cartoons for themselves, and unite with other Muslims online to express their outrage. Street protests broke out in countries far from Denmark. A new, and unprecedented, global consciousness of religion now exists. As each of these examples illustrates, any discussion about contemporary religious change *must* take into account processes associated with globalization. I take this approach with the discussion of Christianity, Islam, Hinduism and Buddhism in the chapters that follow.

CONCLUSION

Beginning with Weber and Durkheim, social scientists have sought to make sense of religious change by emphasizing the interconnectedness of religion, culture and society: as society changes, so religion will also change. Few scholars, past or present, disagree with the proposition that prior to the modern era, religion was the organizing motif of Western societies, and was its most important institution, and that this is no longer the case, particularly in Europe, Canada and Australia. What was it about society that produced this transition? For almost a century, scholars believed that aspects of modernization were inimical to religion. In the 1990s, a cohort of American scholars challenged this assumption, and argued supply and demand for religion was a better predictor of religious change, not just in America, but also in Europe. Neither perspective won over its detractors, in part because one model could not explain every country in the West.

The sociological enterprise remains undiminished, and scholars continue to monitor religious change worldwide, and look towards social factors in explaining this change. Scholars are moving away from grand theories of religious change towards more nuanced explanations of religious decline, stability and revival. Moreover, scholars are recognizing the importance of globalization in the dynamics of religious change. Part II of this book takes this piece-by-piece approach to explaining religious change. Prior to this applied analysis, it is necessary to round out Part I of this book with a discussion of social research methods.

Points to ponder

Examine the papers by Stark (1999) and Bruce (2001). What do you think of this scholarly exchange? What difference has globalization made to your life?

Next steps ...

A balanced and thorough account of rational-choice and secularization theories is Detlef Pollack and Daniel Olsen's edited collection, *The Role of Religion in Modern*

Societies (2008). Rob Warner's *Secularization and its Discontents* (2010) is an excellent, in-depth introduction to debates about secularization. Books discussing globalization and religion include Peter Beyer's *Religions in Global Society* (2006) and Robert Wuthnow's *Boundless Faith: The Global Outreach of American Churches* (2009).

Web

The Social Science Research Council (SSRC), has a blog, 'Immanent Frame' http://blogs.ssrc.org/tif/ which discusses religion, secularism, and society.

5

studying contemporary religion: methods and data

After reading this chapter you will:

- understand the different ways social scientists collect data on religion;

- know where and how to access empirical data on religion; and

- be familiar with the requirements for the conduct of ethical research on religion.

In their book *Souls in Transition: The Religious and Spiritual Lives of Emerging Adults* (2009), scholars Christian Smith and Patricia Snell report that 78 percent of Americans aged 18–23 believe in God, 63 percent think God is a 'personal being involved in the life of people today' and 29 percent feel 'extremely or very close to God' (Smith and Snell 2009: 119). A later chapter in the book quotes a young woman, 'Heather', talking about her relationship with God. Heather says: 'God to me is almost like just someone for you, like a friend per se that you can talk to.' These pieces of information were obtained from data collected and analyzed personally by the researchers (in collaboration with others). How many young people did they need to survey in order to work out the proportion of American teens and young adults who believe in God? How were they able to elicit the quote from Heather? Are their findings reliable? Could such a study be conducted in other countries?

This chapter examines how the empirical study of religion proceeds. Discussion begins with an overview of the two ways in which social scientists study religion, namely qualitative and quantitative techniques, and the main characteristics of these approaches. The remainder of the chapter is practical in focus, showing the reader how to access and generate data on religion.

A brief note before beginning: research methods are very important for those interested in the social scientific study of religion. Later chapters of this book include quantitative and qualitative data, so it is important the novice researcher understands how these data were collected. That said, not everyone finds discussion about data necessary, or thinks of themselves as empiricists, and so some readers may wish to skip this chapter.

QUANTITATIVE AND QUALITATIVE APPROACHES TO THE STUDY OF RELIGION: THE BASICS

The empirical study of religion typically follows the broad divide that characterizes the social sciences: quantitative and qualitative approaches. This section introduces the novice researcher to the aims, data-collection methods and ways to present findings for each of these approaches. The reader already familiar with the basics of these techniques can move to the second section of this chapter, which outlines the various kinds of data on religion that are publicly available.

Quantitative approaches: the search for certainty

Both qualitative and quantitative approaches in the social sciences seek to describe the social world, and understand relationships within the social world. However, they go about this in very different ways.

Quantitative research can assist scholars to answer descriptive questions about the world of religion, such as: What proportion of Americans believe in God? What proportion of Britons are Hindu? Are the current generation of Australian youth less religious than those of earlier generations? Quantitative research also can reliably answer questions about the relationship between religion and other social factors, such as: Are American men more or less likely than American women to believe in God? Are British Hindus more likely to be born outside or inside Britain?

How it works

Quantitative research has a mathematical (statistical) basis for the collection, analysis and reporting of data. To quantify the data, a researcher asks questions of people in a structured way, organizes the answers to these questions into different response categories, assigns each category a numerical value and then uses statistical techniques to analyze and report on these numbers.

Data

Researchers of all kinds collect data. Data are observations about the social world that are generated by the researcher ('data' is a plural word). The data in quantitative social research are *numbers* and numbers are used to represent *words and ideas*. Specific questions put to people, and their answers, are known as **variables** (because the answer to the question varies, e.g. 'yes', 'no', 'maybe'). All the questions and all the numbers used to represent the answers in any given study are called a **data set**.

Here is an example of how quantitative researchers in the field of religion use numbers to represent ideas and words. Scholars of religion often are interested to find out what proportion of the population believes in God. One recent US study, the National Study of Youth and Religion, sought to determine, among many things, the proportion of US teens (aged 13–17) who believe in God (see the case study in this chapter for a full description of this research project).

CASE STUDY

NATIONAL STUDY OF YOUTH AND RELIGION

One of the most detailed, impressive and important studies to have been conducted on personal religiosity is the US National Study of Youth and Religion (NSYR) which commenced in 2001 and concluded its third wave in 2008. This research examines the religious and spiritual lives of American teens and young adults. The extensive published research has examined the factors that influence faith development (or not) among young people and the impact faith has on other aspects of life. It has also provided an in-depth picture of the ways in which American youth are religious, nonreligious and spiritual. The findings of the study are reported later in this book, but of interest here are the methods used in this landmark study (for a full description of the methods, see Smith and Denton 2005; Smith and Snell 2009; Pearce and Denton 2011).

Several methodological features are worth noting. The NSYR is a **panel** study. As far as possible, participants in the research project were studied again at different stages (waves) across the span of the project. The age range of participants in the first wave was 13–17 years old. By the third wave of the project these youth were aged 18–23. The NSYR also had a **mixed methods** approach, combining both a national survey and in-depth interviews. There were three national telephone surveys, and each survey was followed up by a series of in-depth qualitative interviews with selected survey participants.

The national survey component began with the first wave in 2002 and 3290 young Americans took part. In order to obtain this sample, the researchers used a computer system that randomly generated telephone numbers. Each of these numbers was called and the householder was asked if any youth aged 13–17 lived there; if so, the oldest of these was invited to participate in the survey. For the second and third waves of the study the researchers attempted to re-interview as many first-wave participants as possible. The third wave had 2532 returning survey respondents. The full survey questionnaire can be downloaded from the NSYR website (see below).

Once the first survey was completed, the researchers checked their sample against national census data to see how closely it matched the actual population on factors such as gender, age distribution and region of residence. In order to correct any imbalances between the sample and the actual population, the data were **weighted**. This means that the statistical results for any group that is over or underrepresented in the sample is adjusted to reflect its true proportion in the population.

Interviews for the national survey were conducted over the telephone using a CATI system (computer-assisted telephone interviewing). Anyone who has worked in market research would have used such a system. The interviewer reads questions as they appear on the screen and records the respondent's answers into the system. Respondents are taken down different paths depending on their answers. If the young person is a Muslim, then questions reserved for Muslims are put to them.

The in-depth interviews were conducted mainly face-to-face and sought more detailed answers than is possible in the survey. A team of 17 people conducted the interviews and the results are reported extensively in the many books written about this study.

The NSYR was an expensive enterprise and was mounted with the assistance of several major philanthropic bodies in the United States. It is a landmark study and has produced new insights into young people's lives.

Want to know more? Visit the NSYR website for reports and copies of the survey questionnaires: http://www.youthandreligion.org

To carry out this research, they asked a large group of US teens and young adults about their belief in God using the following question:

QUESTION 126: Do you believe in God, or not, or are you unsure? The person asking this question listened to the respondent's answer and then placed the answer into one of four categories:

ANSWER CATEGORIES:

1. Yes

2. No

3. Unsure/don't know

4. Refused

Each of these responses was assigned a number (i.e. yes = 1, no= 2 etc.) and fed into a computer program. Each different number within a variable is called a '**value**'.

Once every person in the study has been asked the question, and the answer assigned a number, the researcher can compute the results. In this case (the belief in God question), they found that 84 percent of their sample of US teens believed in God, 12 percent were unsure and 3 percent did not believe in God (my calculation, using their data). (NB. The figures for belief in God quoted at the start of this chapter come from the same study but refer to young adults aged 18–23.) The calculation and presentation of results for just one variable is called **univariate analysis**. Examples of this kind of analysis include the calculation of frequencies, percentages, and the mean, median and mode for any given variable.

Once this basic information is known, the researcher can dig deeper and begin to explore the relationships between variables. For example, they might ask, 'Are females more likely than males to believe in God?' In answering this question, the researcher is looking to see how differences within one variable might *affect* differences in the other variable. The variable that does the affecting (gender) is called the **independent variable**, and it has two different categories, male and female. The variable that is affected (belief in God) is called the **dependent variable**, and in this case has four different categories (yes, no, unsure and refused). With our example, we are asking whether gender differences are related to different beliefs about God. The researchers in the NSYR found that when it comes to belief in God, girls were significantly more likely than boys to believe in God (87 percent of girls compared to 82 percent of boys). This calculation is called **bivariate analysis** because it makes use of two variables. Techniques used to conduct bivariate analysis include cross-tabulations and correlations.

If it is discovered that being female increases the likelihood that a person believes in God, the researcher will offer various explanations – both empirical and theoretical – as to why this might be the case. The NSYR team, looking at a whole range of religious variables where females were more religious than males, were content to note that this pattern is typical worldwide (Smith and Denton 2005: 277). Some of these reasons are discussed in Chapter 11.

A person's gender is one factor that might influence belief in God, but it is almost certainly not the only factor. For example, place of residence, age, socio-economic status, parents' religiosity and frequency of church attendance, among other factors, could all influence whether or not a person believes in God. Statistical techniques are available to assess the relative influence of different social factors on a dependent variable; this is known as **multivariate analysis**. In this kind of analysis, there is a single dependent variable (e.g. belief in God), and multiple independent variables (e.g. age, school-type, religious attendance). Techniques used to conduct this kind of analysis include multiple regression and logistic regression. Such analysis is found in major religion journals such as the *Journal for the Scientific Study of Religion*, and the *Sociology of Religion*.

Quantitative scholars of religion collect all kinds of data. Among the most common types are measures of religious affiliation (whether a person belongs to a religious group, e.g. Catholic, Hindu, Buddhist), religious practice (e.g. attendance at services of worship, prayer, reading of sacred scripture) and religious belief (e.g. belief in God, belief in miracles, belief in reincarnation). These kinds of basic data are considered later in this book, but there are many other more complicated and interesting measures of religion. Scholars often will create scales, which are dependent variables that combine several measures of religiosity. There are scales for measuring how religiously orthodox a person is, how religiously committed a person is, and scales that measure a person's concept of God, among others (see Hill and Hood 1999).

Data collection and analysis

Data in quantitative research are collected by means of a survey instrument, also known as a questionnaire. This instrument includes all the questions used in the study, and all participants must be asked questions using the same wording, and must be offered the same range of answers. The questionnaire can be administered by the researcher in a number of ways: face-to-face, over the telephone or via the Internet. The most popular technique at present is via the telephone with the assistance of a computer, known as computer-assisted telephone interviewing (CATI). The researcher calls up the respondent, asks the questions (which are flashed up on the computer screen), and then records the answers directly into the computer.

Analysis is done using statistical software packages such as SPSS, STATA and R. I use SPSS in my own work, but this program is expensive, and requires regular license renewal. This makes the open-source, free R package particularly appealing. R is a little more complicated to use, but it's free. No great mathematical skill is required to use these programs. What is required is an understanding of the various analytical techniques, and their related rules, and skill using the software. These techniques can be readily learned and some books are suggested at the end of this chapter.

Sampling

Data in quantitative research is collected from either a **defined population** (e.g. everyone enrolled in a university course, all the children in a school, every resident in a country) or a portion of a defined population (e.g. US or Australian adults). In either case, every person is asked the same question, and every person's answer is counted. When every person in the population is surveyed, this is called a **census**. Census data are the most accurate of any data because the entire population is counted.

Unless you are a national government it is too costly and complicated to conduct a census on large populations. There is no way, for example, the NSYR team could have questioned every single US teen. In such situations, a segment of the population is studied. When a portion of a population is surveyed, this is called a **sample**. Samples can be obtained using **probability** or **non-probability** sampling methods. This difference between these sampling methods is extremely important.

To create a probability sample, every member of the population must have an equal chance of being selected to participate. An example of this is the random selection of 1000 names from a telephone book. The researcher would calculate how many names are in the book, and then devise a system for ensuring that every single person in the book has an equal chance of being selected. This might involve numbering the book from beginning to end, then using a computer program to randomly select participants' numbers.

A non-probability sample involves selecting anyone who is able to be selected conveniently. This means that all the members of a population do not have an equal chance of being selected. An example of this would be the researcher selecting the first 100 names to appear in the telephone book. The rest of the population had no chance of being selected.

If a probability sample is used in a survey, the findings can be mathematically generalized to the wider population from which the sample was drawn. Provided the sample is large enough, these generalizations are theoretically very accurate. (These determinations have been made by mathematicians who work in the field of probability theory.) Well-devised probability samples are known as **representative** samples because they mathematically represent the larger population.

Findings done from analysis of a probability sample are called **estimates**. Remarkably, the responses to any given question from a probability sample of around 1500 people can be generalized to a population of millions with an accuracy of about 2.5 percent on either side of the estimate. A larger sample is needed for estimates to have that level of accuracy if bivariate or multivariate analysis is to be used.

Findings from a non-probability sample cannot be mathematically generalized to a larger population. If an undergraduate psychology class were surveyed, there is no mathematical basis to suggest the findings would be representative of the entire population of psychology undergraduates worldwide. That said, a huge non-probability sample – say 10,000 conveniently selected English teenagers – while not strictly *mathematically* generalizable to the whole teenage population, is still large enough that the researcher could convincingly argue that it is representative of that population. When looking at findings from a survey it is extremely important to check whether the study had a probability or non-probability sample, the sample size, and the non-response rate (the people asked to participate in the study who refused to do so).

Presentation of findings

Quantitative data are usually presented in tables, charts and graphs. Examples in this book can be found in Chapters 6, 7 and 8.

Qualitative approaches: the search for meanings

We have seen that quantitative approaches are centered on numbers. With qualitative research, there is not a number in sight. Qualitative methods have a different way of describing and understanding the social world.

Returning to the example used above, belief in God, we already know the proportion of US teens who say they believe in God. But how do they *understand*

God? As a type of person? Gendered? All-powerful? Interventionist? A higher being? Qualitative methods can help scholars understand the meanings people attach to religious beliefs, practices and affiliations.

How it works

While quantitative studies are concerned with the measurement and causal explanation of religious matters using statistical techniques, a different type of analysis is undertaken when employing qualitative methods. Qualitative techniques have a meaning-centered basis, and are more concerned with understanding subjective human experiences. The aim is to understand what different aspects of religion mean to people, how they make sense of these, and the context in which these meanings are produced.

Data

Whereas the data in quantitative research is structured and numeric, in qualitative research it is unstructured, and the focus is on language and meanings rather than numbers. The data that are used include transcripts of people's words, audio and video recordings, photos and pictures. Data can be collected *in situ*, which involves watching and recording human interaction (sometimes participating too). Data can also be collected during interviews and focus group meetings. Sometimes these data collection methods are combined. Hood and Williamson's (2008) ground-breaking study of Appalachian snake-handling churches involved both videotaping snake handling and in-depth interviews with church members.

Data are analyzed in a more impressionistic, subjective fashion, but qualitative researchers strive for rigor in their analysis. This might include coding data, which involves looking for recurring themes and sorting material accordingly. Qualitative analysis software programs, like NVivo, can assist in qualitative analysis by looking for strings of words and then allowing the researcher to code these phrases into different categories.

Data collection

The data-collection techniques used in qualitative research include in-depth, face-to-face interviews (both structured and unstructured), telephone interviews, email interviews, open-ended responses to surveys, visual material created by the research participants (drawings, charts), and verbal responses to visual stimuli. The researcher may also engage in observation, or participant observation, and take photos, videos or field notes.

The use of these methods results in sets of data that are substantially richer in their descriptiveness compared to the more conventional survey approach. There is no computation or mathematical assessment of this data (the data are more free-form); the focus is on the meanings people have about their experiences, feelings and beliefs.

Sampling

If the qualitative study involves studying a group of people, researchers usually deploy a **purposive sample**. People are selected on the basis that they can provide information about the research problem under investigation. Data from a purposive sample is not statistically generalizable to a wider population, but it may be indicative of what the wider population thinks, believes and how they act. There is no set number required for a purposive sample, but researchers often decide on a sample size by considering the parameters of the broader population that is being studied. To understand and be able to make reasonable claims about a large, diffuse and dispersed population a substantial sample is required (e.g. a project examining the beliefs and practices of US teens). Due consideration must be given in the sample to race, gender and geographical differences. Researchers in the first wave of the NSYR interviewed more than 250 teens face-to-face. They felt this gave them sufficient qualitative insight into the religious and spiritual lives of US teens. If the study were concentrating on a much smaller population, such as American snake-handling Pentecostals, a correspondingly smaller sample is required. If an event is being studied, for example, a pilgrimage to a holy place, an observer needs to collect enough material and to participate in the event in order to feel satisfied they have properly understood what is taking place.

Presentation of findings

This usually involves the publication of excerpts of interview transcripts, and photos, if relevant. This book makes use of qualitative data to illustrate various arguments, and examples of original photos and interview material can be found in later chapters.

So which is best? Qualitative or quantitative? The selection of one method or the other depends on the problem the investigator is researching. Blending methods has many advantages. I recently conducted a study of Australians' beliefs about the afterlife (see Singleton 2012, 2013). I was particularly interested to see if once-dominant, traditional views of heaven as a place of communion with God had been supplanted by more 'fashionable' ideas, such as the belief in reincarnation. In addressing the research problem, I wanted to make authoritative claims about the population as a whole, but also to understand what particular beliefs meant to people. I began with survey data, and using a representative data set, calculated national patterns of belief in the afterlife. It was surprising to discover how many people believed in reincarnation. This warranted further investigation – what did people *mean* when they said they believed in reincarnation? And how did they come to hold such beliefs? I needed qualitative material to explore the variety and character of afterlife belief. To that end, I conducted more than 50 face-to-face interviews. The judicious use of mixed methods provided a more satisfactory investigation of the problem at hand. Having discussed the basics of these methods, attention now turns to do-it-yourself (DIY) research.

DIY RESEARCH: QUANTITATIVE STUDIES IN RELIGION

Given the size and cost of conducting large-scale survey research, getting hold of national-level statistics might seem like a bridge too far for the average researcher, but there are plenty of data out there if you know where to look. There are several kinds of quantitative data in the study of religion, all of which are publicly available. These are:

1. census data for specific countries;

2. cross-national and national surveys with religion questions; and

3. major religion surveys and opinion polls.

These data are available to scholars and students as a **secondary source** and consist of findings published in journals, websites and reports or data sets that are available for a researcher to download and analyze. This section presents an overview of these data sources.

Census data for specific countries

A census is the collection of data from every member of a defined population. It is not a sample, because every member is counted, whereas a sample involves counting a segment of the population. The population can be of any size – every person enrolled in a university subject, or every person living in the UK. The most common kind of census used in the study of religion is a national census. Typically, a census is conducted at regular intervals (every five or ten years). This enables the mapping of various demographic changes over time: how much a population is increasing or decreasing, patterns of ageing, or changes in ethnic composition.

English-speaking countries that ask a religion question in their census include Australia, Ireland, New Zealand, Papua New Guinea, England, Wales and Scotland. Unfortunately the United States law does not allow a census question to be asked about religion. Great Britain collected data on religion for the first time in 2001, while Australia has been collecting data on religion since the first national census in 1901 (even longer for some states). Ireland has data dating back to 1881.

Census data are very reliable, as almost every member of the population is counted. Of course, people may not answer questions truthfully, but the kinds of sampling errors found in surveys are not an issue with a census. Census data in the countries noted above are collected by respondents completing a paper form, or in some cases, online.

The censuses in Australia, Ireland, New Zealand and the United Kingdom ask only about religious affiliation. Religious affiliation refers to whether or not a person identifies as 'belonging' to a religious group. For example, the 2011 census questionnaire used in England asked: 'What is your religion?' and offered 'tick-a-box' categories, covering the major world religions (e.g. Christian, Jewish, Muslim etc.), those with 'no religion' and 'any other religion' where people could record their own response. (Famously, thousands of people in the 2001 UK census noted their religion as 'Jedi', a reference to the mythical religion of the *Star Wars* films). Similarly, the 2011 Australian Census asked 'What is [your] religion?' Australians have 11 categories they can tick, including several Christian denominations, major world religions, other (an open category) and no religion. The religion question is optional, but those who do not respond are still counted and assigned into the 'inadequately described/not stated' category. The Australian Bureau of Statistics does not report publicly on the kinds of responses people record in the 'other' category, but in 2006 there were thousands who noted their religion as Jedi.

People assign themselves to one group or another based on personal preference. Data on religious affiliation cannot tell us about the meaning or importance of these ties, or even about how religious a person might be (this is better measured by considering religious practice and belief). We know that the number of people who regularly attend religious services is far lower than the number of those identifying with a religion (see Hadaway et al., 1993). Nonetheless, census data on religious affiliation is useful in several major ways, as we will see in the next chapter.

In any given census year, researchers can determine national patterns of religious affiliation. Because the census also collects data on a range of other demographic and economic variables, analysis can also be conducted to establish a profile of various religious groups or to determine the relationship between social factors and religious identification. Longitudinal census data also can provide an accurate picture of religious change, particularly when data have been collected across a long period of time.

There are limitations with census data. Most importantly, only one question on religion is asked and thus only a limited picture of religion can be constructed for any given country. The other limitation is that only a few countries collect religion information in their census, so widespread cross-national comparison of census data is not possible. These limitations can be overcome through the use of other kinds of surveys.

Census data availability

Table 5.1 shows where and what kind of census data on religion are available. At each website it is necessary to search for data from different census years (e.g. choose either the England census from 2001 or 2011).

Table 5.1 Various national census programs that have data on religious identification

Country	Census website	Features
Australia	www.abs.gov.au/census	Follow links for data on religion 1901–2011; conduct analysis online for 2006 and 2011 censuses
Canada	www.statcan.gc.ca/start-debut-eng.html	Follow links for census data on religion 1871–2011
Ireland	www.cso.ie/en/census	Follow links for data on religion 1881–2011
New Zealand	www.stats.govt.nz/Census.aspx	Follow links for data on religion 1996–2013
England and Wales	www.ons.gov.uk	Follow links for data on religion from 2001 and 2011 censuses
Scotland	www.scotlandscensus.gov.uk/en/	Follow links for data on religion from 2011 census

Cross-national and national surveys with religion questions

Although less reliable than a census in terms of accuracy, surveys are a better source of data about a wider range of religious items. Many surveys conducted ask up to a dozen questions about religion, but the main focus of the survey is not religion per se. These are either cross-national (comparison between countries) or national (data for just one country) surveys. With any survey, it is always important to check several things about how the data were collected: Is it a random sample? Is the sample of sufficient size for accurate estimates to be made? What is the non-response rate? Beyond this, individual surveys have strengths and weaknesses. Below is a discussion of various surveys that feature a good range of religion questions.

Cross-national survey programs

There are several major cross-national survey programs that ask religion questions, among a range of other topics. Cross-national survey programs collect data from representative national samples in many different countries, but use the same questions. This allows for ready comparison between countries.

The major programs are the World Values Survey (WVS), the International Social Survey Programme (ISSP) and the European Social Survey (ESS).

The **WVS** (which began as the European Values Survey) is a recurring survey program that has been conducted in 97 countries. To date, six waves have been completed (first wave was 1981–2, most recent was 2011–12). Not all countries have been included in each wave. The surveys are administered by a local team of researchers, using questions asked worldwide about attitudes and values, as well as a few on religious life. The last wave included questions on **religious affiliation**, **religious practice** (attendance at services of worship, frequency of prayer) and **religious salience** (the importance of God in daily life). The data are able to be used for cross-national and longitudinal comparison. The sample sizes tend to be small for various countries (in the vicinity of 1000) so the margin of error around various estimates needs to be noted.

The **ISSP** is mainly focused on Europe, but takes in countries in North America, South America, Asia and Oceania. Different research organizations in individual countries add ISSP modules to their own survey programs (for example the British Social Attitudes Survey and the Australian Survey of Social Attitudes regularly include ISSP modules). Modules on religion have featured in 1991, 1998 and 2008. The 2008 module asked about **attitudes towards religions, religious affiliation, religious** and **spiritual beliefs** (belief in God, nirvana, reincarnation), **religious practice** and **religious salience**. The range of religion data collected in the ISSP is broader than that of the WVS. The data lend themselves to cross-national and longitudinal comparison.

The **ESS** was started in 2001 and several waves have been conducted since then. It covers 30 European countries, so its scope is broad. The survey asked about **religious affiliation, religious attendance** and **importance of religion to the individual**. The data lend themselves to cross-national and longitudinal comparison.

Table 5.2 provides information about where to access data from these three programs.

When downloading data sets, it is important that all accompanying material (dealing with sampling, weights, fair use etc.) is downloaded and read.

Table 5.2   Cross-national survey programs that have data on religion

Survey	Website	Features
World Values Survey (WVS)	www.worldvaluessurvey. org	Online analysis available; links for downloading full data set for use in SPSS, STATA etc.
International Social Survey Programme (ISSP)	www.issp.org	Online analysis available; links for downloading full data set for use in SPSS, STATA etc.
European Social Survey (ESS)	www.europeansocial survey.org	Online analysis available; links for downloading full data set for use in SPSS, STATA etc.

National surveys

Obviously, data for individual countries can be readily accessed via the ESS, WVS and the ISSP surveys (just select the country of choice and filter the rest). If one is seeking specific data for a specific country, it is also valuable to visit the website for country-based survey programs (some of these participate in cross-national programs, others do not). Major ongoing research studies (English-speaking nations) that regularly feature religion questions are listed in Table 5.3.

Table 5.3   National survey programs that have data on religion

Country/survey	Website	Features
Australia – Australian Survey of Social Attitudes (AuSSA)	http://aussa.anu.edu. au	Links for downloading full data set for use in SPSS, STATA etc. Registration required to use
Great Britain – British Social Attitudes Survey (BSA)	www.britsocat.com/ Home	Links for downloading full data set for use in SPSS, STATA etc. Registration required to use
USA – General Social Survey (GSS)	www3.norc.org/ GSS+Website	Links for downloading full data set for use in SPSS, STATA etc. Registration required to use
Canada – National Household Survey (NHS)	www12.statcan.gc.ca/ NHS-ENM/index-eng. cfm	Links to reports

Opinion polls (short surveys with representative samples) are conducted regularly around the world and sometimes feature religion questions. These are usually commissioned by media companies who report the findings on TV and in newspapers but do not make the data available to other researchers. Organizations like Ipsos Mori, AC Nielson and Gallup sometimes publish findings on their websites.

Major religion surveys

Arguably the best resource for empirical data on religion are studies that are focused directly on religion. These ask a greater range of questions about religious identification, belief and practice. The largest of these have been done in the United States (where funding is readily available for religion surveys). Major ones are listed in Table 5.4.

Table 5.4   Major US religion surveys with downloadable data sets

Survey	Population surveyed, year/s	Data available from
American Religious Identification Survey (ARIS)	US adults; three waves 1990, 2001, 2008	http://commons.trincoll.edu/aris/. Follow links to download data for 1990 and 2001 waves. Various reports available for all three waves.
PEW Forum US Religious Landscape Survey	US adults; 2008	www.pewforum.org/US-Religious-Landscape-Survey-Resources.aspx. Various reports available.
National Study of Youth & Religion (NSYR)	US teens and young adults; three waves 2002, 2005, 2008	www.youthandreligion.org has information about the surveys and publications (several books, reports). Go to: www.thearda.com/Archive/NSYR.asp for data sets.
Baylor Religion Surveys	US adults; three waves 2005, 2007, 2010	Go to www.thearda.com/Archive/NatBaylor.asp for data sets from first two waves

There are other good sources of facts and figures on religious matters. Highly recommended is the Pew Research Center's Forum on Religion and Public Life, www.pewforum.org, which has excellent data and reports on world religions, global religious trends, and religion and politics, among other things. (In this book, I make considerable use of reports produced by the Pew Research Center's Forum on Religion and Public Life. For the sake of brevity, I will refer to the organization as the Pew Forum. In the bibliography, however, these reports are listed using the full name.) Another excellent source of information on religious demography is Todd Johnson and Brian Grim's *The World's Religions in Figures: An Introduction to International Religious Demography* (2013).

DIY RESEARCH: QUALITATIVE STUDIES IN RELIGION

Very little qualitative data in religion are released to the public, or even shared among communities of scholars. This is often because the data are too specific, or that releasing the material might give away too much about the participants and lead to their being identified. To that end, the researcher seeking qualitative material almost always has to obtain it personally. Many books and university courses are available that cover every aspect of qualitative research, including study design, sampling, data collection and analysis. Some helpful books are noted at the end of this chapter.

There are some issues which need to be considered when doing qualitative research in the study of religion. If the researcher is conducting fieldwork or participation observation, or asking questions in an in-depth interview, it is most likely to relate to something about which people are protective or private. People take their religion seriously! To that end, research must be conducted with respect for the subjects.

A good example is a project I set for my sociology of religion students. I send them into the community to study the rituals enacted in different services of worship. There are several things I ask students to do in order to allow those being studied to go about their business in peace. Most importantly, observers need to be sensitive to the context in which they are studying. I advise students to be aware of and observe dress codes and seating arrangements – some religions seat men and women separately, or require members to wear particular garments or hats. To be allowed into a service of worship might involve adhering to these rules. I also tell students to take mental notes rather than jotting everything down, and to avoid talking during the service. Being discreet is important.

Attending a service might also require participation. I leave it up to students to decide how much they want to participate, but also to be aware of the rules that govern participation, and to participate only as appropriate. For example, if they are attending a Catholic Mass, but are not Catholics, it is inappropriate to take Holy Communion.

Participant observation is a two-way street. A researcher will have thoughts and feelings about participating in something that they may not agree with or support. This also has to be considered. Students might attend a Pentecostal service, in which the whole congregation is expected to sing loudly, sway and clap. Some student observers find it awkward to participate, so I encourage them to stay seated and quiet.

In other situations students are really keen to embrace the experiential part of a religious service, such as the students who go to a Spiritualist church and allow a medium to contact their deceased relatives. In each situation, it is important that the researcher not express private thoughts without first being asked to do so and to participate only to the extent they feel comfortable.

Almost all research conducted by students and professional scholars is governed by a code of ethics and researchers usually need to obtain ethical approval (for example, from a university ethics committee) prior to the conduct of research. Furthermore, consulting a code of ethical conduct is an excellent way for researchers to ground themselves in the requirements for conducting research on religion. I recommend the *Australian Code for the Responsible Conduct of Research*, a document which covers every aspect of the research project. This is available at: http://www.nhmrc.gov.au/guidelines/publications/r39.

This chapter concludes Part I of this book. Part II makes use of the theoretical and methodological insights discussed in this and the previous chapters in order to present a dynamic account and explanation of religious change around the world. This journey begins in so-called 'post-Christian' nations.

Points to ponder

Imagine you were asked to participate in a study that sought your understanding of what happens after you die. What expectations would you have of the researcher? Organize a survey that examines the religious and spiritual beliefs of your university class. What kinds of questions would you need to ask in order to create a religious profile of each respondent?

Next steps ...

A good general introduction to social science methods is Bernard Russell's *Social Research Methods: Qualitative and Quantitative Approaches* (2012). A very helpful, short guide on how to interpret data is Peter Nardi's *Interpreting Data: A Guide to Understanding Research* (2006). Julie Pallant's *SPSS Survival Manual* (2010) is the most accessible 'how-to' SPSS guide I have seen. A book that usefully discusses ethical research is Joan Sieber and Martin Tolich's *Planning Ethically Responsible Research* (2012). The monumental *Measures in Religiosity* by Peter Hill and Ralph Hood (1999) is a must-have for the advanced researcher looking to conduct original survey research on religious topics. A journal with helpful and interesting articles on conducting religious research is *Fieldwork in Religion*, www.equinoxpub.com/FIR.

Web

The University of Kent has a website which focuses on research on religion: http://www.kent.ac.uk/religionmethods/index.html.

part two

winds of change: religion and spirituality in a globalized world

6

post-christian nations? christianity's decline in great britain, australia and canada

After reading this chapter you will:

- have explored data showing religious decline in Great Britain, Canada and Australia;

- be introduced to competing explanations for such patterns, including contemporary secularization theories; and

- be aware of other religious trends in these countries.

How do you imagine your funeral? A church service which follows a traditional, Christian funeral liturgy (order of service)? Or something completely different? A ceremony held in a funeral home, with no obvious religious symbolism or content, and where proceedings are directed by a civil celebrant? In lieu of a sermon, will there be a DVD presentation of photos of your life, set to one of your favorite tunes? Might friends and family be invited to stand up and share their favorite stories about you? Or, because of your family's background, will you be 'farewelled' according to the customs of a religion such as Islam, Hinduism or Buddhism?

Funeral services in Great Britain, Australia and Canada traditionally have been the preserve of the Christian church. Indeed, the church was the place where most people formally and ritually celebrated life's most important rites of passages; birth, death and marriage. Increasingly, however, people are turning elsewhere to mark these significant events.

A recent magazine article described modern funeral trends in Australia (Pryor 2012). The article described how funerals now are held mainly in funeral homes and every aspect of the service is managed professionally by a funeral company (usually a multinational company). The ceremonies are designed to be uniquely personal, and as a celebration of a life. Most services are presided over by civil celebrants. The article described a service held at a funeral home to commemorate the death of one partner of a same-sex couple, where guests were presented with fronds from the couple's favorite tree fern. The ceremony featured a DVD about the deceased's life, along with a breathing and meditation session (Pryor 2012: 31).

Recently I interviewed some clergy and civil celebrants and asked them about the character of the funeral services they conducted (see Singleton 2012). I was told that funerals, even for highly religious people, now are mainly about commemoration of the deceased. When addressing the mourners, celebrants do not dwell on matters of faith, salvation or the afterlife. One Baptist minister told me about his involvement in services managed by funeral companies and staged in funeral homes. He said:

> [in funeral homes] There's no such thing as a Christian funeral anymore, it is a secular service with a few Christian prayers and words tacked on so people are quite happy, 'You're Christian, you're Baptist, fine, do your Baptist bits but it has to be done in an hour so we can get through to the next one.' They're all run by funeral directors. In the end, the church, or religious community or family aren't the primary brokers of the process anymore.

Some clergy are not happy about the marginalization of the church from funerals. An outspoken Anglican archbishop recently gave a talk in which he railed against the 'vulgar egotism' and 'deadly individualism' of personally tailored funerals (Pryor 2012: 31). He said, 'All seems designed to avoid the truth that the person is gone, that death is horrible, that bodies turn to dust, that the person has not one chance in hell of avoiding hell based on the quality of their lives' (Pryor 2012: 31). It is not likely that many Australians would want a funeral that dwelt excessively on the Christian view of death, judgment, salvation and hell. Society, it seems, has moved on from such themes. Funerals now are largely a secular celebration of life, rather than a celebration of faith. (For an excellent account of the changing nature of funerals, see Walter 1996.)

The Christian church's diminished role in rites of passage is indicative of a significant drift away from Christianity in Great Britain, Australia, Canada and other parts of Western Europe. Societies once dominated by Christian symbols, rituals and institutions are now described regularly as 'post-Christian' (e.g. Hunt 2004; Bauzon 2008) or 'secular' societies. How did such a change come about?

Part I of this book described how earlier generations of sociologists, from Weber to Berger, thought they were witnessing the slow, steady decline of Christianity in modernizing societies, especially Western Europe. This was the accepted sociological orthodoxy until it was challenged in the 1990s by American 'rational choice' scholars, particularly Rodney Stark (1999), who insisted that religious participation had been low for centuries in Western Europe. He and his colleagues argued this low demand for religion was the product of a depressed religious marketplace. However, the data supporting the idea of a religious market was equivocal at best, and Stark's assertion about continuously low rates of religious participation in Europe was refuted by other scholars. Critics concluded that the religious economies model could not explain effectively patterns of European religion. Thus, by the turn of the twenty-first century, attempts to sustain grand sociological theories of religious change – ones that could explain global patterns – were increasingly problematic.

Recently, data on religion have improved and these show a very clear pattern; in Britain, Australia and Canada, levels of religious affiliation, attendance and belief have dropped markedly since the 1960s. This trend has prompted a qualified return of theories and explanations for religious decline. This time, analysis examines closely the cultural and historical circumstances of particular societies. As foreshadowed in Chapter 4, two explanations for the decline in Christianity in Great Britain, Australia, Canada and other parts of Western Europe will be presented. These are socio-historical accounts which point to a 'cultural revolution' in the 1960s as having a deleterious effect on Christianity, and revitalized secularization theories which argue that present trends are the inevitable outcome of centuries of modernization.

To be sure, the 'decline of Christendom' is not the only significant religious change to have occurred in post-Christian societies (the use of this phrase does not imply that Christianity will disappear in these countries, rather it is a convenient term to refer to countries that have a similar trajectory of recent Christian decline). Pentecostal and evangelical congregations have attracted new members, while Islam, Buddhism and Hinduism have also grown significantly. Arguably, none of these compares in magnitude to the decline of Christianity in traditionally Christian countries.

POST-WAR RELIGION IN GREAT BRITAIN

Until fairly recently, church records of membership, marriages and baptisms were the main data sources used by sociologists to measure religious change across a long period of time (Bruce 2001; McLeod 2007). This data, however, did not always capture the opinions and behavior of the entire population. Now, more representative and complete data are available via the national census, and various national and church life surveys (see Chapter 5). This section uses these data to examine changing patterns of religious affiliation, attendance and belief in Great Britain. In the analysis that follows, particular attention is given to changes *post the 1960s*. The argument is not that this was the beginning of the decline (some scholars, as will be seen, believe this to be the case). Rather the focus of analysis is the 1960s to the present day and is more concerned with personal religious behavior than religion's involvement in the public sphere, as the former can be more readily quantified and measured.

Recent religious affiliation, attendance and belief in Great Britain

Religious affiliation

Examining longitudinal data on religious affiliation is one of the key ways to measure religious change. Voas and Crockett (2005: 18) note, 'Declared affiliation is a poor measure of religiosity in absolute terms – many British people identify themselves as "Christian" or "Anglican" or "Catholic" despite having no real connection with any church – but it is a useful indicator when examining change over time.' Religious affiliation refers to whether or not a person identifies as 'belonging' to a religious group.

Beginning in 2001, the census in Great Britain has been collecting data on religious affiliation. (The following discussion includes only England and Wales, as the 2011 census data released from the UK Office of National Statistics included only these two countries. Scotland is releasing its data separately.) In 2001, 71.5 percent of the population in England and Wales identified with a Christian denomination. This decreased significantly in the decade to 2011. A summary is presented in Figure 6.1.

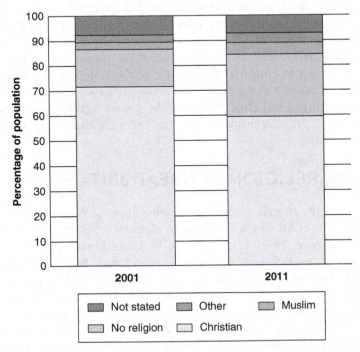

Figure 6.1   Change in religious affiliation, 2001–2011, England and Wales
Data Source: Office for National Statistics (2010: 4)

Three major trends are worth noting. Between 2001 and 2011 there has been:

- A *substantial increase* in the proportion of the population declaring no religious affiliation, from 14.8 to 25.1 percent;

- A *large decrease* in the proportion of the population identifying with the Christian religion, down from 71.5 to 59.3 percent;

- Continuing growth of the Muslim population, from 3 percent of the population to 4.8 percent.

Figure 6.1 shows percentages only, and this is a good way to see the size of groups relative to the population as a whole. The majority of people in England and Wales still identifies with a Christian denomination, but this is a shrinking majority. The next-largest group is of those who do not identify with a religion, and it is a growing minority, as are Muslims and those who identify with religions apart from Christianity. While the proportion of Muslims, Hindus and other religions is increasing, it still represents only a small proportion of the total population.

The 'no religion' group has grown very rapidly. A way to evaluate effectively the speed and magnitude of change is to calculate how much specific groups have increased or decreased in size between censuses. The England and Wales census data show that the *number* of people with no religion almost doubled in the decade from 2001 to 2011, from 7,709,267 people to 14,097,229, an increase of 83 percent. In the same period, the number of people who identify with a Christian denomination fell from 37,338,486 people to 33,243,175, a decrease of −11 percent. Islam has grown rapidly in the same decade, almost doubling in size from 1,546,626 people to 2,706,066, people, an increase of 75 percent. Simply put, the census data show one of the fastest-growing categories in England and Wales is of those who claim no religious identification.

The decline in the proportion of the population identifying as Christian continues an ongoing trend. Voas and Crockett (2005; see also Crockett and Voas 2006) examined data from different waves of the British Household Panel Survey (BHPS) and the British Social Attitudes Survey (BSA) and found religious affiliation has been in decline since the early 1980s (when their data starts). It is important to keep this trend in mind. Williams et al. (2009), using data from different waves of the European Values Survey (EVS – part of the World Values Survey), also found religious affiliation in Britain has been in decline in recent decades.

Another trend worth noting briefly is to do with church membership (not quite the same as affiliation). The Christian Research Organization in Britain has mapped denominational changes across many decades. It found that while there is a decline in membership with the larger, established denominations, smaller, independent evangelical and Pentecostal churches have grown in membership since the early

2000s (Christian-research.org: NB. full access to data on their website can only be obtained by becoming a member.) (See also Jenkins 2007.)

Religious attendance

Questions about religious attendance are a staple of many national survey programs and a much better measure of how serious people are about their religion. As with the data on religious affiliation, attendance at Christian services in Britain has been in general decline in recent decades. Data from the 2008 BSA (ISSP module) show that 9 percent of the population claim to attend services of worship weekly or more often. Fifty-one percent of the population *never* attend a religious service, while a further 11 percent attend once a year, or less than once a year (my calculations). (It should also be remembered that people routinely overestimate their level of religious attendance.) The low rates of attendance indicate that many of those who affiliate with a Christian denomination have only a nominal association.

Scholars, using surveys such as the WVS and the BSA have detected a decline in attendance in recent decades (Crockett and Voas 2006; Williams et al. 2009; Norris and Inglehart 2011). Voas and Crockett (2005: 17) note, 'it is universally accepted that churchgoing has been declining for at least four decades'.

Religious belief

Religious belief also appears to be in general decline. Crockett and Voas (2006: 567) note: 'The evidence also points to an erosion in religious belief over the past several decades.' Certainly, in the 1990s, an idea that had considerable cachet among scholars and other interested observers was that of 'belief without belonging' (BWB), proposed by eminent British sociologist, Grace Davie (Davie 1990, 1994). This refers to the 'persistence of [belief in] the sacred in contemporary society despite the undeniable decline in churchgoing' (Davie 1994: 94). Davie noted that although measures of religious belief, such as belief in God, had declined in the decades up until the early 1990s, they had done so at a *slower* rate than measures of religious affiliation (Davie 1990: 455). Davie argued there was a persistence of nominal religious belief in the absence of regular church attendance.

In two journal articles, Voas and Crockett (2005; see also Crockett and Voas 2006) explore the magnitude and character of BWB in Britain. Based on a sophisticated statistical analysis, they argue:

> The only form of BWB that is as pervasive as Davie suggests is a vague willingness to suppose that 'there's something out there', accompanied by an unsurprising disinclination to spend any time and effort worshipping whatever that might be. As soon as one focuses on belief in the teachings of the church, one finds belonging to go with it. (Crockett and Voas 2005:24)

This is an important point: for the majority of people, religious beliefs are perhaps just religious opinions and may not make that much difference to everyday life (see Mason et al. 2007, 2010).

People in Great Britain have not turned away completely from supernatural belief. Quasi-religious and other folk beliefs – reincarnation, clairvoyance, belief in a higher power – are held by a reasonable proportion of the population (Voas 2009: 161). However, as Davie notes, 'the content of belief is drifting further and further from the Christian norm' (cited in Brown 2009: 5). And again, these beliefs, in most cases, do not make much difference to a person's everyday life (Mason et al. 2007).

One further point ought to be mentioned. An important recent finding from British sociologists is that religious decline is generational in character; younger age cohorts are less likely than older age cohorts to attend, affiliate or belong. Crockett and Voas (2006: 581) note:

> Religious decline in twentieth-century Britain was overwhelmingly generational in nature; decade by decade, year by year, each birth cohort was less religious than the one before. Religious affiliation, almost universal among those born at the start of the twentieth century, is found in less than half those born in the 1970s. The falls in regular attendance and in the perceived importance of religious belief [among the young] have been equally striking.

In summary, the data show a drift in Great Britain away from Christian affiliation, orthodox religious belief and regular church attendance. Importantly, studies show that young people are the vanguard of this decline. The population of Great Britain is best characterized now as nominally Christian, with a steadily growing population of people who affiliate with religions apart from Christianity and an even larger and faster-growing group, young people especially, who do not affiliate with any religion at all.

And Western Europe?

Are the broad patterns identified in Britain typical of other parts of Europe? There is considerable diversity in the religious life of countries across Europe (Greeley 2003; Draulans and Halman 2005; Halman and Draulans 2006; Norris and Inglehart 2011). Each country has its own story to tell, and this ought to be taken into account in any analysis.

There are some interesting similarities as well, particularly in Western Europe. Using data from various waves of the World Values Survey (WVS), Norris and Inglehart (2011: 86) find 'Traditional religious beliefs and involvement in institutionalized religion (i) vary considerably from one country to another; and (ii) have steadily declined throughout Western Europe, particularly since the 1960s.'

Sociologist of religion David Voas (2009), used data from the highly reliable European Social Survey (ESS) to search for common patterns in European religion. Based on his analysis, he argues:

> While there are indeed many interesting variations in European religion – countries may be high or low in affiliation, attendance, and belief – there is also a single, inescapable theme. Religion is in decline. Each generation in every country surveyed is less religious than the last, measured by the best available index of religiosity. Although there are some minor differences in the speed of the decline (the most religious countries are changing more quickly than the least religious), the magnitude of the fall in religiosity from the early to the late 20th century has been remarkably constant across the continent. (Voas 2009: 167)

The decline of religion has not necessarily resulted in a rise in the number of 'die hard' atheists. Rather there has been the emergence of what Voas calls 'fuzzy fidelity'. This term describes those who have a loose loyalty towards Christianity: 'They believe in "something out there", pay at least lip service to Christian values, and may be willing to identify with a denomination. They are neither regular churchgoers (now only a small minority of the population in most European countries) nor self-consciously non-religious' (Voas 2009: 161).

Other patterns manifested in Great Britain are also evident throughout Europe. Mainly as a consequence of recent, large-scale immigration, there has been a sharp increase in the number of Muslims living in Europe. Some Christian churches also have been revitalized by the migration of Christians from the developing world (see Jenkins 2007).

There has been a tendency among some scholars to describe Western Europe as an 'exceptional case' in the global religious landscape (see Davie 2002; Berger et al. 2008). However, as Norris and Inglehart (2011: 88) note: 'the erosion of religiosity is not exclusive to Western European nations; regular churchgoing also dropped in the last two decades in affluent Anglo-American nations such as Canada and Australia'. Indeed, as shown in the next two sections, the patterns of decline in Australia and Canada are very similar to those found in Great Britain.

RELIGION IN AUSTRALIA

The first white settlers in Australia (circa 1780s) brought their religious preferences with them from England, Scotland and Ireland. When the various states of Australia became a federation in 1901 the constitution enshrined a separation of church and state. That said, a high proportion of the population affiliated with a Christian denomination in 1901 (96 percent). This eroded across the next 100 years. Can Australia still be thought of as a country of Christians?

Religious affiliation, attendance and belief in Australia

Australia enjoyed something of a 'modest religious boom' in the 1950s (Hilliard 1997: 211). According to Hilliard (1997: 211) 'In the mid-1950s in every denomination all the measurable indices of religious life – church membership, Sunday school enrolments, the number of new congregations, church income and enrolments in theological colleges and seminaries – had gone steadily upwards.' From the mid-1960s onwards, however, this trend was reversed.

Religious affiliation

The best way to map changes in religious affiliation is via data from the Australian census, which has been collected nationwide at regular intervals since 1901. Table 6.1 presents selected census data on religious affiliation from 1901 to 2011 and illustrates many important changes in Australia's religious composition.

Table 6.1 shows the percentage of the population in any given census year which identified with a particular group (e.g. in 2011, 17 percent of the population claimed to be Anglican, 25 percent Catholic, 19 percent 'Other Christian' etc.). Each column contains data for one group or category (e.g. Anglican; Catholic etc.) and each row represents a census year (e.g. 1901, 1993). The most helpful way to make sense of this

Table 6.1   Religious affiliation of Australians 1901–2011 (percentage of the population)

Census year	Religious affiliation						
	Anglican %	Catholic %	Other Christian %	Total Christian (inc. Anglican, Catholic, other Christian) %	Other religions %	No religion %	Not stated/ inadequately described %
1901	40	23	34	96	1	0	2
1933	39	20	28	86	1	0	13
1947	39	21	28	88	1	0	11
1961	35	25	28	88	1	0	11
1971	31	27	28	86	1	7	6
1981	26	26	24	76	1	11	11
1991	24	27	23	74	3	13	11
1996	22	27	22	71	4	17	9
2001	21	27	21	68	5	16	12
2006	19	26	19	64	6	19	11
2011	17	25	19	62	7	22	9

Note: Percentages have been rounded. Percentages in rows may not add to 100 because of rounding. The column 'Total Christian' adds together Anglicans, Catholics and other Christian groups.

Data source: Australian Bureau of Statistics census data for various years.

table is to read down each column and see how various groups and categories have changed between 1901 and 2011. Here is a summary of the major trends:

- In 1901, 96 percent of the population affiliated with a Christian denomination, and by 1971 this was 86 percent. By 2011, only 61 percent identified as Christian;

- The percentage of the population identifying with the largest Protestant denomination, the Anglican Church, has dropped dramatically. In 1971, 31 percent of the population identified as Anglican; in 2011 it was just 17 percent;

- 'Other Christian' groups have declined from 28 percent in 1971 to 19 percent in 2011. More detailed information about specific denominations is not presented in this table, but further analysis shows traditional mainline denominations, including the Presbyterian and Methodist (now Uniting) Churches, have declined since the early 1970s;

- Further analysis (not shown in the table) shows some smaller independent, evangelical and Pentecostal churches and some other conservative denominations and sects have grown in recent decades;

- The proportion of Catholics has remained constant since 1971, when 27 percent of the population identified as Catholic. In 2011, it was 25 percent. Catholics are now the largest Christian denomination in Australia;

- The category 'Other religions' (which includes Muslims, Hindus, Buddhists, and Jews) has grown dramatically since 1971 and now represents 7 percent of the population;

- In 2011 22 percent of the population said they had no religion. In 1901, it was less than 1 percent, and in 1981, 11 percent.

There is also a pronounced age cohort effect evident in the 2011 census. My own analysis of census data shows those aged 40 or older are significantly more likely than those aged under 40 to identify with a Christian denomination, while those aged under 40 are much more likely than those aged over 40 to claim no religious identity.

The main story evident in this table is the decline since the 1970s in affiliation with mainstream Protestant Christianity and the increase in the proportion of those declaring 'no religion'. The majority of the population has always identified as Christian, and this is still the case, but increasing numbers of people do not see this religious identity as important or relevant. If identification is declining, is the same true of religious beliefs and practices?

Religious belief and practice

Several recent national surveys reveal that attendance at religious services in Australia is low. The 2009 *Australian Survey of Social Attitudes* found only an estimated 14 percent attend religious services *nearly weekly* or more often (8 percent attend weekly or more), while 46 percent never attend. Regular weekly attendance is in decline overall, down from about 24 percent of the adult population in 1966 (Mol 1971), and even higher in the 1950s (Kaldor et al. 1999a). There has also be a decline in traditional religious belief since the 1960s (Mason et al. 2007). In summary, the patterns manifested in Australia are very similar to those of Great Britain. As in Britain, younger age cohorts are less likely than those of older age to hold religious beliefs or attend services regularly (Mason et al. 2007: 311).

RELIGION IN CANADA

Religion in Canada is described by scholars as fitting somewhere between Western Europe and the United States; not as decisively secularized as the former, and not as religious as its nearest neighbor (see, for example Warf 2006). Certainly Canada has its own distinctive religious history (see Choquette 2004; Scott 2012). The indigenous peoples of Canada had their own religions. Following white settlement, substantial Protestant and Catholic communities emerged. The French-speaking province of Quebec has been a traditional stronghold of Catholicism, while Protestantism has prevailed elsewhere. That said, the patterns noted above are also evident in Canada. Roger O'Toole (2006: 8) notes: 'Canadian religion exhibits its own characteristic features at the same time as it manifests many of the typical patterns associated with the religious activities of contemporary post-industrial societies.'

Religious affiliation and attendance in Canada

Religious affiliation

Helpfully, reliable data about religious affiliation are available via the Canadian census and the National Household Survey, both administered by Statistics Canada. Table 6.2 illustrates important changes between 1901 and 2011.

Table 6.2 can be read in the same way as Table 6.1. Each column contains data for one group or denomination (e.g. Catholic; United Church of Canada etc.) and each row represents a census year (e.g. 1933, 1941 etc.). The overall proportion of the population identifying with a Christian denomination dropped from 90 percent in 1981 to 67 percent in 2011. The proportion of the population identifying with the Catholic church decreased markedly between 1981 and 2011. In this period, there was also a decrease in the proportion of the population identifying as Protestants, particularly the United Church of Canada, which dropped from 16 percent of the population in 1981 to 6 percent in 2011. The proportion of those with no religious affiliation grew from 7 percent of the population in 1981 to 24 percent in 2011. The pattern of religious change in Canada is almost identical to that of Great Britain and Australia.

Table 6.2   Religious affiliation of Canadians 1931–2011 (percentage of the population)

	Religious affiliation					
Census year	Catholic %	United %	Other Christian %	Total Christian (inc. Anglican, Catholic, other Christian) %	Other religions %	No religion %
1931	40	19	37	96	<1	<1
1941	42	19	35	96	<1	<1
1951	43	20	32	96	<1	<1
1961	46	20	30	96	<1	<1
1971	46	17	28	91	<1	<1
1981	47	16	27	90	3	7
1991	46	12	25	83	4	13
2001	43	10	24	77	6	16
2011	39	6	22	67	8	24

Note: Percentages have been rounded. Percentages in rows may not add to 100 because of rounding. The column 'Total Christian' adds together United, Catholics and other Christian groups. The Catholic group does not include 'Ukrainian Catholic'.

Data source: Statistics Canada census data for various years.

As in Australia and Great Britain, there is an age cohort effect associated with being nonreligious. According to Statistics Canada (2003: 9) in 2001

> people who reported they had no religion tended to be younger than the general population. Almost 40 percent were aged 24 and under, compared with 33 percent of the total population. Their median age was 31 years, below the overall median age of 37 for the general population.

The other major change noted in the table above is the rapid increase in the followers of other religions. Between 1991 and 2001, the numbers (not proportions) of Buddhists grew by 84 percent, Muslims by 129 percent, Sikhs by 89 percent and Hindus also by 89 percent. These groups combined represented 6 percent of the population in 2001.

Religious attendance

Reliable data about religious attendance has been collected for some time in Canada. Drawing on waves of General Social Survey data (GSS), Eagle (2011) finds the proportion of weekly attenders has dropped from 31 percent in 1986 to 18 percent in 2008.

The foregoing analysis reveals strikingly similar trends in several post-industrial countries. The reasons why these changes have taken place is discussed later in this chapter. The next section discusses briefly the fortunes of the Catholic Church in the past few decades.

EXCURSUS: CRISIS IN THE INSTITUTION OF THE CATHOLIC CHURCH?

The state government of Victoria, Australia, conducted recently a 'Parliamentary Inquiry into the Handling of Child Abuse by Religious and other Organizations'. Submissions were heard from the Victoria Police, victims' groups and non-governmental organizations (NGOs). Australia's two highest-ranked Catholic clerics appeared before the inquiry to answer questions. One of the clerics, Cardinal George Pell, 'admitted the Catholic Church had put pedophile priests "above the law", covered up abuse and moved abusers' (Zwartz 2013). Responding to other questions, 'He denied that he was like Pontius Pilate, washing his hands of the abuse problem, or that the $30 million hostel that the Sydney archdiocese had built in Rome with permanent rooms for him was "a palace"' (Zwartz 2013). This inquiry is just one example where the Catholic Church's handling of clergy sexual abuse has been subjected to scrutiny and criticism.

The Second Vatican Council in the 1960s (see case study, Chapter 3) signaled a new, progressive era for the Catholic Church. In the past two decades, however, particularly in Western Europe, Great Britain, North America and Australia, the Church has endured several crises. While affiliation with the Catholic Church has remained fairly steady or shown modest declines, the proportion of people attending Mass regularly has fallen (see Dixon et al. 2007; Jenkins 2007; Eagle 2011; Christian-research.org). Some of the reasons behind this fall are discussed in the next section.

Falling attendance is just one of the issues facing the Catholic Church in the West. Dozens of instances of sexual abuse perpetrated by priests have been reported (see Plante and McChesney 2011), and priests have been defrocked and prosecuted. In early 2013, Pope Benedict XVI surprised many with his sudden resignation, citing age and health-related concerns. Many press outlets circulated a story suggesting he resigned because of an internal Vatican report which detailed corruption within the Church. Either way, his resignation shook many in the Catholic establishment.

Throughout the West, the Catholic Church has also struggled with decreasing numbers of clergy, with fewer men stepping forward to become priests, while the median age of priests is also increasing (see Young 1998; Gautier et al. 2011). Many potential priests are put off by the Church's requirement that priests be celibate. To make up for the shortfall, the Church is increasingly bringing to the West priests from places such as India and Viet Nam. The Church so has far declined to ordain women and has given no indication that the celibacy requirement for priests will be changed. In this regard, the Catholic Church is largely out of step with prevailing social trends in the West. Some former Catholics report that issues such as 'the irrelevance of the Church to life today' and 'the misuse of power and authority in the Church' have been a catalyst for their leaving the Church or for no longer attending Mass (Dixon et al. 2007: vi).

MAKING SENSE OF RECENT RELIGIOUS CHANGE

The foregoing analysis of census and other data shows similar patterns of religious change in Great Britain, Australia and Canada since the 1960s. In summary:

1. An overall decline in affiliation with Christian denominations;

2. Declining religious attendance;

3. An substantial increase in the proportion of those who do not identify with a religion;

4. A small increase in affiliation with some kinds of Christian denominations, particularly evangelical and Pentecostal churches;

5. The growth of Hinduism, Buddhism and Islam.

In this section, a variety of explanations for these patterns will be discussed.

Growing religions: why?

The growth of religions such as Islam, Hinduism, and Buddhism in Britain, Western Europe, Australia and Canada is almost entirely due to migration, and higher birth rates among these groups, and is not because of the conversion of Christians or those with no religion. Canada, Britain and Australia expanded their migration programs in the decades after the 1950s, allowing in more migrants from a more diverse range of countries.

For example, after the Second World War, groups of migrants came to Australia, first from majority Catholic countries like Italy, then Muslim countries such as Lebanon and Turkey. This was followed by migration from Buddhist and Hindu countries (e.g. Viet Nam, China, Sri Lanka, India) (see Bouma 2006). According to Bouma (2006: 56) 'with the increase in their numbers came the establishment of well-organized communities ... these are not just ethnic communities, but religious communities'.

This is true also of Canada in the last few decades, where 'large numbers of new Canadians arrived from many countries in Europe, Asia, Africa, and Latin America' (Choquette 2004: 377). A Statistics Canada report (2003: 8), commenting on the 2001 Census, observes:

> Immigration was a key factor in the increases for all these groups [i.e. Hinduism, Buddhism and Islam]. The proportion of immigrants entering Canada with these religions increased with each new wave of arrivals since the 1960s. Of the 1.8 million new immigrants who came during the 1990s, Muslims accounted for 15%, Hindus almost 7% and Buddhists and Sikhs each about 5%.

In Great Britain, the story is the same, with the growth of Hinduism, Islam, Sikhism and Buddhism all explained by migration (see Dobbs et al. 2006). In Chapters 9 and 10, these patterns are explored in depth.

It is worth mentioning briefly the Christian 'success story' identified above: the growing evangelical and Pentecostal churches. Why have these churches grown when other, mainline Protestant denominations have declined? For the most part, these congregations and denominations also have been boosted by immigration (see Jenkins 2007). For reasons explained in Chapter 8, the kinds of churches prospering in the developing world are typically the same kind growing in Great Britain, Canada and Australia. Newly arrived migrants are disproportionately attracted to these churches rather than to traditional mainline Protestant denominations. Data from various Australian *National Church Life* surveys also show that another source of growth for Pentecostal churches is from people 'switching in' from other Christian denominations, Catholic and Protestant (Kaldor et al. 1999b). That said, *specific* congregations in the mainline churches, especially those in the inner city, have been re-invigorated by large groups of Christian migrants.

Christian decline: why?

The data reviewed above show that church-going in Canada, Britain and Australia is for the most part increasingly confined to a small, ageing proportion of the population. Young people are less likely than older people to attend church, or identify themselves as Christian. How might this be explained? As indicated in Chapter 4, explanations point either to a 'cultural revolution' in the 1960s, or the enduring effects of modernization as the probable causes of Christianity's decline. Both arguments will be presented below.

The death of Christian Britain (and Australia and Canada)?

Writing about Britain, social historian Callum Brown (2009) argues a cultural revolution in the 1960s is the root cause of recent decline. According to Brown (2009: 9), between 1800 and 1963 Britain was a 'highly religious nation', and that appreciable religious decline has happened only recently. He argues Christianity reached something of a high watermark in the 1950s. Brown (2009: 5) finds: 'Between 1945 and 1958 there were surges of British church membership, Sunday school enrolment, Church of England Easter Day communicants, baptisms and religious solemnization of marriage, accompanied by immense popularity for evangelical "revivalist" crusades.'

What contributed to this brief revival? Perhaps people were looking for comfort and security in the wake of the war's devastation, and before that, the grim times of the 1930s economic depression. In the 1950s Britain was recovering slowly from the impact of the war and a new era of consumerism was beginning. Sales of household items such as washing machines and TVs soared. Most significantly, there was a 'baby boom' – a sharp increase in the birth rate – meaning the average family size was growing larger. (Children born between 1946–65 are called Baby Boomers.) Religion seemed like a happy corollary to people's newfound domestic bliss. Then came the 1960s, when according to Brown, 'the death of Christian Britain' began.

In Brown's view, the death of Christian Britain was caused largely by a 'cultural revolution' in the 1960s that shook Britain (and the Western world). Brown (2009: 176) documents the many far-reaching cultural changes of that decade:

In the 1960s, the institutional structures of cultural traditionalism started to crumble in Britain: the ending of the worst excesses of moral censorship (notably after the 1960 trial of *Lady Chatterley's Lover* and the ending in 1968 of the Lord Chamberlain's control over British theatre); the legalization of abortion (1967) and homosexuality (1967), and the granting of easier divorce (1969); the emergence of the women's liberation movement, especially from 1968; the flourishing of youth culture centered on popular music (especially after the emergence of the Beatles in late 1962) and incorporating a range of cultural pursuits and identities (ranging from the widespread use of drugs to the fashion revolution); and the appearance of student rebellion (notably between 1968 and the early 1970s).

In short, 'traditional' values and institutions were under assault. According to Mason et al. (2010: 110), 'The "cultural revolution" which ensued across the West entailed a wholesale rejection of past traditions and the authority derived from them. Religious, civil and parental authority were attacked as oppressive'.

How did the 'cultural revolution' precipitate Christianity's decline? The church of the 1960s was the upholder of traditionalism and morality, and in dynamic and revolutionary times young people – the swelling ranks of Baby Boomers – were no longer interested in tradition. Instead, it was a time when young people started to 'tune in, turn on, and drop out', and engage in experimentation and rebellion. The Boomer generation which came of age in the 1960s and early 1970s turned away from the church.

Scholars suggest other post-1960s social changes have impacted also on church attendance (see Evans and Kelley 2004). It is an indisputable fact that in the early post-war years churches, with their associated sporting clubs and regular dances, played a role in the community that went beyond simply meeting people's religious needs. The church was a place to socialize and meet prospective marriage partners. From the 1960s, social needs could increasingly be met elsewhere, particularly as teens and young adults could now afford cars.

The Boomers were the first generation to turn away en masse from the church. In subsequent decades, the Boomers, *particularly women*, stopped socializing their own children into Christian culture (this is an important part of Brown's argument). Such an explanation appears to account, in part, for the patterns of generational decline identified above. As McLeod (2007: 2) notes '[into the '70s and beyond] there was a serious weakening of the process by which the great majority of children were socialized into membership of a Christian society'.

Callum Brown is not the only historian to consider the dramatic effect of the 1960s on Christianity. Others, including Hugh McLeod in his book, *The Religious*

Crisis of the 1960s (2007), acknowledge the profound effect of 1960s culture on religion, arguing 'In the religious history of the West these years may come to be seen as marking a rupture as profound as that brought about by the Reformation' (McLeod 2007: 1). (To be sure, McLeod argues the time period of this 'rupture' is about 1958–74, what he calls 'the long 1960s'.)

Moreover, Britain was not alone in feeling the effects of the 1960s revolution. Similar patterns occurred in Australia and Canada, where researchers attribute, in part, the recent decline of Christianity among present-day youth to the failure of Boomer parents to pass Christianity on to their children (Mason et al. 2007; Bibby 2009). Eminent Canadian sociologist Reg Bibby (2009: 185) argues, 'Boomers … have not been as inclined as the older generations to hold beliefs or expose their children to religions.' In summary, contemporary youth in Britain, Canada are Australia are being raised in cultures which are decidedly post-Christian or secular.

Revitalized secularization theory: Britain, Western Europe, Canada and Australia

The '1960s cultural revolution' thesis is not the only view of why Christianity is in decline. The recent data have allowed proponents of 'classical' secularization theory the opportunity to restate the fundamental principles of their arguments (see Voas 2008; Bruce and Glendinning 2010; Bruce 2011). The most fully realized articulation of revitalized secularization theory is to be found in Steve Bruce's *Secularization: in Defence of an Unfashionable Theory* (2011).

According to these scholars (whose focus is mainly on Britain), church affiliation and attendance began to decline slowly from the late 1800s, as a corollary of modernization (Voas 2008; Bruce and Glendinning 2010). Until a few decades ago, this decline was incremental rather than rapid. It has accelerated more recently. What hastened the decline? Steve Bruce and Tony Glendinning (2010: 107) agree with Brown that 'much of the [post 1960s] decline of the churches is explained not by adult defection but by a failure to keep children in the faith'. However, they think this stems from 'the disruptive effects of the 1939–45 war on family formation', rather than the 1960s cultural revolution. It was during the war years when families, mothers in particular, struggled to socialize children into the faith, thereby hastening the decline evident in recent decades (see also Voas and Crockett 2005; Crockett and Voas 2006). Bruce and Glendinning note (2010: 108):

> To the extent that the late 1950s and 1960s did see a marked failure of the family transmission of religious commitment, part of the explanation must lie with the parents of the defecting generation. That dating draws our attention to the social dislocation caused by the Second World War.

With the post 1960s decline in attendance and affiliation explained, revitalized secularization theories, like earlier iterations of the theory, point to the centrality of modernization in causing two centuries of religious decline. Bruce and Glendinning (2010: 108) argue:

> the sociological tradition that leads from Karl Marx, Max Weber and Emile Durkheim, via Bryan Wilson and Peter Berger, lists as compound causes [of secularization] the rationalization, religious diversification, and increasing egalitarianism and individualism that have accompanied industrialization, democratization and economic growth … Although one can imagine some sort of threshold effect with these causes, the general assumption is that the declining plausibility of religion (and hence abandonment of the churches) will have been gradual and that at least some symptoms of it will be visible in the nineteenth century.

Another interesting and provocative example of the re-invigoration of the secularization model using the most up-to-date data is Norris and Inglehart's *Sacred and Secular: Religion and Politics Worldwide* (2011). Focusing on a larger number of countries and taking into account recent change, they argue:

> 'modernization' (the process of industrialization, urbanization, and rising levels of education and wealth) greatly weakens the influence of religious institutions in affluent societies, bringing lower rates of attendance at religious services, and making religion subjectively less important in people's lives. (2011: 25)

Modernization achieves this because it brings with it 'existential security' – fewer travails, greater material comfort – and people thus have less need for a 'sacred canopy' in their lives. Those people with a more precarious existence, particularly those living in less secure societies in the developing world, have a heightened need for the comfort and security of religion.

Which of these various explanations is correct? As Mason et al. (2007: 57) observe, there is a tension between explanations of religious change which chronicle the myriad contingent historical factors at work in recent religious decline (e.g. McLeod 2007; Brown 2009) and those which posit more general, longer-term social-structural causes linked to modernization (e.g. Bruce 2011; Norris and Inglehart 2011). Nonetheless, Mason et al. (2007: 57) argue the different types of explanation are the 'fruit of different methods, each of which brings to light a different aspect of reality; and each has its kernel of truth'. At present the former approach is arguably more widely accepted by scholars.

Certainly, there are different views about the causes of recent religious change. However, there is little doubt that while the cultural ascendency of Christianity was challenged in the late nineteenth and early twentieth centuries (see Chapter 4), secular culture began to emerge with vigor in several countries from the 1960s onwards. Historian Hugh McLeod (2000: 289) argues: '[a] fine balance between the forces of religion and secularity remained characteristic of Western Europe until the 1960s.

Only then did the balance tip more decisively in a secular direction'. There are enough similarities between Britain, Australia and Canada (possibly excluding Quebec) to suggest the same, or very similar, kinds of causes and effects are at work.

Others scholars also are thinking creatively about the factors behind religious decline. One example is French sociologist, Danièle Hervieu-Léger, whose work is the subject of this chapter's case study.

DANIÈLE HERVIEU-LÉGER: RELIGION AS A CHAIN OF MEMORY

What do the theorists examined in depth so far – Durkheim, Weber, Marx, Berger, Luckmann, Wilson – have in common? All are white, European men. This bias reflects the state of the sociology of religion up until the late 1960s and early 1970s. Sociology, as with public life generally, was dominated by men. One of the many cultural changes that took place in the 1960s was the emergence of the second wave of feminism (the first wave dates to the early twentieth century when women campaigned for the right to vote in elections). Inspired by books such as Betty Friedan's *The feminine mystique* (1963), women campaigned tirelessly against sexual discrimination in public and private life. Many rights for women were attained, including paid maternity leave, equal pay for equal work, and sexual discrimination legislation.

Since the 1960s, conterminous with the second wave of feminism, women increasingly have been making important contributions to the sociology of religion. Prominent British scholars include Eileen Barker, famous for her work on new religious movements (see Barker 1984), and Grace Davie, one of the foremost scholars of religious change in Britain and Europe (see Davie 1990, 1994, 2002).

One of the leading voices of continental sociology of religion is Danièle Hervieu-Léger, well-known for her thoughtful and provocative account of religious change, *Religion as a Chain of Memory* (2000), first published in French in 1993 (*La religion pour mémoire*). In this book, Hervieu-Léger rethinks aspects of secularization. As with Luckmann's *The Invisible Religion* (1967) and Berger's *The Sacred Canopy* (1967), Hervieu-Léger begins by describing the elements of religion, before proceeding to consider how religion is affected by modernity. Hervieu-Léger suggests religion ought to be understood as a distinctive, communal 'way of believing'. Religion is where people follow a 'body of convictions – both individual and collective – which are not susceptible to verification, to experimentation' (2000: 72). Importantly, these kinds of belief are passed on from one generation to the next. In this sense, religion is a chain of memory – a tradition of beliefs – shared in a continuous, unbroken line from sometime in the past to the present. A tradition of belief survives and reproduces itself insofar as 'mention of the past and memories ... are consciously shared with and passed on to others' (2000: 123).

When a group collectively observes a long-held traditional rite – like a Catholic funeral service or Anglican christening – the chain of memory is reproduced and

(Continued)

(Continued)

reaffirmed. Critically, however, modernity has fractured the continuity of this chain of memory: 'Industrialization, urbanization, the spread of trade and interchange mark the waning of the social influence of religion and the piecemeal destruction of *communities, societies and even ideologies based on memory*' (my italics) (2000: 127). Hervieu-Léger conceives of secularization as 'a crisis of collective memory'.

In explaining her argument she cites the example of French Catholicism. Hervieu-Léger notes declining attendance among French Catholics, especially the young, where only 2.5 percent of those aged 18–24 regularly attend Mass (2000: 131). In explaining Catholic decline, Hervieu-Léger argues 'rather than attribute the fall in conventional religious observance to ... the growth of rationalism instilled by science and technology, one should look at the complex redistribution taking place in the sphere of believing' (2000: 132). She notes there has been a failure to transmit the collective memory of religion, a 'breakdown in the imaginative grasp of continuity' (2000: 132). In traditional Catholicism, the village parish 'represented *the* society of memory', linking people symbolically in a chain 'stretching from past to future' (2000: 132). Now, modernization, with its associated individualism, urbanization and mobility, has 'put an end to the [local] parish which ... served to sustain the Catholic identity of the French'. In effect, modernization has fractured French Catholicism's chain of memory, and contributed in part to Catholicism's diminishing place in French society.

Of the scholars considered in this chapter, perhaps Brown gives too little credence to developments before the 1960s, while arguably Bruce and Glendinning dismiss too readily the far-reaching impact of the 1960s cultural revolution. As will be shown in the next chapter, Christianity did not pass through the 1960s unscathed.

CONCLUSION

This chapter mapped several decades of religious change in Britain, Australia and Canada. The biggest story is that of traditional Christianity's decline: people, young people especially, are increasingly turning away from Christian identification and practice. This is evidence of secularization, if we understand that to be the process by which religion has come to play a less important role in people's lives within particular, post-Christian societies. As Turner notes (2011: 150), the concept of 'secularization, provided we remain imaginatively responsive to the diversity of modern religion, can still be safely applied to the modern world'.

This chapter, however, has also shown that secularization is just one of a number of religious trends occurring in Western societies. Limited Christian revival is occurring, particularly evident in the growth of Pentecostal and independent churches, while Islamic, Hindu and Buddhist communities also are growing. Societies can be secularizing and experiencing religious growth at the same time. Later chapters consider more fully the processes behind this growth.

For opponents of secularization theory, the United States – the world's largest Christian nation – has always been the country which challenges the axiom that modernization equals secularization. Christianity appears vibrant and vital in that country. How did American religion ride out the 1960s and beyond? This is discussed in the next chapter.

Points to ponder

Chat to someone who was a teenager or young adult in the 1960s (this may well be your parents). Ask them what life was like for young people then. Did it really feel like there was a sense of change, upheaval or cultural revolution? Did they turn away from the church then? Share your findings with others and try and formulate a picture of life in the 1960s.

Next steps ...

For an interesting account of religious life in Australia, read Gary Bouma's *Australian Soul* (2006); for a discussion of Canada, try the edited collection *The Religions of Canadians* (Scott 2012); for Britain, Callum Brown's *Religion and Society in Twentieth-century Britain* (2006); and for Western Europe, Philip Jenkins' *God's Continent: Christianity, Islam, and Europe's Religious Crisis* (2007) and Grace Davie's *Europe: The Exceptional Case: Parameters of Faith in the Modern World* (2002). To fully understand the complex arguments about recent secularization, I suggest also reading Callum Brown's *The Death of Christian Britain* (2009), Hugh McLeod's *The Religious Crisis of the 1960s* (2007) and Steve Bruce's *Secularization: In Defence of an Unfashionable Theory* (2011).

Documentaries

The UK's *Office of National Statistics* has a Youtube.com channel with the short graphic film, *Religion in England and Wales*(https://www.youtube.com/watch?v=tXdZJoXux C8andlist=UUFAmuev5BtHEh3o-WxgFA3gandindex=13). A four-part Australian documentary series, *The Making of Modern Australia*, has a wonderful episode, 'The Australian Soul', which depicts many of the issues discussed in this chapter. Britain's Channel Four produced the eight-part series *Christianity: A History*. Episode eight, 'The Future of Christianity' focuses on the 1960s changes in Europe, among other topics.

Web

A website produced by the University of Manchester, British Religion in Numbers, is full of useful information: http://www.brin.ac.uk.

7

one nation under god? american 'exceptionalism'

After reading this chapter you will:

- be introduced to the variety and vitality of religion in the United States;

- be familiar with major, recent developments in US religion; and

- understand the sociological causes of these developments.

On the first Sunday of February every year more than 100 million Americans turn on their TVs to watch the biggest event on the US sporting calendar, the Super Bowl. The Super Bowl is the pro-football national championship playoff, held between the National Football Conference champion and the American Football Conference champion. The three most-watched TV shows in US history all are recent Super Bowls. In 2013, Super Bowl XLVII, a 30-second, nationwide commercial spot was estimated to cost up to $3.8 million. Advertisers during Super Bowl XLVII included Mercedes Benz, Ford, Doritos, Coca-Cola, Subway, Walt Disney Corporation and the Church of Scientology.

The Church of Scientology's commercial did not air nationally, but was shown in selected TV 'markets' in America. The commercial ran for a minute (it can be found on Youtube.com, or the Church's official website, www.scientology.org). It begins by addressing certain kinds of individuals: 'the curious, the inquisitive, the seekers of knowledge, to the ones who just want to know about life, about the universe, about yourself …' As it continues, it stresses the importance of 'knowledge' for successful living, presumably the kind of religious knowledge found in Scientology.

The Church of Scientology is known widely for its celebrity adherents, including actors Tom Cruise (*Mission: Impossible*), John Travolta (*Pulp Fiction*) and Elisabeth Moss (*Mad Men*). Despite its high profile, few people know much about this religion. Religious studies scholar Hugh Urban (2011: 2) notes: 'With a tight system of security and a complex, esoteric hierarchy of teachings, Scientology is surely one of the most impenetrable and least understood new religions.' It teaches that a 'thetan' – an 'immortal spiritual being with unlimited potential … reincarnated in countless forms over many lifetimes' (Urban 2011: 70) – is part of each human, in a manner roughly analogous to the human soul. Followers proceed through a series of steps by which they gain further knowledge of and insight into thetans. Some critics decry Scientology as a 'cult', while its followers have fought a long battle in the United States to have it recognized as a religion (for an excellent account see Urban 2011).

The Church of Scientology was founded by US science fiction writer, L. Ron Hubbard, in the 1950s, and is one of several new US religions or sectarian religious movements to have emerged in the last 200 years. Other notable examples include Pentecostalism, Jehovah Witnesses, Christian Science, Spiritualism, Satanism and Mormonism. Some of these are movements within Christianity, while others, like Scientology, Satanism and Spiritualism, are entirely new religions. The United States arguably has been the world's most prolific source of major new religions and religious movements in recent history. Attracting thousands, and in some cases, millions, of adherents, each has taken its place in the US religious firmament alongside Catholicism, dozens of Protestant denominations, Native American religions, New Age religions and, increasingly, Islam, Hinduism and Buddhism. The result is a monumental and vibrant 'religious marketplace'. There is vigorous competition among religions for adherents, legitimacy and cultural relevance, which may explain Scientology's Super Bowl commercial. TV is just one of the mediums employed by religions to promote their message.

With such religious variety and vitality, the United States appears largely to have resisted the kind of religious decline witnessed recently in Australia, Western Europe and Canada. Americans report consistently higher levels of attendance, belief and belonging than almost any other post-industrial nation. ('Post-industrial' refers to countries whose economies are centered more on service provision and technology than on manufacturing or agriculture.) This level of religious interest has important implications for the widespread applicability of secularization theories. However, as everywhere else in the world, religion in the United States has been transformed in recent decades. Established, 'mainline' Protestant denominations are losing members, while a huge influx of migrants has changed the demographic profile of Catholicism, and caused religions like Islam and Hinduism to grow. 'Strict' forms of Christianity, particularly Pentecostalism and evangelicalism, also have prospered. These changes have redefined the religious landscape of the United States, but also, by virtue of the country's influence, brought change to religion elsewhere around the world.

This chapter examines recent religious change in the United States. It begins with a brief examination of the history and diversity of US religion, followed by a review of current patterns of affiliation and belief. It focuses then on several recent major trends: the drift of young people away from Christianity, the migrant impact on religion, the birth of the spiritual marketplace and the growth of conservative forms of religiosity.

RELIGIOUS DIVERSITY IN THE USA: ONE NATION, MANY GODS?

Modern America has been characterized by religious diversity and competition since the beginning of white colonization. In his eminently readable book *A History of Christianity in the United States and Canada*, historian Mark Noll (1992: 7) makes the observation that 'almost as soon as there were European settlers in North America, there were also several varieties of Christianity'. Anglicans, Puritans and Quakers, among others, came from different parts of Europe in the 1600s and 1700s and settled in eastern parts of the United States (Gaustad and Schmidt 2002; Noll 1992). They established communities based on religion and religious values, and were desirous of religious freedom (the right to practice religion without any government interference or restriction). Among the most notable early religious immigrants were the Puritans, a radical Protestant sect from England. Seeking religious freedom, they arrived from the 1620s and established several colonies in Massachusetts. Noll (1992: 39) notes Puritans 'enjoyed the liberty to plant a congregational form of worship and instill a deep pious sense of community'.

America initially was dominated by traditional European Protestant groups, but this did not remain the case for long. In the 1730s, the Great Awakening – a country-wide surge in piety – contributed to the growth of other Protestant denominations, including distinctive Baptist denominations. The 1800s witnessed what is known as the Second Great Awakening, along with the rise of autonomous African-American churches, the growth of Catholic communities, and the founding of new sects such as the Mormons. In the twentieth century, the mass migration of Catholics from Latin America and Europe, the rise of Pentecostalism and the post-war arrival of waves of Buddhist and Muslim migrants have all influenced the religious mosaic of the United States. The result is a country that has been described as more religiously diverse than any other (see Eck 2001), or more appropriately, one which exhibits the greatest diversity within Christian denominations. Importantly, the religious vitality and fervor that characterized the early Puritan colonies remain evident in many parts of contemporary America.

A large-scale study of US religion conducted by the Pew Forum in 2007 surveyed a representative sample of 35,000 people and captured the variety of US religion. The Catholic Church is the single largest denomination (approximately a quarter of the population identifies as Catholic) but, as will be seen below, it is extremely diverse. The Protestant denominations represent three distinct traditions: 'mainline' Protestant churches, evangelical Protestant churches and historically black Protestant churches (Pew Forum 2008: 10).

Mainline Protestant refers to the larger, traditional denominations, many of which were founded in Europe. Examples include the Lutheran, Presbyterian, Episcopalian (Anglican) and some Baptist churches. These denominations tend to have a liberal and progressive doctrine and use traditional forms of liturgy in their worship. The Episcopalian church, for example, has progressive views about the ordination of gay and female clergy. **Evangelicals** are those denominations and Christians who, according to Lindsey (2007: 4) 'hold a particular regard for the [inerrancy of the] Bible, embrace a personal relationship with God through a "conversion" to Jesus Christ, and seek to lead others on a similar spiritual journey'. Evangelicals are theologically conservative and routinely opposed to homosexuality, abortion and the ordination of women. **Black Protestant churches** were founded by African-Americans in the nineteenth century to meet the religious needs of the black community. They played, and continue to play, a significant role in community welfare and civil rights activism. These denominations typically have a musical worship style, known as gospel music, and tend to be theologically conservative. The Pew Forum (2008: 5) estimates approximately 26 percent of the US population affiliates with an evangelical Protestant denomination, 18 percent with a 'mainline' denomination and 7 percent with a black Protestant church.

Within the three larger Protestant groupings there is stunning variety. According to the Pew Forum (2008: 13):

> American Protestantism is very diverse. It encompasses more than a dozen major denominational families, such as Baptists, Methodists, Lutherans and Pentecostals, all with unique beliefs, practices and histories. These denominational families, in turn, are composed of a host of different denominations, such as the Southern Baptist Convention, the American Baptist Churches in the USA and the National Baptist Convention.

Beyond the various Protestant groupings there is also much religious variety. The case study for this chapter looks closely at some interesting US churches and other religions.

A COOK'S TOUR OF AMERICAN RELIGIONS

Named after the English travel agent, Thomas Cook, a Cook's tour is a brief tour in which only the main attractions of a country are seen. In this case study, you go on a brief tour around the United States, stopping at different places along the way to see religious traditions which are either unique to or originated in that country. Find a detailed map of the United States and refer to it as you read.

(Continued)

CASE STUDY

(Continued)

The tour starts in New York State, in the upper eastern part of your map. Look for the city of Buffalo.

1. Situated 60 miles south of Buffalo in upstate New York is the pretty Spiritualist community of Lily Dale, home to about 40 registered mediums. Spiritualism is America's home-grown, talk-to-the-dead religion (see Chapter 2). Each summer, thousands flock to the town for personal consultations, Spiritualist services and mediumship training. A good book about the town is Christine Wicker's *Lily Dale: The Town that Talks to the Dead* (2003). Web: www.lilydaleassembly.com

2. The African-American Abyssinian Baptist church is found in Harlem, New York City. There can be witnessed a service with powerful preaching and extraordinary gospel music in the tradition of the black Protestant churches. Videos can be watched on the church's website www.abyssinian.org. A recent book by scholar Anthony Pinn, *The African American Religious Experience in America* (2005) traces the rise of the black Protestant movement.

3. 160 miles to the west of New York City is Lancaster county, Philadelphia. This is home to a community of Anabaptists known as the Amish. These are a group of conservative Protestants who eschew the trappings of modernity. They speak an old version of Dutch as their first language, and the majority live as farmers. Theirs is a simple lifestyle, and they often reject modern conveniences such as cars, refrigerators or TV. The community is incredibly tight-knit and little has changed in the centuries since they emigrated from Europe. An excellent book about being raised Amish is Richard Stevick's *Growing Up Amish* (2007). This book traces the many issues which confront Amish youth when they come of age. They partake in Rumspringa, taking leave of their sheltered, communal life to live with outsiders. At the end of this time, they are offered the choice to leave the Amish community (and be ex-communicated) or return and be baptized into the church.

4. Further to the south-west, in the rural regions of Tennessee and Kentucky, among several Southern states, can be found serpent-handling churches. These churches literally interpret a sentence in the Christian Bible that says followers of Jesus will pick up snakes with their hands. This practice, which is illegal, is done during regular church services on Sundays, and can result in snake bites, illness and sometimes death. An outstanding sociological and psychological assessment of these rural church communities is Hood and Williamson's (2008) *Them that Believe: The Power and Meaning of the Christian Serpent-handling Tradition*. Videos and information can be found at: holiness-snake-handlers. webs.com.

5. Heading south-west to Texas, the extraordinary Lakewood church is encountered. www.lakewoodchurch.com. This is a 'megachurch' with a congregation of more than 20,000. The church complex is a former sports arena purchased for $7.5 million in the early 2000s. Megachurches are churches with congregations

in excess of 2000 people and most are in the Pentecostal or evangelical tradition. They began in the United States and no other nation has as many. Worship in these churches typically is very contemporary, with professional-standard musicianship, and preaching which focuses largely on personal issues. Sermons can be watched on the website. Scott Thumma and Dave Travis' book, *Beyond Megachurch Myths: What We Can Learn from America's Largest Churches (2007)* is arguably the authoritative account of megachurches.

6. Heading north-west to Utah, and in the capital, Salt Lake City, the headquarters of the Church of Jesus Christ and the Latter Day Saints, also known as the Mormons, is found. This denomination is one of the fastest growing Christian denominations in the world. Started in the 1830s by Joseph Smith, the Mormons have a sacred text, the Book of Mormon, which is read in conjunction with the Christian Bible. The Mormon church was founded in New York State and was seen as heretical by mainstream Christians. Mormons did, after all, argue there are two holy texts, and they believed in polygamy (since disallowed in the Mormon church, but practiced still by small, breakaway groups). After much persecution, they headed west and established their headquarters in Salt Lake City. Mormons are an accepted, highly religious and growing presence in the United States and many other countries around the world. Matthew Bowman's *The Mormon People: The Making of an American Faith* (2012) is an accessible history of this US religion.

7. Further to the west is Los Angeles, home of the Church of Scientology, the new religion described in the introduction to this chapter. Highly recommended is Hugh Urban's *The Church of Scientology: A History of a New Religion* (2011) for a balanced, informative investigation of this high-profile religion.

This little tour demonstrates just some of the variety found within US religion.

Why is there such religious *variety* in the United States? In Chapter 4 rational-choice theories of religious change were introduced. These theories purport to explain the dynamics of the religious marketplace, in particular, the reasons why some countries have a 'stagnant' religious culture and others are vibrant. Roger Finke and Rodney Stark's *The Churching of America 1776–2005* (2005) is a book which applies these theoretical insights to explain the variety of US religion. The authors argue that no state religion, or quasi-state religion, was ever established in America, unlike the situations in Western Europe. Given these 'unregulated' conditions, various religions and denominations were able to flourish. Finke and Stark (2005: 3) argue: 'As the state and local regulation of American religion declined, a growing supply of energetic clergy actively marketed their faiths, new churches arose without resistance, and a rich variety of new religious options emerged.' Finke and Stark's book charts such movement in great detail and arguably describes the most persuasive empirical application of rational choice theories. Not only is the United States religiously diverse, as discussed in the next section, it is demonstrably more religious than almost any other post–industrial nation.

HOW RELIGIOUS IS AMERICA TODAY? PATTERNS OF RELIGIOUS AFFILIATION, BELIEF AND PRACTICE

US law does not permit the census bureau to include a question about religious affiliation (religious identification), or any form of religious behavior, so census data on religion are not available for America. As discussed in Chapter 5, this is the most accurate kind of data. US social scientists, however, have long collected reliable, generalizable data about religious affiliation and other religious matters. This section considers patterns of religious affiliation, belief and practice in the contemporary United States based on this data.

Religious identification

A survey series with accurate data on religious affiliation is the *American Religious Identification Survey* (ARIS) which has been administered in 1990, 2001 and 2008 (see Kosmin and Keysar 2006, 2009a). Each wave of this national survey has questioned more than 50,000 adults. Such a large sample means the researchers can make highly accurate estimates about the population as a whole, particularly for smaller groups which usually have insufficient numbers in surveys to allow accurate estimates to be made.

Using ARIS data, Table 7.1 shows the religious self-identification of US adults in 1990, 2001 and 2008.

Table 7.1   Religious self-identification of the US adult population 1990, 2001, 2008

	1990		2001		2008	
	Estimated number of people	%	Estimated number of people	%	Estimated number of people	%
Catholic	46,004,000	26.2	50,873,000	24.5	57,199,000	25.1
Other Christian	105,221,000	60.0	108,641,000	52.2	116,203,000	50.9
Total Christians	151,225,000	86.2	159,514,000	76.7	173,402,000	76.0
Other religions	5,853,000	3.3	7,740,000	3.7	8,796,000	3.9
Nones	14,331,000	8.2	29,481,000	14.1	34,169,000	15.0
DK/refused	4,031,000	2.3	11,246,000	5.4	11,815,000	5.2
Total	175,440,000	100.0	207,983,000	100.0	228,182,000	100.0

Source: Kosmin, Barry A., and Keysar, Ariela. (2009a) *American Religious Identification Survey* (ARIS 2008), *Summary Report*. Hartford, CT: Institute for the Study of Secularism in Society and Culture.

Table 7.1 shows that in 2008, 76 percent of US adults identified with a Christian denomination, 3.9 percent identified with religions apart from Christianity, and 15 percent did not identify with a religion. At the broadest level, the United States can be characterized as a Christian nation.

This table also highlights some interesting trends. First, the proportion of the population which identifies as Christian has *decreased* by 10 percent between 1990 and 2008. Mainline Protestant denominations have borne the brunt of these losses. Kosmin and Keysar (2009b) note 'Ninety percent of the decline comes from the non-Catholic segment of the Christian population, largely from the mainline denominations, including Methodists, Lutherans, Presbyterians, Episcopalians/Anglicans, and the United Church of Christ.'

This trend replicates patterns found in Western Europe, Canada, and Australia, where there has been a drift away from identification with established mainline Protestant churches.

Why are the mainline Protestant denominations losing adherents? Social researchers Tom Smith and Seokho Kim (2005) have examined this question in depth, and propose several reasons for the 'shrinking Protestant majority'. One is immigration trends, and the fact that the majority of recent immigrants are not mainline Protestants, but identify with other Christian denominations, other religions or no religion – which reduces the mainline Protestant 'share' of the population (Smith and Kim 2005: 221). Other reasons include poorer retention rates – people leaving to go to other churches, people leaving altogether – among mainline Protestant denominations.

Generally in recent decades the evangelical Protestant denominations and sects have done better than the mainline Protestant denominations in retaining their members and growing their churches (Smith et al. 1998; Finke and Stark 2005; Pew Forum 2008). Finke and Stark (2005), proponents of the rational-choice perspective, argue that mainline Protestant decline and evangelical Protestant growth are related. In their view, mainline Protestant decline has occurred because such churches do not demand much of their members, whereas the growing denominations are 'high demand'. Congregants in high demand churches are required to attend more regularly, and to give generously of their time and resources. People accept these high demands because of the 'rewards' accrued by such participation (e.g. blessings from God, strong support networks). In turn, high-demand churches do better at fostering commitment and retaining members.

Smith and colleagues (1998) also consider why evangelical churches have grown in recent decades and in explanation, point to aspects of evangelical doctrine. The evangelical movement is comprised of conservative, 'Bible-believing' Christians, who maintain a sharp worldview: there are 'us', those who are 'saved' and following correct religious doctrine, and 'them', liberals and non-Christians who deviate from biblical standards. Smith and his colleagues (1998: 89) argue the movement prospers because of this tension: 'evangelicalism … thrives on distinction, engagement, tension, conflict, and threat'.

It should be noted that churches which attract new migrants also have prospered in recent decades. Finke and Stark (2005: 240) argue: 'Supporting a tight-knit ethnic and religious community and often supported by conservative religious teachings, many of the new congregations generate high levels of member commitment.'

A final trend to note is the increasing proportion of religious 'nones' (a US phrase for people who do not affiliate with a religion). This has increased from 8 percent of the population in 1990, to 15 percent in 2008. The most pronounced growth took place between 1990 and 2001, when the number of religious nones in the United States grew by 106 percent (Kosmin et al. 2009: 20). This, too, is consistent with patterns found in the countries discussed in the previous chapter. In sum, the pattern of religious affiliation in the United States in recent decades mirrors to some extent the situations in Canada, England and Wales and Australia; a decline in mainline Protestant affiliation and an increase in religious nones. The United States, however, remains decidedly more religious than the post-Christian countries.

Religious belief and practice, American style

Americans are among the most religious Westerners, if this is measured by belief and practice. In order to illustrate this point, Table 7.2 compares countries on a number of religious variables using data from the 2008 International Social Survey Program (ISSP) religion module.

The data in Table 7.2 are self-estimates of religious belief and behavior. Following the publication of a famous paper that compared self-reports of religious attendance with headcounts of church attendance (see Hadaway et al. 1993), most social scientists agree that people tend to overestimate their religious practices. Berger et al. (2008: 12) note 'survey data on religion are always somewhat suspect. Given the respective cultural contexts, Americans may exaggerate their religiousness ...

Table 7.2   Adult population of selected countries: belief in God, belief in hell, frequency of prayer, attendance at services of worship and religious self-description (percentage of population)

	Country					
Item	Philippines %	USA %	Ireland %	Great Britain %	Australia %	Germany %
Believes in God	96	87	77	42	43	49
Believes in hell	81	71	49	28	29	20
Prays weekly+	90	69	55	21	23	24
Attends services of worship nearly weekly+	71	37	51	11	14	16
Describes self as 'extremely/very religious'	27	26	13	7	9	9

Note: Survey participants may hold more than one of these beliefs/engage in these practices so the columns in this table add to more than 100 percent.

Data source: 2008 International Socal Survey Program (ISSP) survey for various countries. Figures have been rounded. Figures quoted are from analysis done by the author. Those who carried out the original collection of the data bear no responsibility for this analysis.

Europeans may exaggerate their secularity.' Nonetheless, these data are taken from the same survey and meaningful comparison can be made.

Each column shows data from one country, e.g., the first column has data for the Philippines, and shows 96 percent of Filipinos believe in God, 81 percent believe in hell, 90 percent pray weekly or more often. The next columns show data for America, Ireland and so on. The best way to read this table is to read across each row, comparing data from one country to the next on the same item (i.e. the first row is belief in God, second row is belief in hell). I have chosen the countries deliberately: the Philippines is a highly religious developing country, with a Catholic-majority population. Ireland has a very strong Catholic heritage. Great Britain, Australia and Germany are typical of the 'post-Christian' nations I discussed in the previous chapter.

This table shows that, on every measure, Americans are more religious than Britons, Germans or Australians, and on all but one measure, more religious than the Irish. For example, 87 percent of Americans believe in God, compared to 77 percent of Irish, 42 percent of Britons, 49 percent of Germans and 43 percent of Australians. On more decisive measures of religious practice, there is a similar pattern: 69 percent of Americans claim to pray weekly or more often, compared to 55 percent of Irish, 21 percent of Britons, 24 percent of Germans and 23 percent of Australians. It should be noted that the United States is not uniformly religious, and there is notable regional variation with respect to religious affiliation and attendance. Southern states (e.g. Mississippi, Alabama, Louisiana) for example, are more religious than states in New England (e.g. Vermont, New Hampshire) (see Rogers 2013).

Why is the United States more religious than other large, post-industrial countries? Proponents of rational choice theories of religion, like Finke and Stark (2005; see also Stark and Finke 2000) argue America's religious variety and 'free-market' competition of religions (discussed in the previous section) contribute to religious vitality. How do variety and deregulation lead to vitality? How this works was explained in detail in Chapter 4, with reference to the example of fast food. Simply put, competition and aggressive marketing induce more participants to make use of a product or service. Without competition, suppliers become lazy and consequently service only a small, committed – 'rusted on' – portion of the market. Using the rational-choice perspective to read the US religious situation, Finke and Stark (2005: 6) note: 'religious freedoms increased the involvement of the people'. The more active churches there are, busily seeking members, the greater the level of religious participation.

Other scholars typically identify myriad historical, social and cultural factors contributing to US religious vitality (see Berger et al. 2008 for such an explanation). Many point to America's early days, observing that religion had a special place in society. This was apparent to French scholar Alexis de Tocqueville who, in the nineteenth century, wrote

there is no country in the world where the Christian religion retains a greater influence over the souls of men [sic] than in America; and there can be no greater proof of its utility and its conformity to human nature than that its influence is powerfully felt over the most enlightened and free nation of the earth. (cited in Graebner 1976: 263)

This theme was explored a century later in one of the most well-known sociological discussions of the link between US culture and religion, Will Herberg's *Protestant-Catholic-Jew: An Essay in American Religious Sociology* (Herberg 1960). According to Herberg (1960: 3), 'American religion and American society would seem to be so closely interrelated as to make it virtually impossible to understand either without reference to the other.' Religious communities, by dint of historical and cultural circumstances, 'serve as a context for self-identification and social location in contemporary social life' (Herberg 1960: 36). He continues, the 'principle by which men [sic] identify themselves and are identified, locate themselves and are located in the social whole is neither "race" (except for Negroes [sic] and those of Oriental [sic] origin) nor ethnic-immigrant background (except for recent arrivals) but religious community' (Herberg 1960: 36). While Herberg perhaps underestimates the importance of various markers of social identity (such as class, education, race and gender), he is essentially correct in noting the enduring primacy of religious identity in the American social imaginary. In the 1950s Herberg argued the three major religious categories were Protestant, Catholic and Jew. In later decades, categories of conservative, evangelical, liberal and nones appear to have increased importance (see Putnam and Campbell 2010; Wuthnow 1996), but people are often still defined and define others by their 'religious preferences'.

In summary, the United States exhibits greater religious *variety* and *vitality* than Western Europe, Canada and Australia for myriad reasons: religion always has been a culturally significant marker of personal identity, and played an important part in the migrant and African-American experience. Religious freedom, aggressive evangelization and an ever-expanding array of churches have helped sustain this vitality, as has the presence of denominations and churches which are variously high demand, strict and theologically conservative. Americans may overestimate the level of their own personal religiosity, but this reflects the fact that religion uniquely has animated American life for centuries.

Is religious attendance in decline?

In the previous chapter it was noted that attendance at religious services has declined in Western Europe, Canada and Australia from the 1960s to the present day. Is this true of the United States? The answer is 'a little'. Robert Wuthnow (2007: 51) notes: 'polls and surveys suggest that attendance levels at religious services among the full adult population of the United States have remained fairly constant for at least thirty years. Constant, but with some erosion in recent years.' Putnam and Campbell (2010: 79) note 'streams of evidence suggest that Americans have become somewhat less observant religiously over the last half century'. Presser and Chaves (2007: 421) find: 'the best evidence – from time-use studies – suggests that weekly attendance at religious services declined between 1950 and 1990, and has remained stable since then'. While the proportion who attend weekly has remained fairly stable for the past two decades, Lipka (2013), using Pew Forum data, finds: 'The percentage of Americans who say they 'seldom' or 'never' attend religious services … has risen modestly in the past decade. Roughly three-in-ten U.S. adults (29%) now say they seldom or never attend worship services, up from 25% in 2003.' As discussed below, this trend is more pronounced among younger age cohorts.

To sum up this overview of religious identification, belief and practice in the United States (and to draw to a close various arguments about secularization which have been played out across several chapters) we see that the United States is more religious than other post-industrial nations. And yet there is a small, discernible decline in religious attendance, and an increase in the proportion of religious nones.

Proponents of 'revitalized' secularization theory, in particular Steve Bruce (2011), interpret this as showing secularization is occurring in America, in much the same way as it has in Europe – a corollary of the many changes wrought by modernization. Against such an argument, Putnam and Campbell (2010: 76) observe: 'if we are witnessing such a process in the United States, at this rate it will take a couple of centuries to reduce American religious observance to the current European levels … we are skeptical about bold assertions of secularization in America'. Others are caustic about efforts to apply the secularization paradigm to the United States (see Finke and Stark 2005). Nonetheless, some US scholars are taking these patterns of decline seriously (see the next section).

Most US social scientists who are cognizant of recent moderate Christian decline do not, on the whole, interpret recent trends as evidence of a generalized, linear process linked to 'modernization', but as a specific effect of social and cultural changes occurring mainly in the 1960s and impacting on particular segments of society more than others (Taylor 2007; Wuthnow 2007; Putnam and Campbell 2010). So where to for theories of widespread secularization?

Secularization appears to describe Europe, Canada and Australia more appropriately and directly than America, and for the most part, this is the present scholarly consensus. Putnam and Campbell (2010: 71) note: 'the bedrock fact [is] that America is now and always has been an unusually religious country'. Very few scholars argue the United States is in the grip of decisive secularization. But this does not mean religious life has remained unchanged in recent decades, or a secular culture does not exist (see Taylor 2007). Laurence Moore (1994: 4) observes 'if secularization inadequately describes … the United States, the mere statistical counter-assertion that organized religion remains important obscures much that has happened over time'. The remainder of this chapter considers important changes that have taken place in recent decades: a youthful drift away from religion, the immigrant reshaping of American congregations, the rising political influence of the evangelical movement and the emergence of the spiritual marketplace. There are many stories to tell about contemporary American religion.

THE CHANGING FACE OF AMERICAN RELIGION: THE 1960s AND BEYOND

The decade or so after the end of the Second World War was something of a 'golden age' for Christianity in America. Putnam and Campbell (2010: 83) note: 'Virtually all experts agree … that the period from the late 1940s to the early 1960s was one of exceptional religious observance in America.' It was in the 1950s that the phrase 'One Nation under God' was added to the United States Pledge of Allegiance and 'In God We Trust' became the national motto. Evangelist Billy Graham began his crusades and was hugely successful, drawing millions to evangelical rallies across the country. It was a religiously buoyant time.

The social mood shifted perceptibly in the next decade, and traditional institutions – family, politics and religion – all seemed to be affected. A cultural revolution was taking place. Putnam and Campbell (2010: 91) argue:

> The Sixties represented a perfect storm for American institutions of all sorts … In retrospect we can discern a mélange of contributing factors: the bulge in the youngest age cohorts as the boomers moved through adolescence and into college, the combination of unprecedented affluence and the rapid expansion of higher education, 'the Pill,' the abating of Cold War anxieties, Vatican II, the assassinations, the Vietnam War, Watergate, pot and LSD, the civil rights movement … the antiwar movement, the women's liberation movement, and later environmental and gay rights movement.

These, and other post-1960s social, technological and cultural changes, such as massive migration, rising individualism and rampant consumerism, have reshaped US religion irrevocably. As documented in Chapter 3, by the end of the 1960s, social scientists, commentators and theologians already had discerned some of these changes. In the remainder of this chapter, post-1960s religious developments are explored in detail.

'Youth disaffection from religion'

Recent scholarship reveals a pattern of 'youth disaffection from religion' in the United States (Putnam and Campbell 2010: 120). In his book, *After the Baby Boomers*, Robert Wuthnow (2007: 62) notes: '[The data] show that young adults in the late 1990s were significantly less likely to attend church regularly than young adults in the early 1970s.' Christian Smith and Patricia Snell (2009: 91) find the current generation of 'emerging adults' is 'less likely than older adults to pray daily and attend services weekly. They affiliate with their faiths less strongly.' Putnam and Campbell (2010: 120–32) also find major differences between age cohorts, with younger people much more likely than older people to be religious nones (see also Smith and Snell 2009: 89).

In the previous chapter, it was noted that this kind of age cohort decline is thought to have occurred because of the failure of Baby Boomers to pass religion on to their children, and to the fact that those raised after the 1960s had come of age in a vastly different culture, one which was inimical to religion and religious tradition. US scholars point to similar explanations, eschewing the 'modernization' explanations of classical secularization theory (see Taylor 2007; Wuthnow 2007; Smith and Snell 2009; Putnam and Campbell 2010). Putnam and Campbell (2010: 126), writing about the nones, for example, find 'some of them are the children of boomers who had discarded formal religious affiliation a generation ago'. In their view, young people are retreating from religion also because of their own progressive, relative morals (an inheritance from their Boomer parents) and a dislike of the overt moralizing of religious conservatives. Charles Taylor (2007: 495) suggests 'the generations which have been formed in the cultural revolution of the 1960s are in some respects deeply alienated from a strong traditional model of Christian faith'.

Robert Wuthnow (2007) points to various social factors causing the youthful drift from the churches, most notably, marriage patterns. In America, young adults are remaining single for longer and having fewer children, and having them later in life, which in turn has an impact on church attendance, as children and marriage are strong predictors of more frequent attendance (Wuthnow 2007: 66). These changes are linked to broader cultural shifts in the ways in which people view the institution of marriage. Each of these explanations has merit.

Religion and immigration

American always has been a nation of religious immigrants, but in recent decades, and as in Australia, Canada, and Europe, migration is reshaping the US religious landscape. According to a recent Pew Forum report (Pew Forum 2012a: 52), the United States is:

> The world's No. 1 destination for Christian migrants, who make up an estimated 32 million (74 percent) of the 43 million foreign-born people living in the United States. The U.S. is also the top destination for Buddhist migrants (including many from Vietnam) and for people with no particular religion (including many from China). The U.S. is the world's second-leading destination for Hindu migrants, after India, and for Jewish migrants, after Israel. Among Muslim migrants, however, the U.S. ranks just seventh as a destination.

What effect do these migration patterns have on America's religious composition? According to the ARIS data (see Table 7.1), religions other than Christianity represented 4 percent of the population in 2008; the numbers of people who identified with other religions had increased by 50 percent since 1990 (Kosmin and Keysar 2009a: 4). For the most part, this growth is not from conversion, but immigration and high birth rates among these religious groups. According to the Pew Forum (2008: 8), among 'Muslims, roughly two-thirds … are immigrants … and Hindus, more than eight-in-ten … are foreign born'. Chapters 9 and 10 explore this growth in greater detail.

Established religious traditions, particularly of Christian denominations, also are being transformed from *within* by waves of migration (see Warner 2005). According to the ARIS data (see Table 7.1) Catholics represented 26 percent of the population in 1990 and 25 percent of the population in 2008. In those years, huge numbers of US adults ceased to identify as Catholic. However, Catholics have remained the single largest denomination, due almost entirely to a significant influx of Latino immigrants (Kosmin and Keysar 2009a, b). The Pew Forum (2008) estimates that today about a third of US Catholics are Latino.

The Latino influence on the Catholic Church in the United States is explored in a recent book by Timothy Matovina, *Latino Catholicism* (2012), who claims that waves of migrants from different Spanish-speaking countries have reshaped the character of US Catholicism in recent decades. Matovina (2012: 246–7) finds: 'Latinos have much to offer US Catholicism. Their youthfulness is a source of revitalization for Catholic faith communities. Their leadership has extended Catholic involvement in faith-based community organizing … Their ritual and devotional traditions incite embodied prayer and faith.'

Seekers in the spiritual marketplace

The 1960s was a time when many teens and young adults shunned the strictures of organized religion. Many, however, still were interested in spirituality. Fueled by the massive 1960s mood of 'counter-culture', there was something of a 'spiritual awakening' in the late 1960s and 1970s, in which emerged new and unprecedented alternatives to Christianity. Alternative spiritual groups, like the Krishna Consciousness Society (the Hare Krishnas), the Unification Church (Moonies) and the Sri Chinmoy movement all founded communities or centers at this time. Other newer religions, like Satanism, also appeared. The New Age movement, encompassing practices as diverse as reiki healing, past-life therapy and yoga, began to flourish. This plethora of spiritual alternatives has been dubbed the 'spiritual marketplace' (Roof 1999). Such options became popular also in Great Britain, Australia and Canada.

Writing in the 1960s, scholar Thomas Luckmann noted that people, freed from the domination of organized religion, increasingly were formulating their own 'symbolic universes'. This theme of **religious individualism** is picked up in a very interesting and influential book by sociologist Wade Clark Roof, *The Spiritual Marketplace: Baby Boomers and the Remaking of American Religion* (1999). Among Baby Boomers Roof discerned the emergence of a 'quest culture', in which people no longer sought identity from a group (like a church), but instead engaged in a personal, individualistic 'quest for an authentic inner life and personhood' (1999: 7). In late modern society, people now are 'seekers', looking for the authentic religious expression that is right for them. For many people, this might involve searching – 'shopping' – outside the bounds of traditional, organized religion, looking towards alternative spiritualities, or the vibrant, 'life-centered' forms of religion offered by new evangelical or Pentecostal churches.

Another sociologist, Robert Wuthnow, argues something similar in his book, *After Heaven: Spirituality in America Since the 1950s* (1998). He argues people's expression of spirituality – that is, the relationship a person has with the transcendent – has changed. Once spirituality was about 'dwelling'. This is the kind of spirituality embedded in organized religion, and the places and organizations of organized religion. People once were loyal to those organizations and institutions. Now, spirituality is about seeking. In this kind of spirituality, people seek moments and encounters with the sacred. This involves greater range of selection and a search for authenticity. In other words, 'try whatever works'. (Recent studies suggest the 'seeker culture', especially when it comes to alternative spirituality, is largely the preserve of Baby Boomers – see Chapter 13.)

If people are seeking forms of spirituality to meet individual needs, how does the religious market – the supply-side – respond? In the 1960s Peter Berger noted that religions, no longer able to take a 'clientele' for granted, had to market their wares to prospective consumers. An excellent study which examines the marketing of religion is Mara Einstein's *Brands of Faith: Marketing Religion in a Commercial Age* (2008). She argues 'religious products ... have become branded in much the same way that consumer products have been branded' (2008: xi). These newly marketed religious products and services are described as 'faith brands' and 'exist to aid consumers in making and maintaining a personal connection to a commodity product' (Einstein 2008: xi). The Scientology commercial discussed at the beginning of this chapter is one such example.

Another curious 'innovation' in US religion related to this recent religious commodification, is the burgeoning 'Christian market'. Everyday products, services and goods are 'Christianized'. One can listen to Christian rock music, see Christian movies, read Christian novels and magazines and buy Christian candy and soft-toys. (See for example, 'scripture candy' from Alabama: http://www.scripturecandy.com/.)

It is a parallel world in which the Christian consumer can live. The market for these Christianized products is driven largely by evangelical Christians, who have created a distinct subculture serviced by evangelical universities, TV stations and publishers. With estimates suggesting there are anywhere between 20 million and 60 million evangelicals in America, it is a huge market. Book series, such as the apocalyptic novels, *Left Behind*, have sold millions of copies.

Evangelicals and religious politics

While evangelical Christians have created a distinct subculture, they have also in recent decades been very active in mainstream politics. Evangelical 'para-church' organizations, such as the *National Religious Broadcasters*, the *Moral Majority* and *Focus on the Family* have mobilized the evangelical vote to influence political decision-making around key areas of evangelical concern: abortion, same-sex relationships, drug use, family formation and school education (see Chapter 12 for a discussion of creation science and intelligent design). This politicized involvement has been dubbed the 'Christian Right'. Well-resourced, vociferous and highly organized, the Christian Right has enjoyed remarkable political influence, particularly during the Republican presidencies of Ronald Reagan and George W. Bush. Despite the United States having a constitutional separation of church and state, religious organizations have influenced voter preferences and political policy.

Commentators view the rise of evangelical politics as a religious reaction to the liberalism of society since the 1960s, when evangelicals increasingly felt embattled by rising cultural pluralism, relativism and secularism (see Smith 1998 et al.; Putnam and Campbell 2010). According to Putnam and Campbell (2010: 120), 'To many religious Americans, this alignment of religion and politics represented a long-sought consummation ... [however] Many other Americans were not so sure.' Indeed, as shown in Chapter 12 , there is an emerging atheist movement in the United States, partly a reaction to the evangelical movement.

CONCLUSION

The modern United States is a religiously vital country, yet one that has experienced considerable religious transformation in the past few decades: perhaps not widespread secularization, but many changes, including a noticeable drift of youth away from the church. Mainline, traditional Protestant denominations are in decline, while immigration has altered considerably the religious profile of the United States. Additionally, the forces of consumerism and individualism have become part of the expression of US faith. New, powerful forms of conservative Christianity have emerged. By virtue of its international standing and influence, US religion affects other places around the world. Its global reach is explored in the next chapter.

Points to ponder

Debate the proposition that 'secularization is not occurring in the United States'. Think carefully about how you might define secularization, and whether the patterns found in the United States replicate the European, Australian and Canadian experience.

Next steps ...

Robert Putman and David Campbell's *American Grace: How Religion Divides and Unites Us* (2010), provides a masterful, accessible overview of recent religious change. Alan Wolfe's *The Transformation of American Religion* (2003) takes a closer look at the everyday, lived religion of Americans. Courtney Bender's *The New Metaphysicals: Spirituality and the American Religious Imagination* (2010) considers the terrain of contemporary US spirituality.

Documentaries

The US Public Broadcasting Service makes many interesting films about US religion. I recommend the six part series from 2010, *God in America*, http://www.pbs. org/godinamerica/view/. Also recommended is the 2007 series *The Mormons*, a wonderful history of this growing sect www.pbs.org/mormons/view/. Both of these can be watched online. Those living in the United States can also watch online the PBS documentary *The Amish* www.pbs.org/wgbh/americanexperience/films/amish/player/. Britain's BBC also made recently an intimate documentary about an Amish family, *The Amish: A Secret Life*, www.bbc.co.uk/programmes/b01lk6vn.

Web

Pew Research Center's Forum on Religion and Public Life www.pewforum.org is an outstanding clearinghouse for information on US religion.

8

christian vitality?
asia-pacific, africa and
latin america

After reading this chapter you will:

- be introduced to global developments in Christianity in the past 100 years;

- be aware of the regions and countries in which Christianity is growing rapidly; and

- understand the sociological explanations for such developments.

Many years ago I traveled to the Central American country of El Salvador. El Salvador had been in the grip of civil war since 1980 and when I arrived, in early 1993, a ceasefire had been in place for 12 months. The civil war was between left–wing guerrillas, who drew much of their support from poor rural areas, and the ruling military, who controlled the cities. After the war, a period of reconstruction had begun. I had the opportunity to visit a communal farm, 'Alegría', in the countryside. This community had been established by one of the Episcopalian Churches in the capital, San Salvador. The church sent workers and money (sent from churches overseas) to this rural community to help it recover from the devastation of the war. On the day I arrived a gift of money had been presented to the farmers enabling them to purchase a water pump, and create a supply of fresh water from a nearby river.

The association between the established churches and the poor is particularly significant throughout Latin America. Many in the Catholic, Baptist and Episcopalian churches are influenced by the theological tradition of 'liberation theology', a school of thought developed in the 1960s by theologians in the Latin

American Catholic Church. Liberation theology 'emphasizes spiritual as well as social, political and economic liberation' (Evans 1992: 135. For an account of liberation theology see Tombs 2002). The practical outworking of this theology includes, for example, education, health services and advocacy provided by the church for the poor.

In El Salvador, this outreach to the poor put some leaders of the established churches at odds with the ruling military government. This was the case in many Latin American countries in the 1970s and 1980s, where the 'theology of liberation ... came into conflict with powerful military dictatorships, which began persecuting the church' (Robert 2000: 54). Scholar Dana Robert (2000: 54) notes 850 bishops, priests and nuns were killed in Latin America in these decades. In El Salvador, many clergy and church workers were targeted by 'death squads' for allegedly assisting the left-wing rebels. Some were tortured and released, others were killed. I visited a house next to the university that had been home to six Catholic priests. One night in 1989, the priests, their housekeeper and her daughter were dragged into the garden and shot in the head. The house is now a memorial to the slain. I met other clergy who had been tortured by the death squads. One of them, a Baptist minister, had been dragged away and bundled into a car after leading a Sunday morning church service. His young daughter was left behind on the street, wondering if she would ever see her father again.

Later on my trip I met an Episcopalian priest who gave me a tour of the capital San Salvador. Along the way he pointed out a newly established Pentecostal church. Pentecostalism, as I will argue in this chapter, is a rising movement in world Christianity. The priest commented that this new congregation was populated mainly by wealthy and elite Salvadoreans. Pentecostal churches are a growing presence in El Salvador, and are now finding favor among the rising middle class (see Offutt 2010). In addition to their worship services, such churches are establishing schools and other social services.

The example of El Salvador is typical of recent religious changes throughout Latin America. In this part of the world, Christianity, particularly the Catholic Church, has been an established part of society for centuries, but in recent decades changes have occurred that have transformed the religious culture, as well as politics and the wider society. First, liberation theology challenged the religious and political status quo and now Pentecostalism is changing the face of religion in this region. Latin America is not alone in experiencing prodigious religious change in the last few decades. Christianity, particularly Pentecostalism, is growing phenomenally in Asia and Africa. This has implications both for local communities and for the future of world Christianity. Examining the causes of these changes and understanding their implications is the focus of this chapter.

The chapter begins with a demographic overview of a century of Christian change. From there, discussion focuses on Pentecostalism; what it is, and what its ascendancy means in the context of both local and global culture. The case study in this chapter examines the growth in Papua New Guinea (PNG) of one of the world's largest Pentecostal denominations, the Foursquare Church.

Before this, I should add a note about terms. In the past it has been common in academic and popular parlance to divide the world into the categories 'first' and 'third' world or 'developing' and 'developed' world. It is now common to use the terms *Global South* and *Global North* instead. These terms divide the world into regions either economically developing or becoming more industrialized (South) or post-industrial and highly developed (North). Regions and countries in the Global North include North America, Europe, Australia, Japan and New Zealand, with the rest of the world making up the Global South (Pew Forum 2011a: 13). These terms are not geographically precise; Australia and New Zealand (together known as Australasia), part of the Global 'North', contain some of the most southern points of land in the world. Nor are the categories perfect; some countries counted as part of the Global South, like South Korea, Hong Kong, the Gulf States, Taiwan and Singapore, are industrially advanced or oil rich, and whose citizens enjoy a good standard of living, while parts of the Global North (e.g. areas in Eastern Europe) are relatively poor.

Given these inaccuracies, why use such terms at all? As will be seen in this chapter, the terms are very helpful in showing *where* in the world Christianity is growing (many parts of the Southern hemisphere) and where it is declining or staying constant (most parts of the Northern hemisphere). To that end, Australasia, although in the south, religiously is like countries in the north, and counted as such. I use the terms Global South and North in this chapter; elsewhere in this book, I prefer to use terms like 'the West', 'Asia', 'the East' or the 'Middle East'.

CHRISTIANITY'S 'GONE SOUTH': THE RADICAL SHIFT IN WORLDWIDE CHRISTIANITY

Christianity is the world's largest religion, with an estimated 2 billion adherents worldwide in 2010 (Pew Forum 2011a: 9). Christianity was founded in the Middle East, was originally a Jewish sect, and its first followers were persecuted by the Roman Empire. Within a few centuries, its fortunes changed; in 312 CE the Roman Emperor Constantine declared it the religion of the Roman Empire, and its ascendancy to being the world's biggest religion began (McLeod 2003: 1). Over the next few centuries it grew mainly in Europe.

As Christianity moved into Europe, its expression and character changed from its specific Jewish and Mediterranean origins. According to historian Philip Jenkins (2002: 6)

In art and popular thought, Jesus became a blond Aryan ... and Christian theology was reshaped by West European notions of law and feudalism. European Christians reinterpreted the faith through their own concepts of social and gender relations, and then imagined that their culturally specific synthesis was the only correct version of Christian truth.

At the start of the twentieth century, the majority of the world's Christians lived in the Global North. Christianity's demographic, intellectual, political and cultural center was Europe and North America. By century's end, however, this situation had changed dramatically.

In 1910, approximately 32 percent of the world's population identified as Christian. Since then, the proportion of the world's population identifying as Christian has not increased significantly. In 2010, an estimated 35 percent of the world's population was Christian (Pew Forum 2011a: 9). While the *proportion* of the world's population which is Christian has changed little in 100 years, a monumental geographic change has taken place in the same period of time. The proportion of the world's Christians who live in the Global South has increased significantly, while the proportion who live in the Global North has shrunk markedly. Christianity worldwide has turned upside down, and has literally 'gone South' (Jenkins 2002: 3).

Several research centers recently have published estimates of where the world's Christians live, and how this has changed over the past 100 years (e.g. Johnson and Ross 2009; Pew Forum 2011a). A recent report by the Pew Research Center's Forum on Religion and Public Life (the Pew Forum), *Global Christianity: A Report on the Size and Distribution of the World's Christian Population* (2011a), helpfully and reliably maps these demographic changes, using historical data generated by the Center for the Study of Global Christianity (at Gordon-Conwell Theological Seminary), along with its own recent estimates. Using these data, Figure 8.1 shows the distribution of the world's Christians in 1910 and 2010.

The percentages in Figure 8.1 show religious affiliation. As discussed in Chapter 5, not everyone who identifies with a religion attends services of worship regularly, or even believes in God. Nonetheless, data on religious identification can be helpful in mapping patterns of change. In 1910, 66 percent of the world's Christians lived

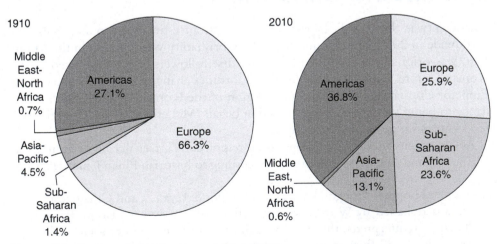

Figure 8.1 Regional distribution of Christians

Source: Pew Forum (2011a: 9). Percentages may not add up to 100 because of rounding.

in Europe. By 2010, that had dropped to 26 percent. In that time, Christianity has grown significantly in sub-Saharan Africa, Latin America and the Asia-Pacific region. In simple terms, the majority of the world's Christians live in the Global South. (That said, the single country with the most number of Christians is the United States.)

Why has Christianity gone South? We know from the previous two chapters that in the regions of the Global North, **Western Europe**, **Australasia** and **North America**, the proportion of the population identifying as Christian decreased between 1910 and 2010, and although the number of Christians has grown in real terms, this growth has been slower compared to elsewhere around the globe. **Latin America** has remained largely Christian across the last 100 years, and today the majority of the population in countries there identify as Christian. Importantly, the rate of population growth in Latin America has generally outstripped population growth in the Global North. In effect, more Christians are being born in Latin America than in the Global North.

Add to this the prodigious growth in the number of Christians in sub-Saharan Africa and the Asia Pacific. In **sub-Saharan Africa 100** years ago, the majority of people identified with or practiced local religions, and only a minority were Christians (9 percent of the population in sub-Saharan Africa). Now the majority of the population (63 percent of the population in sub-Saharan Africa) are Christian (Pew Forum 2011a: 15). People there have converted, and consequent children are born into Christian families. It is a similar story in the **Asia-Pacific**, where the Pew Forum (2011a: 15) estimates the proportion of the population identifying as Christian has grown from 2.7 percent of the population in 1910 to 7 percent of the population in 2010. Again, the overall population growth in these regions generally outstrips the population growth in the Global North. Through a combination of higher birth rates, and an increasing number of adherents, Christianity now has more followers in the Global South than the Global North.

Why Christianity? Explaining the acceptance of Christianity in the Global South is a complex task, and individual countries have their own story to tell. However, there are some commonalties. In majority Christian countries (where the majority of the population are Christians – countries like Brazil, Papua New Guinea, the Philippines and South Africa), Christianity typically was an inheritance (or imposition) from the age of European colonization. This has since been nurtured by effective missionary activity and evangelism, the nationalization of churches (churches administered by locals rather than foreigners), and the lack of effective competition from other religions. As will be seen below, dynamic styles of Christianity are also a factor in recent conversion. In minority Christian countries (e.g. China, India, Viet Nam), vigorous evangelism and the loosening of state restrictions on Christianity are all important factors in the growth of Christianity.

There are further reasons for Christianity's success in the Global South. Religious leaders in the Global North often complain about the spiritual poverty of secularized societies, and the challenge of evangelizing to those who live in materialistic cultures. In the Global South, particularly in sub-Saharan Africa and the Pacific, Christianity, when introduced, has ready belief and acceptance and takes the place of or accompanies an already powerful traditional spiritual worldview. It is easy for many of these people to accept the supernatural claims of Christian teaching. (It should also be noted the introduction of Christianity has typically had a detrimental effect on indigenous religions and customs, with Christianity viewed by missionaries as the only true religion.) Religion also provides social acceptance, personal meaning, material opportunities, social services and community. The need for these can be heightened in societies experiencing rapid social transition, as is the case in many countries in the Global South. The next section explores some of these factors in greater detail.

Importantly, the shift in world Christianity is more than a simple demographic change. A distinctive *style* of Christianity is prevailing in the Global South. According to Jenkins (2002: 7):

> [the] denominations that are triumphing … are stalwartly traditional or even reactionary by the standards of the economically advanced nations. The churches that have made the most dramatic progress in the Global South have either been Roman Catholic, of a traditional and fideistic kind, or radical Protestant sects, evangelical or Pentecostal:

In the next section, I look at the example of Pentecostalism to consider why a 'dynamic' style of Christianity is prospering in the Global South, and the implications for the future of Christianity worldwide.

THE GROWTH OF 'DYNAMIC' CHRISTIANITY: THE CASE OF THE PENTECOSTALS

Christianity has grown dramatically in the Global South across the past 100 years, and the kinds of Christianity that are prevailing tend to be theologically conservative, experiential (focused on observable religious experiences) and biblically orthodox (the Bible is generally seen as the authoritative word of God). This is best exemplified by the growth of Pentecostalism.

Worldwide, Pentecostalism is now among the fastest-growing movements within Christianity. The Pew Forum (2006: 1), in its report, *Spirit and Power: a 10-country Survey of Pentecostals*, notes the 'major strands of Pentecostalism now represent at least one quarter of all Christians … ranking second only to Catholicism in the number of followers [worldwide]'. An estimated 584 million people worldwide are Pentecostal, representing 8.5 percent of the world's population (Pew Forum 2011a: 67). Internationally, the Assemblies of God is the largest Pentecostal denomination, but there are other well-known international denominations, such as the Foursquare Church and United Pentecostal Church International.

The Pentecostal movement began with the Azusa Street Revival in Los Angeles in 1906 and spread across America. The Azusa Street revival was a remarkable event.

People in the Azusa Street Christian Mission openly began to experience the 'gifts of the Holy Spirit', such as speaking in tongues (explained below). A spontaneous movement at first, it soon became formally organized and Pentecostal denominations were formed (see Robbins 2010). It boomed in the United States and remains a large movement there; about 5 percent of the US adult population belong to a Pentecostal denomination (Pew Forum 2006: 94). (It should be noted that Pentecostalism has emerged in the Global North as a potent religious force, attracting adherents away from established, older denominations, and finding strong support among immigrant communities.) Many of the world's major Pentecostal denominations, such as the Assemblies of God and the Foursquare Church, are headquartered in the United States.

The expansion of Pentecostalism in the Global South has been remarkable, and it is now the dominant strand of Protestantism in many nations (remembering that the Latin American countries and the Philippines are majority Catholic), having overtaken other more established Protestant denominations. For example, in present-day Brazil, which has a majority Catholic population, about seven out of ten Protestants are Pentecostals, while in Kenya, which has a majority Protestant population, about 50 percent of Protestants are Pentecostals (Pew Forum 2006: 4). In the Pacific and Latin America, much of the membership of the Pentecostal churches is being drawn from traditional 'mainline' denominations, such as the Catholic, Anglican, Lutheran and Baptist traditions (Ernst 2006).

Who are the Pentecostals?

Scholars of Pentecostalism note the incredible diversity worldwide among Pentecostals, and the diffuse movements encompassed by the term (see Anderson 2004, 2010; Yong 2010). Indeed, Pentecostal theologian Amos Yong (2010) prefers to spell Pentecostalism with a lower-case 'p' to signify the broadness of this movement. A helpful overview of the many strands is provided by Allan Anderson (2010). I will summarize these briefly.

The term '**Pentecostal**' refers to churches which place a strong emphasis on the so-called 'gifts of the spirit' (e.g. speaking in tongues, miraculous healing), hold the doctrine of 'baptism in the Holy Spirit' (discussed below), make use of contemporary music in their worship, and have a theology and preaching that is focused more on the application of the Bible to one's everyday life than on exegesis of Christian scripture (exegesis is a detailed examination of the meanings of religious texts).

Closely related to Pentecostalism is the **charismatic** movement. The term 'charismatic' applies to individuals and groups within larger mainline denominations who are favorably disposed towards the Pentecostal spiritual practices and accept other Pentecostal doctrines, such as baptism in the Holy Spirit. Charismatic congregations, small groups and individuals can be found in the Episcopalian and Anglican Churches, Catholic, Baptist, Lutheran and Churches of Christ denominations, amongst others. The Pew Forum (2006: 1) observes Pentecostal and charismatic groups often are together referred to as '**renewalists**', because of their shared belief in the spiritually renewing gifts of the Holy Spirit.

In the literature, one also will encounter the terms 'classic Pentecostalism' and 'neo-Pentecostalism'. Classical Pentecostalism refers to the older forms of Pentecostalism found in the most established Pentecostal denominations, mainly in America. Neo-Pentecostalism refers to 'newer independent Pentecostal churches that embrace contemporary cultures, use contemporary methods of communication ... and often have a prosperity emphasis' (Anderson 2010: 32).

The gifts of the spirit, important in Pentecostalism, are a range of ecstatic phenomena. The gifts traditionally include speaking in tongues, being slain in the Spirit, prophecy, visions and miraculous healing. Speaking in tongues (also known by the technical name glossolalia) involves speaking in an unknown, yet realistic-sounding, language of which the speaker has no previous knowledge (Singleton 2002: 354). It consists of indecipherable strings of words and phrases which sound more language-like than simple 'gibberish'. Samarin (1972: 2) defines it as 'a meaningless but phonologically structured human utterance believed by the speaker to be a real language but bearing no systematic resemblance to any natural language'. It is important to emphasize that the language spoken by a tongues speaker is not a known language. Before becoming a tongues speaker, a person has no prior knowledge of this language and will not develop any comprehension of what is being said as they continue to speak in tongues, though they will almost certainly become familiar with the sound of the language and use the same language as the practice is continued (see Singleton 2002 for a detailed discussion).

Other ecstatic behavior can be witnessed in Pentecostal churches, including being 'slain in the spirit'. This entails spontaneous, uncontrolled shaking and, sometimes, falling. Many Pentecostal churches routinely have moments in the service where congregants may speak in tongues or are invited to the front of the church to experience 'God's power' and so may be slain in the spirit.

Contemporary worship styles and music are very important to Pentecostals. According to Miller and Yamamori (2007: 23), the 'engine of Pentecostalism is its worship'. The music is loud and modern, and has much in common with contemporary rock music. Worshippers are encouraged to allow their bodies freedom, to be unrestrained and exuberant. There is plenty of waving of arms, swaying, clapping and other movement. Pentecostal churches have a very functional appearance and there is little use of traditional religious imagery (e.g. stained glass, altars etc.). The service is not as structured as those in mainline denominations, and usually there is no formal liturgy or the celebration of Holy Communion.

Theologically, Pentecostal churches usually are evangelical. Evangelical Christians place a strong emphasis on the infallibility and literal interpretation of Scripture, hold the doctrine of salvation through grace rather than works (a place in heaven cannot be earned; it is a gift from God) and place little emphasis on liturgical or sacramental aspects of faith. Most Pentecostal and charismatic Christians are evangelical, although not all evangelicals are charismatic.

The doctrine of being 'baptized in the spirit' is central to Pentecostal teaching. Baptism in the Holy Spirit refers to a 'second blessing' or spiritual experience, following conversion, in which the believer is empowered by the Holy Spirit to enjoy a deeper and more profound Christian life. According to Black (1991: 107), Pentecostals see baptism in the Holy Spirit as 'distinct from, and usually later than the experience of being born again [accepting Jesus Christ as a personal savior], and quite distinct from the experience of baptism in water'. Other doctrines and teachings favored by Pentecostals include most controversially the 'prosperity doctrine' – the idea that God rewards the faithful with material wealth and better life outcomes (e.g. greater social status, better housing, better 'fortune' or 'luck').

Explaining the growth of Pentecostalism

Why has Pentecostalism prospered in the Global South? Jenkins (2002: 72) cautions against totalizing, universal explanations as to why Pentecostalism has grown and points to the importance of local factors in making sense of religious change. That said, he also notes there are some common features for the reasons why this religious movement has so much traction worldwide. Below is a summary of various explanations posited by different scholars, all or some of which may be factors explaining growth in different locations. (For overviews see Ernst 2006; Jenkins 2002; Miller and Yamamori 2007.)

Adaptability

In the first instance, it is a form of religious expression particularly adaptable to local conditions. Beyer (2006: 148) observes 'Pentecostalism has proven attractive to a wide variety of peoples in different cultural settings. It is easy to adopt and above all easy to adapt.' It is certainly true in Pentecostalism that new congregations can be established rapidly, and are not mired in bureaucracy or beholden to ecclesiastical hierarchy. Ernst (2006: 713) notes 'the fastest growing segment of Global Christianity is ... small independent Pentecostal or evangelical groups that rarely identify themselves with any particular denominational establishment'. Individuals and small communities 'moved by the spirit' can readily establish their own church, and lay persons often are able to serve in pastoral roles. On drives through the PNG countryside I have spied many 'pop-up' new churches.

Worship style, spirituality and theology

Pentecostalism is dynamic religion: it is contemporary, alive and energizing. This is often in contrast to the staid, liturgical and traditional styles found in the mainline churches. The widespread use of contemporary gospel music and an exuberant worship style are seen as critical to Pentecostalism's appeal (Cox 1995; Beyer 2006; Miller and Yamamori 2007). Preachers teach about the reality of supernatural intervention in everyday life, and offer the prospect of supernatural healing, widely practiced in the Pentecostal and charismatic traditions (see Singleton 2001b).

Although not preached in every Pentecostal church, the prosperity doctrine appeals to many. Material goods are not shunned but actively sought by the faithful, and wealth is seen as a sign of God's blessing (Meyer 2010: 147; see also Coleman 2000 for a good description of the prosperity doctrine). Many Pentecostals believe God will improve their material circumstances if they are faithful and give generously (including providing a portion of their income to their church).

Effective evangelism

Pentecostal churches have also proven to be very effective at evangelizing. Meyer (2010: 157) notes:

> Traveling crusades … books, tapes and DVDs and the beaming of televangelist radio and television programs have been central to capturing broad audiences. Likewise there are a host of Pentecostal banners, sign boards, stickers, and sounds that index the presence and power of Pentecostal churches.

In the PNG town where I lived when writing some of this book, it was very common to come across a Pentecostal preacher with a loudspeaker proclaiming the gospel; at the market, the main park near the airstrip or along the main road in town. Worship services could be heard blasting out on Saturdays and Sundays. All of this religious dynamism means that Pentecostal churches are particularly effective at drawing in religious 'switchers' from mainline traditions, or appealing to those who are unchurched.

Urbanization and social dislocation

Jenkins (2002) notes one important social consequence of modernization is the expansion of urban centers, and the subsequent migration of people from rural areas to cities looking for work. This move can come at a cost: Miller and Yamamori (2007: 22–23) note in many parts of the Global South people find themselves socially dislocated as they move from rural to urban locations.

Pentecostal churches in the Global South particularly have been diligent in their outreach and evangelization to those living in the margins (Roberts 2000: 56). Pentecostal churches provide a range of health, welfare and educational services. Jenkins (2002:74) notes these churches provide: 'a social network that would otherwise be lacking, and help [in teaching] members the skills they need to survive in a rapidly developing society'. Commentators note also Pentecostalism can lead to individual betterment as believers abstain from destructive behavior, such as drinking, and become more focused on looking after themselves (Miller and Yamamori 2007: 32).

At the same time, as the example of El Salvador shows, Pentecostalism appeals to more well-to-do people because it facilitates, and is associated with, upward social mobility (Miller and Yamamori 2007: 32). According to Miller and Yamamori (2007: 21) 'Pentecostalism was born among lower-class people, and much of its amazing initial growth was due to its connection with impoverished people ... But over the last few decades in particular, Pentecostalism has attracted a new class of more afflu-ent and educated people.'

In like manner Offutt (2010: 391–2) argues: 'Pentecostal churches are blossoming in middle- and upper-middle-class neighborhoods across the Global South ... highly visible churches are attracting urban professionals and university students. They sit in pews with their social peers and listen to pastors that are also socially mobile.' Many preachers like to openly display their wealth as evidence of the prosperity doctrine.

Gender

Church traditionally has appealed more to women than men (see Chapter 11). Pen-tecostalism has been noted as being particularly receptive to women's spiritual and practical needs. Jenkins (2002: 75–6) puts it this way: 'membership in a new Pente-costal church means a significant improvement in the lives of poor women, since this is where they are more likely to meet men who do not squander family resources on drinking, gambling, prostitutes and second households'. In conversations I had with religious professionals in PNG I was told many married women are attracted to these congregations in the hope that by joining the church their recalcitrant hus-bands might follow and clean up their lives.

In sum, we see a range of social and cultural factors explain the particular appeal of Pentecostalism. Some of its appeal is due to particular elements in Pentecostalism which are not always found in other churches, especially its dynamic and con-temporary approach to worship. At the same time, Pentecostal churches have been organized in their evangelism and effective in their ministry to those living on the margins of modernizing societies.

EXCURSUS: THE DYNAMICS OF CONTEMPORARY CHRISTIANITY: AFRICA AND CHINA

The focus in the chapter thus far has been on the global rise of Pentecostalism. To provide a larger view of world Christianity, this section explores briefly the impact and character of Christianity in Africa and China, two regions in the world where Christianity is growing rapidly.

Engaged Christianity in Sub-Saharan Africa

Like many African countries, Zambia is in the grip of a HIV/AIDS epidemic. A 2011 estimate from the United Nations suggested about one million Zambians had HIV/AIDS, in a population of 14 million (www.unaids.org). In a recent newspaper interview, a Zambian church minister, Reverend Pukuta Mwanza, observed: 'So, the reality of HIV/AIDS became so prevalent [in Zambia] … that there was a common saying: "If you are not infected, you are affected"' (Falsani 2013). Mwanza is executive director of the Evangelical Fellowship of Zambia, which is the peak body of evangelical churches in the southern African country. One of its stated aims is 'To empower the poor, marginalized and vulnerable persons and households' (Evangelical Fellowship of Zambia, nd). This social concern is a hallmark of African Christianity, in both European-founded denominations and African-established churches.

As noted above, Christianity now dominates the religious landscape of most Sub-Saharan countries. (The countries in Saharan Africa are Muslim-majority countries. e.g. Egypt, Morocco.) A few countries in Sub-Saharan Africa have Muslim majorities (e.g. Mali and Senegal), some have a roughly even mix of Muslims and Christians (e.g. Nigeria, Chad), however, most are majority Christian countries (e.g. South Africa, Botswana, Zambia and Rwanda) (Pew Forum 2010). There is considerable variety in the kinds of Christianity found in Sub-Saharan Africa.

The 'mainline' Christian denominations are an important presence. An inheritance from the age of colonialism, they have grown prodigiously in the twentieth century, and today there are large populations of Catholics, Anglicans, Lutherans and other conservative Protestants in Sub-Saharan Africa. Gifford (2008) notes these traditional, mainline churches make an enormous contribution to the provision of education, health care and social services.

African Christianity is not simply an inheritance of European colonization and missionizing. Christianity, remarkably, had been a presence in Africa for almost two millennia: the Ethiopian Orthodox church was established perhaps as early as the first century AD. It became the state religion of Ethiopia in the fourth century AD. This is not the only form of African Christianity which owes little to European colonization. In the early twentieth century several vibrant churches emerged, established by Africans rather than European missionaries. These include the Zionist Christian, Nazarite Baptist and Aladura churches. More recently, independent Pentecostal and charismatic churches have emerged (see Meyer 2004). These indigenous African churches are known collectively as African Independent Churches. Kalu (2003: 89) suggests that most of the Pentecostal churches in Africa 'did not originate from the revival in Azusa Street in the United States and [were] not a product of missionary enterprise'. Moreover, the uptake of Christianity has not obliterated indigenous folk religion entirely, and the spirituality of many African Independent Churches is an admixture of folk religion and Christianity.

Christianity is growing quickly in Africa. One estimate suggests that 22,800 Africans become Christian every day (Gifford 2008: 276). Like other places in the Global South, in recent decades it has been Pentecostal and charismatic Christianity which has grown most rapidly, drawing in both converts to Christianity, and 'switchers' from the mainline denominations. According to the pre-eminent scholar of African Pentecostalism, Ogbu Kalu (2007: 9), 'All Christian forms are growing in Africa, but Pentecostalism enjoys the fastest growth rate.'

As noted above, one of the main reasons Pentecostalism is prospering in the Global South is because of its ability to address pressing, local needs. This is true of Africa. Kalu (2003: 88) observes:

> The ordinary Pentecostal in Africa is less concerned with modernity and globalization and more about a renewed relationship with God … empowerment by the Holy Spirit and protection in the blood of Jesus as the person struggles to eke out a viable life in a hostile environment.

A prominent dimension of the theology of many African Pentecostal churches is the 'prosperity gospel', which is a 'set of doctrines promising believers both physical health and material success on earth' (Robbins 2004: 122). Foremost among those who benefit from God's providence are the church pastors themselves. Gifford (2008: 286) observes: 'Pastoring these newer churches has brought not just a living, sometimes considerable wealth, but also fame and status.' Significantly, this emphasis on prosperity sits alongside increasing Pentecostal social engagement (see Miller and Yamamori 2007).

Christianity's 'greenfield'? China

Pentecostal congregations in the West have embraced the possibilities of the Internet. The website of the monumental Lakewood Church in Houston, Texas, has video sermons, podcasts, an online shop (music, books) and links to Twitter, YouTube and Facebook (they have their own smartphone app too). Australia's largest church, Hillsong, has a similarly slick website, which even streams Hillsong's own TV show. (See Hillsong.com and Lakewoodchurch.com.) A large church in China is following suit. The Beijing International Christian Fellowship (BICF), a growing independent Pentecostal church of several thousand members, has comfortably embraced the digital age, with a website almost as fancy as its Western counterparts (bicf.org). Interestingly, a tiny disclaimer at the bottom of the homepage notes: 'Due to local government regulations, the Fellowship is open to foreign ID holders only.' The BICF is for foreign nationals, or ethnic Chinese who have the right kind of documents. Herein lies the paradox of Christianity in China: it is growing quickly, but subject also to government regulations and restrictions.

China has its own significant indigenous religions (see Chapter 1), but like most parts of the globe, Christianity is present there as well. Until the nineteenth century, Christianity's fortunes waxed and waned in China. In that century, there was extensive and vigorous missionary activity and the numbers of Chinese Christians grew substantially. Christian growth was halted dramatically by the Communist regime in 1949. At that time, there were approximately 700,000 to 1 million Christians in China (Yang 2005: 426). Initially, Christianity was brought under state control, however: with the 1960s 'Great Proletarian Cultural Revolution' religion was officially banned and Christians were harshly persecuted (Yang 2005: 427). Some churches continued operating in secret ('underground' churches). This ban was later dropped, but Christianity is still technically regulated by the Communist state, and Chinese Christians are supposed to follow one of three official church movements. In practice, it is a little more fluid and many Chinese are members of one of many underground or unofficial churches. The Pew Forum (2011a: 97) estimates there are now 67 million Chinese Christians, about 5 percent of the population, the majority of whom are Protestants. Scholars note that Pentecostalism is an important part of this growth (see Cox 1995; Anderson 2000).

Earlier in this chapter I examined why Pentecostalism is finding favor the world over. Prominent scholar of religion in China, Fenggang Yang (2011) has examined why Christianity *generally* is flourishing in spite of a regime that is antipathetic to religion, and in a country that is becoming more modernized and prosperous – conditions which are, in the view of some scholars, supposed to neutralize religious growth. Applying some of the insights of the market economies thesis (see Chapter 4), Yang argues that 'heavy regulation of religion will lead not to religious demise but, rather, to complication … a tripartite religious market with different dynamics' (2011: 86).

Yang (2011: 88) suggests that the heavy regulation of religion in China has seen three 'religious markets' emerge: the red market, which is state-sanctioned religious activity (e.g. one of the official Church movements); the black market, which is officially banned religious activity (e.g. membership of the unofficial branches of the Catholic church); and a gray market, which is religious activities with an ambiguous legal status (e.g. yoga practice, or Chinese spiritual practices like *Qigong*). Government regulation in China has not eradicated religion, rather, it caused the black and gray markets to swell and prosper to meet the religious and spiritual needs of the population. According to Yang (2011: 123), the gray market 'is not only huge but volatile … a fertile ground for new religious movements'. Pentecostalism finds its niche in the unofficial religious markets, one which is growing rather than stultifying.

GLOBAL OR AMERICAN CHRISTIANITY?

While Christianity's demographic center is no longer the Global North, the United States has more Christians than any other individual country. These two dynamics do not, in the view of Wuthnow and Offutt (2008: 213) 'operate in isolation from one another'. In particular, there is debate among scholars whether the rise of Pentecostalism and other evangelical churches constitutes the 'Americanization' of Global Christianity (see Brouwer et al. 1996; Noll 2009; Anderson 2010). That is, American-style theology and practice have become the new world standard, replacing earlier European hegemony. There is little doubt the American influence on religion in the Global South is obvious and direct. Pentecostalism spread throughout Latin America, Asia and, to an extent, Africa, in the first instance through the evangelizing efforts of American churches which established congregations in overseas localities (see Noll 2009). Today, American-founded Pentecostal denominations are in many countries and American leadership continues to nurture these congregations. Other, American, non-Pentecostal Christian movements are also prospering in the Global South, including the Church of Jesus Christ and the Latter Day Saints (Mormons) and the Seventh-Day Adventist church, and much of this success is the result of the evangelizing efforts of American missionaries.

Moreover, American cultural influences are found throughout the Global South in Pentecostal worship styles, preaching and theology. PNG is a case in point. American religious influences are immediate and direct. American preachers are broadcast on satellite TV, local congregations have American DVDs, guest preachers come from the United States and contemporary American gospel music is played on local radio, and sung in churches. I have heard PNG Pentecostal pastors preaching in a dramatic, theatrical – almost berserk – manner, echoing the 'fire and brimstone' style of American tent-revival preachers.

American churches continue to focus considerable mission efforts overseas. This enterprise is explored by eminent sociologist Robert Wuthnow in his recent book, *Boundless Faith* (2009). He notes '[in 2001] there were 42,787 U.S. citizens working full-time as missionaries in other countries ... significantly higher than the comparable number in the 1950s' (Wuthnow 2009: 23). Wuthnow (2009: 23) also finds as many as '350,000 Americans had spent two weeks and up to a year abroad serving as short-term mission volunteers, and an estimated one million had served less than two weeks'. Some of these short-term trips involve teenagers (see Trinitapoli and Vaisey 2009). There is little doubt that American Christianity, Pentecostal and otherwise, is highly influential in the Global South.

However, as scholars of globalization have argued, when ideas, resources and cultural practices are transplanted from one location to another, the 'glocalization' of culture occurs; culture is an expression of local and global influences mixing together (see Vasquez and Marquardt 2003). The result in many churches is an adapted, hybrid expression of Christianity – American influences in theology and worship style mixing with and responding to local tastes, preferences and issues. Pentecostal churches in PNG, for example, are reaching out to people who are often very poor, and facing chronic health and wellbeing issues, such as HIV/AIDS, alcohol abuse, domestic violence and male infidelity. Added to this are the persistence of the traditional Melanesian worldview and powerful social obligations and customs. Preaching, theology and outreach programs must necessarily address these issues. American religious practices are not simply transplanted into this distinctive cultural milieu without considerable adaptation.

Since the end of the Second World War, churches throughout the Global South have become nationalized (see Robert 2000), meaning that mostly they are run, and in the case of many independent churches founded, by nationals rather than foreign missionaries. Increasingly churches in the Global South are also exerting their influence beyond their borders. Offutt (2010: 398) notes one particular congregation in El Salvador has a:

2006 foreign outreach budget [which] was $165,000, through which they supported Salvadoran missionaries to India, the Philippines, West Africa, and a number of Latin American countries. Medical or evangelistic mission teams from Josue [the church in question] have gone out to Kosovo, Equatorial Guinea, Honduras, the Niger, Nicaragua, and Vietnam.

The increasingly irreligious Global North is a particular focus of Pentecostal churches in the Global South. Thus we see the phenomenon of 'reverse mission', where missionaries are sent to the Global North to conduct mission work (see Jenkins 2007). Pentecostal Churches in PNG, for example, have sent missionaries not only to neighboring Pacific nations but to nearby Australia as well. Religious migrants from the Global South have also invigorated some traditional congregations in the Global North, or established their own, independent churches.

CASE STUDY

THE FOURSQUARE CHURCH IN PAPUA NEW GUINEA

One of the world's largest Pentecostal denominations is the Foursquare Church. It was founded by a woman evangelist, Aimee Semple McPherson, in 1920s America. Today it counts as many as eight million members worldwide (source: www.religion-facts.com), with congregations in Africa, the Americas, Europe and the Asia Pacific. McPherson was a dynamic preacher and evangelist who built a huge church, the historic Angelus Temple, near downtown Los Angeles. The Temple still can be visited today, and is an early example of a 'megachurch'; a church with seating for thousands. From America, Foursquare evangelists planted churches around the world.

The name 'Foursquare' signifies the fourfold, ongoing ministry of Jesus: he is the savior, baptizer with the Holy Spirit, healer and second-coming king. The Foursquare Church represents these parts of Jesus' ministry with different colors – red, blue, yellow, and purple – and banners and flags with these colors are displayed prominently at the front of their churches. The Foursquare Church, like most other Pentecostal denominations, preaches the doctrine of baptism in the Holy Spirit, and believes in the charismatic gifts of the Holy Spirit (e.g. speaking in tongues).

The Foursquare Church arrived in Papua New Guinea in 1956 with American evangelist Mason Hughes. Its popularity grew and in 1988, the Foursquare Church became nationalized (that is, organized by PNG nationals) (Gibbs 2007: 68). There are now several hundred congregations and perhaps 100,000 or more members nationwide.

On a recent, sunny Saturday morning in the Eastern Highlands of PNG, I had a long conversation with Reverend Kumoro Vira, a Foursquare pastor and the first national president of the Foursquare Church in PNG. He kindly shared with me his thoughts about the Foursquare Church in PNG. Among many topics, we discussed the focus of its ministry, why it is prospering in PNG, and its new missionary activity.

Reverend Vira told me the Foursquare Church in PNG draws new members from among the unchurched and those who previously worshipped in other, mainline denominations, such as the Lutheran and Catholic churches. Foursquare Churches play lively music, sing gospel choruses, and conduct services in *tok ples* (local language) or *tok pisin* (the lingua franca in PNG). Some of the songs are translated

Figure 8.2 A typical house found in the Papua New Guinea (PNG) Highlands
Source: Ceridwen Spark

Figure 8.3 A Foursquare Gospel church service in the PNG Highlands. In this photo the children are receiving a special children's message
Source: Ceridwen Spark

(Continued)

(Continued)

from English, some are their own compositions. He said the baptism in the Spirit and signs of other gifts of the Spirit are an important part of Foursquare ministry: 'It is part and parcel of our ministry. You can go to Assemblies of God and Foursquare and other Pentecostal churches too, like CLC (Christian Life Center) [and see these gifts]. Yes it is part of us, part and parcel of the Pentecostal movement.'

Reverend Vira felt that the Foursquare Church's emphasis on family is a key reason why this movement is prospering in PNG. He told me,

One thing in the Foursquare [is] we emphasize the family ... God is the father and we worship the family kind of God, loving, caring, so we emphasize the family, the importance of family and of course in the ministry, pastors and leaders, we are all family. Sometimes you will see the members of the clergy [in other denominations], my thinking there is a distance, there is a gap. There is the clergy over there and there is a sheep over here but in the Foursquare church we are trying to emphasize we are all family members.

He also felt the Foursquare Church provided a moral and spiritual compass for a society experiencing transition and upheaval, saying:

[our church is showing people] This is the way we behave, this is the way we behave towards our wives and this is the way we behave to our opposite sex when we are young. We don't sleep around, we don't live together, you know its not our culture. So we don't steal, its disgrace to our community, our *haus lain* (extended family) and this sort of thing.

Like many denominations in PNG, the Foursquare Church's ministry extends far beyond worship and they provide important social services, including mobile health clinics in rural areas, schooling and accommodation. One particular example we discussed was a program promoting women's health and wellbeing:

We see that the gospel of Jesus Christ is not for the soul or inner-being only. It's also for the body and that is why we have special programs like [for example] the women's group ... So we have this ministry which specifically speaks to women ... we incorporated this health program for women, like, 'What is HIV?' and you know ... and maternity situations, so women take care of that.

Women sometimes take important leadership roles, such as preaching and leading worship. (This denomination was, after all, founded by a woman.)

The Foursquare Church in PNG is more than a far-flung outpost of an American mother-church. It is proudly national, and most of its pastors and workers are Papua New Guineans. That said, they still affiliate with the church in America, and attend conferences with Foursquare pastors from around the world.

Like a growing number of churches in the Global South, the Foursquare Church in PNG sees its mission field extending overseas. Reverend Vira told me:

> We Papua New Guineans ... we have been a receiving church but now we are sending church ... We have received so we must give, so we are focusing, our focus is now on the Pacific region now. Our first missionary to Australia is in Western Australia ... we have a missionary now in Vanuatu, we have a missionary now in the Solomons [Islands, another Melanesian country] ... we have a missionary in Palau and we have a missionary in Cairns [an Australian city] ... I think we will soon have a missionary in Fiji.
>
> Like many other Pentecostal churches, the Foursquare Church has a global reach. Its Papua New Guinean chapter is a growing and important presence in the country's religious, social and cultural life, and is now exerting its influence further afield.
>
> **Want to know more?**
>
> * The Melanesian Institute, located in Goroka, PNG, is a research institute specializing in religion among the Melanesian people. A range of its publications can be accessed via the website: http://www.mi.org.pg/

It is not just Pentecostal churches from the Global South exerting their influence in Global Christianity. Church leaders from the Global South represent an increasingly influential presence in worldwide denominations, such as the Anglican and Catholic Churches. According to Rubenstein (2004), there are now more Anglican Bishops from Africa and Asia than Britain and America, and their numbers allow them to pass resolutions at international meetings that fit their more conservative theology, such as the denial of ordination for women and homosexuals. In March 2013, the Catholic Church elected Argentinian Cardinal Jorge Mario Bergoglio to be pope (Pope Francis I), the first non-European pontiff in more than 1200 years. Contemporary Christianity worldwide is not American in style, but is truly transnational, with the flow of ideas and resources criss-crossing borders worldwide.

CONCLUSION

This chapter has examined the growth of Christianity in the Global South and considered some of the social, demographic and cultural reasons behind this. It was observed that Pentecostalism is arguably the most significant contemporary movement in Christianity throughout the Global South. Other evangelical or theologically conservative denominations and religious movements are also prospering in the Global South, including the Seventh Day Adventists, the Mormons and charismatic and evangelical streams within the Anglican and Catholic Churches. The influence of the Global North on world Christianity is less pronounced than it was a few decades ago, although the United States remains a truly significant national presence in world Christianity. While the Catholic Church still has its headquarters in Europe, much of its vitality is found in the Global South, in countries such as Viet Nam, the Philippines and India, and Latin America.

All of this growth and change has both local and international religious implications. The local church scene throughout the Global South is increasingly Pentecostal and charismatic in character. Internationally, we are seeing a more concerted mission effort from churches in the Global South to the 'irreligious' Global North, while transnational church organizations are influenced increasingly by the theological preferences of constituencies in the Global South.

Moreover, Pentecostal and evangelical churches are involved increasingly in local politics and seeking to influence public life throughout countries in the Global South. Pentecostal politicians, in places like Nigeria, Brazil and Guatemala, are keen to display their religious credentials and implement social policy that reflects a Pentecostal agenda. This, coupled with Pentecostalism's expanding social services, means its influence is extending far beyond the church door. All of this recent change means that Christianity's future may not look anything like its past.

Points to ponder

What effect might the growth of Christianity have on pre-Christian local customs and ways of life in countries throughout the Global South? Marx called religion the opiate of the masses. Do you think this is true of Pentecostalism?

Next steps ...

The Pew Forum report, *Global Christianity: A Report on the Size and Distribution of the World's Christian Population* (2011a), is a key source of demographic information about the world's Christians. It can be downloaded from the Pew Forum website. An excellent introduction to world Christianity is Douglas Jacobsen's *The World's Christians: Who They Are, Where They Are, and How They Got There* (2011). Donald Miller and Tetsunao Yamamori's book *Global Pentecostalism: The New Face of Christian Social Engagement* (2007) considers the increasing scope of Pentecostal social justice ministries. The book also includes a DVD. Robert Wuthnow's *Boundless Faith: The Global Outreach of American Churches* (2009) examines the transnational networks of world Christianity and has helpful chapters on the Globalization of Christianity. Harvey Cox's *Fire from Heaven: The Rise of Pentecostal Spirituality and the Reshaping of Religion in the Twenty-first Century* (1995) is an accessible account of world Pentecostalism. Ogbu Kalu's *African Pentecostalism: An Introduction* (2008) is an excellent book focusing on Africa, and I also recommend Fenggang Yang's *Religion in China: Survival and Revival Under Communist Rule* (2011).

Documentaries

Britain's Channel Four produced the eight-part series *Christianity: A History*. Episode six, 'Dark Continents', focuses on the Global South. The TV series *Unreported*

World, also shown on Britain's Channel Four, has a short film on Nigeria's millionaire preachers (2011 series, episode 14). Watch online at www.channel4.com/programmes/unreported-world/4od#3268166.

Web

The Gordon-Conwell Theological Seminary is home to the Center for the Study of Global Christianity and their website has many useful resources: http://www.gordonconwell.edu/resources/Center-for-the-Study-of-Global-Christianity.cfm

9

buddhism and hinduism in a globalized world

After reading this chapter you will:

- possess an insight into how globalization is affecting Hinduism and Buddhism;

- understand the patterns and processes of religious migration; and

- be able to explain why 'Eastern' religious ideas are popular in the West.

'Maeve' (not her real name) is a 23-year-old Australian university student. I interviewed her as part of a study on contemporary belief in the afterlife (see Singleton 2012). She thinks that after she dies she might be reincarnated: 'I'm just open to it I suppose. I don't like to think there is nothing.' Maeve is not a religious person; she was raised as a Catholic but no longer considers herself a member of that tradition.

Reincarnation – also known as rebirth or transmigration – is the belief that some aspect of a person, such as the spirit or soul, survives death and is 'reborn' in another human, or in some cases, another living creature. The doctrine of reincarnation is central to Hinduism, which teaches that a person's actions in one life influence what happens upon rebirth. Buddhism also teaches the doctrine of reincarnation; people are trapped on a constant wheel of death and rebirth and must seek enlightenment to break this cycle. None of the Abrahamic religions – Judaism, Christianity or Islam – subscribes to the doctrine of reincarnation.

Even though she was raised Catholic, and lives in a country in which Christianity is the largest religion, Maeve finds Buddhism more appealing: 'I was raised a Christian but I like the beliefs that Buddhists have, just karma and that sort of thing and [it's] just peaceful, I just like the way they work.' Maeve is not alone among Australian youth in believing in reincarnation. A recent national Australian study found 31 percent of people aged 13–24 'definitely' believe in reincarnation (Singleton 2012: 457). This widespread belief in reincarnation is indicative of a broader Western interest in, and acceptance of, beliefs and practices that originate from Eastern religions.

During the late nineteenth century, a handful of Westerners were drawn to the teachings and practices of Hinduism and Buddhism, an interest that accelerated in the 1960s with the growth of the New Age movement. Today it appears the West is 'enchanted' by Eastern religions. Examples of this interest include yoga classes, Tantric massage services, mindful meditation programs, sell-out stadium tours from the Dalai Lama and best-selling books from gurus such as Deepak Chopra. Much of this is 'Buddhism-lite' or 'Hinduism-lite', where people dabble with ideas, practices and concepts drawn from serious religious traditions, perhaps only vaguely aware of their religious roots. But many Westerners also explore these religions deeply, and convert, particularly to Buddhism.

This Western interest in aspects of Eastern religions has coincided with the large-scale migration to the West of Buddhists, Sikhs and Hindus. Sizeable migrant communities of people following these religions now live in Great Britain, Canada, Australia and the United States. These migrants maintain active links and networks with their countries of origin.

This chapter explores recent changes in the Buddhist and Hindu traditions. Particular attention is paid to how migrating religions and migrants settle into new locations. In addition, it considers how and why Eastern religious ideas, practices and beliefs have become popular among Westerners. Consequently, this chapter brings to the fore aspects of the globalization of world religions, showing how this process involves the large-scale migration and settlement of people and their religion, and the flow of ideas and concepts from one culture to another.

THE MAJOR RELIGIONS OF ASIA: CONTEMPORARY EXPRESSIONS

This section describes briefly the central tenets of Buddhism and Hinduism, which are among the world's biggest religions. They are diverse and diffuse: a few short paragraphs cannot do them justice. As noted in Chapter 1, there is even debate about whether and to what extent Hinduism and Buddhism *are* religions. What follows then is a brief sketch that illuminates some of the important elements of contemporary Buddhism and Hinduism.

Religions of the East and West?

The Middle East was the birthplace and cradle of three of the world's major religions – Islam, Christianity, and Judaism, together known as the Abrahamic religions. Christianity is now the largest religion in the Western world (Europe, North America, Australasia). Another important location for the birth and development of religions was South-East, South and East Asia, sometimes referred to as the 'East'. China has produced various Chinese folk-religions, ancestor veneration, and the religious-like philosophies of Taoism and Confucianism. Japan was the birthplace of Shintoism. India was the birthplace of Hinduism, Buddhism, Jainism and Sikhism.

Pioneering sociologist of religion, Max Weber, was especially interested in the differences between Eastern and Abrahamic religions (see, for example, Weber 1958). He argued Abrahamic religions posit a dualism between a perfect creator-God and sinful, flawed humans. Eastern religions do not have this dualism. Rather 'the world [is] viewed as a completely connected and self-contained cosmos ... all the natural world is permeated with spirituality' (Campbell 1999: 41). According to Hamilton (2002: 244), the 'Eastern ethos ... holds a conception of divinity as essentially impersonal and immanent in reality and the Western [i.e. Christian] view of the divine [is] essentially personal, transcendental, separate from and outside the world.'

These differences become apparent when places of worship in the Hindu and Christian traditions are examined. A Hindu temple is designed to dissolve the boundaries between the divine and physical worlds. As far as possible, the site is selected because it is invested with supernatural significance. Deities reside in special places throughout Hindu Asia; a temple is positioned to take full advantage of this. According to Mitchell (1977: 68): 'the gods always play where groves are, near rivers, mountains and springs'. By contrast, a Christian church is a 'house' of worship. It is a place where the faithful gather and worship a God that does not reside on earth. A church site is selected for pragmatic reasons; usually it is a convenient gathering place for Christians who live in close proximity.

Hinduism

There are approximately 948 million adherents worldwide. Modern India is the country where the majority of the world's Hindus live, but large-scale migration from India to other parts of the globe means that sizeable communities can be found in many countries outside South Asia (see next section). Hinduism, unlike the Abrahamic religions, is a polytheistic religion, and posits the existence of many gods (literally thousands of gods). It emerged around 1500 BCE. Hinduism does not have a centrally defined doctrine or a rigid authority structure, although smaller communities which worship specific deities may have such structures. The term Hinduism encompasses a broad range of beliefs, practices and activities and its various practitioners come from culturally diverse backgrounds. **Sikhism**, now an independent religion, emerged from Hinduism in the fifteenth century.

Although Hinduism is a diverse religion, there are a few key doctrines which critically shape everyday Hindu life. Hindus believe in an ultimate reality, *Brahman*, a spirit or essence which unites all existence and is manifested in the many Hindu deities. According to Wuthnow (2005: 41), Brahman is 'ultimately beyond human comprehension ... and thus cannot be accurately spoken of in terms of a person, personal attributes, or other humanly constructed categories'. Hindus subscribe also to the doctrines of *samsāra*, the belief there is an ongoing cycle of life, death and rebirth (rebirth is known as reincarnation); *karma*, the idea of cause and effect, whereby one's actions in this life have consequences in the next; and *dharma*, which are prescriptions for a person's behavior and actions. Hindus may practice *yogas*, which are various spiritual disciplines and practices (e.g. meditation, yoga, temple worship, or pilgrimage to a holy place).

Important parts of contemporary Hinduism are various *sampradayas*. According to Flood (1996: 134) a sampradaya is 'a tradition focused on a deity, often regional in character, into which a disciple is initiated by a guru. Furthermore, each guru is seen to be within a line of gurus ... originating with the founding father.' A well-known sampradaya is the International Society for Krishna Consciousness (ISKCON), also known as the 'Hare Krishnas'. This is one of many sampradayas found throughout the Hindu world.

Hindu nationalism, known also as Hindutva movements, is a prominent aspect of contemporary Hinduism in India. According to Zavos (2010: 5), Hindu nationalism is 'an ideology that seeks to imagine or construct a community (i.e. a nation) on the basis of a common culture – a culture configured by a particular notion of Hinduism'. Hindu nationalist movements have sought to influence Indian political life and have been particularly active in the last few decades. One nationalist party, the Bharatiya Janata Party, held power in India from 1998–2004. The rise of Hindutva movements is a consequence of modern political developments and realities, a response to a perceived 'threat' from outsiders, especially other religions and ethnicities. Peter van der Veer (2009: 274) notes 'one needs to observe that ... Hindu nationalist movements strive for an Indian utopia that leaves little space for Muslims and Christians'.

As part of their political agenda, many Hindutva movements also encourage personal and communal religiousness, and thus strong religious commitment is often a feature of such groups. Moreover, some Hindus living outside India have continued to involve themselves in Indian political affairs through their financial and practical support of Hindutva movements.

Buddhism

There are approximately 468 million Buddhists worldwide, the majority of which live in Asia. As will be seen, however, there has been a major Buddhist diaspora across the globe, particularly in the last 50 years.

Buddhism first emerged from India around the fifth century BCE. According to Buddhist tradition, an Indian prince, Siddhartha Gautama (later called the Buddha), experienced a series of revelations about the nature of existence. His followers moved through Asia (e.g. China, Tibet, Japan and Thailand), and different regional traditions emerged. Leading Buddhism scholar Bernard Faure (2009: 18) argues 'it is perhaps preferable to talk of a Buddhist nebula rather than a unified religion'. Indeed, the notion of a coherent Buddhist religion – 'Buddhism' – is 'a recent construction, dating from the start of the nineteenth century. It was during this era that the neologism first began to appear in texts' (Faure 2009: 24).

Buddhists believe the self can be reborn many times. In strict Buddhist doctrine there are no gods. Some Buddhist groups, however, particularly in East Asia, believe in various gods and demons. In such cases, Buddhist beliefs are mixed with other folk religions.

Buddhism has several important doctrines and beliefs. Buddha revealed 'Four Noble Truths': life is unsatisfactory; suffering has a cause; suffering can be stopped through enlightenment; and there is a path to enlightenment. Enlightenment can be attained by following a set of precepts called the 'Eightfold Path'. These include having right speech (avoiding non-edifying words) and having right action (avoid stealing, killing, and sexual impropriety). Important practices in Buddhism include meditation, which can help the follower remain aware of the conditions of existence.

There are also several major traditions within Buddhism. These include: Theravada (traditions found in Thailand, Laos, Cambodia, Burma, Sri Lanka and Malaysia), Mahayana (traditions found in China, Japan, Viet Nam and Korea) and Vajrayana (Tibetan traditions). Some scholars suggest another identifiable strand is Triyana, which is Western Buddhism.

Contemporary Buddhism: engaged or enraged?

The newspaper headline reads: '"Man of Peace" approves of violence to [Muslims]' (Lloyd Parry 2013). The article describes recent ethno-religious violence in Arakan state, Burma (Myanmar), where a religious minority, the Rohingya Muslims, have been subject to violence and ethnic cleansing. This has been 'organized, incited, and committed by local Arakanese political party operatives, the Buddhist monkhood, and ordinary Arakanese [who are predominantly Buddhists], at times directly supported by state security forces' (Human Rights Watch 2013: 4). The 'man of peace' to whom the newspaper article refers is Buddhist monk Wirathu, who, the article claims, has 'contributed towards an atmosphere in which more and more Buddhists regard Muslims as enemies' (Lloyd Parry 2013).

Some might be surprised to hear of conflict between Buddhists and Muslims in Burma. The common view in the West is that Buddhism is a religion of inward contemplation and perhaps inactivity (Queen and King 1996: vi). Buddhism, however, like other religions, is implicated in everyday, worldly affairs.

Two of the realities of contemporary Buddhism in Asia are what is described by some scholars as 'engaged Buddhism' and 'enraged Buddhism'. First emerging in the nineteenth century (Queen 1996: 20), and popularized by Vietnamese monk Thich

Nhat Hanh in the 1960s, 'engaged Buddhism' refers to Buddhists' 'energetic engagement with social and political issues and crises' (Queen and King 1996: vi). The most conspicuous examples of engaged Buddhism include Nobel Peace Prize recipient the Dalai Lama, who has campaigned internationally for his country of Tibet, and Burmese politician Aung San Suu Kyi who has vociferously and bravely opposed the ruling military in her home country.

Buddhism is involved in politics in other ways. Although not as numerous as Hindu nationalist movements, there has been a rise in Buddhist nationalist political groups in recent decades. They campaign on a religious-nationalist agenda (where religious identity serves as a basis for nationhood). The rise of Buddhist nationalism is connected to ethnic-religious conflict and tensions in specific countries. A notable example is Sri Lanka, where there has been an active Sinhalese-Buddhist nationalist movement opposed to Hindu Tamils (see Bartholomeusz and De Silva 1998; Devotta 2001). Outbreaks of religiously motivated violence, like that in Burma, are described by some commentators as instances of 'enraged Buddhism'. Both engaged and enraged Buddhism are responses to the contemporary social world in which Buddhists live. The remainder of this chapter examines the recent globalization of these religions.

GLOBALIZED RELIGION: HINDU AND BUDDHIST DIASPORAS

According to the Pew Forum (2012b: 10), as of 2010, 99 percent of the world's Hindus and Buddhists live in the Asia-Pacific. Like all the world's major religions, Buddhism and Hinduism have always been faiths 'on the move', that is, characterized by migration. In both traditions, most of this movement took place, and continues to take place, within the Asia-Pacific region (Pew Forum 2012a).

Particularly in the past two centuries, however, communities of Hindus and Buddhists have moved further afield (i.e. outside Asia-Pacific) in increasingly larger numbers, representing something of a 'diaspora', which is the large-scale movement of people, their culture and religion from their homelands to places further afield. King et al. (2010: 36) argue a diaspora involves a 'dispersion across international space, orientation to a homeland, and a clear sense of common identity sustained through ethnicity, language, and religion'. Hindu and Buddhist diasporas have taken place mainly in two main waves: in the nineteenth century and post Second World War.

In his masterful book about Buddhism in America, *How the Swans Came to the Lake* (1986) scholar Rick Fields notes there were 63,000 Chinese in California by the end of the 1860s, drawn by the discovery of gold. Among them were Buddhists who established the first Buddhist temples in America. (Other Chinese were followers of Chinese-folk religions, a syncretic mix that often includes Buddhist elements.) In Australia the first Buddhists, predominantly from China and Sri Lanka, came to

Australia in the 1840s Gold Rush (Halafoff et al. 2012: 10). Scholar Martin Baumann (2001) notes that tiny communities of Buddhists emigrated to Russia and modern-day Serbia from the Asia-Pacific in the early twentieth century. These first Buddhist and Hindu communities in the West were small by contemporary standards.

Today, in the 'Age of Migration', when an estimated 3 percent of the world's population are migrants (King et al. 2010), there has been a significant migration, numbering in the millions, of Hindus and Buddhists around the world. After countries in Asia, the main destinations for Hindus are the United States (which has received 1.4 million of the Hindu migrants alive today), the United Kingdom and Canada (Pew Forum 2012a: 35–6). In the past decade there has also been a sharp increase in the number of Hindu migrants moving to the Gulf States of the Middle East.

The most popular country of destination for Buddhist migrants is the United States, where an estimated 1.7 million have settled (Pew Forum 2012a: 39–41). According to the Pew Forum (2012a: 41): 'Buddhists also have migrated in substantial numbers to Australia (more than 300,000), Canada (nearly 300,000) and Germany (about 200,000).'

The proportion of Hindus and Buddhists living in the West has grown substantially in the past two decades, mainly as a result of migration, coupled with high birth rates and conversion to a far lesser extent. In Australia, for example, census data reveal Buddhism has grown from 1.1 percent of the population in 1996 to 2.6 percent in 2011. Buddhism is now the second-largest religion in Australia after Christianity. Similarly, Hinduism has grown from 0.4 percent of the population in 1996 to 1.4 percent in 2011. Using data from the American Religious Identity Surveys, Kosmin and Keysar (2009a) estimate the proportion of Buddhists in the United States increased from 0.2 percent of the population in 1990 to 0.5 percent in 2008. In Britain, census data reveal Hinduism has grown from 0.98 percent of the population in 2001 to 1.5 percent in 2011. The majority of Hindus and Buddhists in the West are migrants, or children of recent migrants.

It is important to note the majority of migrant Hindus and Buddhists moving to the West are not, in the first instance, migrating for religious reasons. Indeed, sociologist Chetan Bhatt (2000: 562) argues it is 'historically inaccurate … to speak of a "Hindu diaspora" … in the context of the secular processes of South Asian labour and merchant migration from India and Pakistan to East and South Africa, the UK and elsewhere'. In the past 50 years, people have migrated mainly to improve their labor opportunities or to reunite with family who have already migrated, or to flee conflicts and environmental disasters. Most do not migrate for religious reasons, such as to escape persecution or to engage in missionary activity. (That said, some ethnic conflicts do have a religiously motivated element and refugees do flee such conflicts.)

Even if the main reasons for migration are not religious, religion is often an important part of migrants' identity, and they take their religion when they settle in a new country. What happens when they arrive? One way to understand the sociological aspects of the movement of religion and religious people from one place to another is the concept of 'religious settlement', which is explored in the next section.

RELIGIOUS SETTLEMENT

When international migrants leave one country they must settle into another. This has many dimensions: migrants will have to make new friends, join new communities, find work, housing and schooling. Some migrants bring their faith with them. How does this find expression in the migrant process? Gary Bouma, leading Australian sociologist of religion, proposes the concept of 'religious settlement', which describes first, religion's role in the migration process, and second, the processes by which religions move from one location to another. According to Bouma (1996: 51), 'religious settlement' has four essential dimensions:

A. Religion as a source of assistance and support provided to the migrant;

B. Religion and the individual migrant's settlement and identity formation in a new society;

C. Building a religious community in a new place; and

D. The processes by which a new religion, or new variant of an existing religion, finds a place in a society, including the reactions of both communities and the state to the presence of a 'new' religion.

Each of these dimensions is explained below. The discussion focuses mainly on Buddhist and Hindu religious settlement from East to West, but is applicable to other religions and religious migrants.

Points A and B are about religion and the role it plays in helping settle the *individual migrant* into their new country. Religious groups already established in the host country can help settle newly arrived migrants, providing both practical and spiritual support. Hindu and Buddhist faith communities are usually allied to particular ethnic groups, so the temple is often one of the first places of call for newly arrived migrants. It is here they might find practical support. Bouma (1996: 60) observes: 'Religious groups … have helped newcomers to find accommodation and employment … how to get needed professional services and how to educate children.'

Personal faith can assist in the process of migrating. Bouma (1996: 60) reports: 'Interviews with migrants … frequently reveal the role of religion in coping with emotional stresses of settlement.' Bankston and Hidalgo (2008: 56) note a number of studies show the importance of religious institutions in promoting the psychological wellbeing of immigrants, 'affecting the normative adaptation of immigrants to the host country'. Williams (1996: 229), writing about Indian Hindu migrants in America, observes: 'Religion is prominent at stages in the immigrant experience because in the midst of rapid social change it provides a transcendent anchor for memory that relates personal and group identity to the past.'

Point C highlights an important part of religious settlement, specifically the establishment and building up of *new religious communities* in the host country. As more settlers of the same religion and ethnicity arrive in the host country and find each other, new religious communities are formed. Chinese Buddhists who arrived in the United States and Australia during the nineteenth-century goldrushes came together to create religious communities, as have later waves of Buddhist migrants from Cambodia, Laos, Viet Nam and Japan (see Numrich 2008; Rocha and Barker 2010).

Perhaps the most important aspect of settling a religious community into a new place is the building of a religious base; usually a place of worship. This can be expensive and complicated. Funds need to be raised, land bought and temple construction undertaken. McAra (2010: 63), writing about the establishment of Buddhist temples in Australia, notes religious organizations often have to negotiate complex land-use and planning issues, as well as religious prejudice.

The kind of spiritual community that emerges in the host country is never the same as that in the home country. The experience of migrant religious communities is the product of the home religion *adapting* to the conditions and cultural context of the host society. Discussing the transmission of the Hindu Indian tradition into North America, Carman (1996: 15) notes:

> A small immigrant community does not have the luxury of building many different temples for many different groups [as is the norm in India]. Moreover, Indians have followed the example of other immigrants, who often view their ritual center as an appropriate place for domestic rituals and for social gatherings [in a way it may not be in the home country]. Far away from India, various caste and regional differences often seem less important ... [also] Hindus are coming to a new land that is devoid of Hindu stories of previous appearances of Hindu deities.

Wuthnow (2005: 43) notes the immigrant experience has a unifying effect on Hinduism that would not otherwise occur: 'temples ... function as pan-Indian centers, bringing together immigrants from various regions of India and accommodating various deities and styles of worship'. Migrant religions in the host society find themselves in the religious minority, and in societies which are becoming increasingly pluralistic and secular. Bankston and Hidalgo (2008: 56) note that 'responding to the pluralistic setting of the larger society can often intensify the religious practices and ethnic solidarity of immigrant religious institutions'.

Finally, point D refers to the issues migrant religions face settling into the host society. 'New' religions must negotiate the laws, views and customs of the host society. Such issues appear to have become more acute in the past few decades as the number and visibility of religious minorities in the West have expanded dramatically: the host society does not always receive new religions well. New immigrants can be subject to vilification, racism and discrimination on the basis of their religion, a point expanded on in the next chapter. That said, host societies have also adapted positively to swelling migrant numbers and their religious needs. When my children were at pre-school, they celebrated Christmas, along with Vesak (a South-Asian celebration of the Buddha's birthday) and the Hindu festival of Diwali (see below). This reflected the diversity of faiths and ethnicities in the pre-school.

In places that were once predominantly monocultural and Christian, such as Great Britain and Australia, the impact of religious settlement is readily visible (see the case study in this chapter, 'Buddhism and Hinduism in the 'burbs').

BUDDHISM AND HINDUISM IN THE 'BURBS: RELIGIOUS SETTLEMENT IN ACTION ...

The municipality of Maribyrnong (comprising several suburbs, such as Footscray, Braybrook and Yarraville), nestled next to the Maribyrnong River in inner western Melbourne, Australia, is a place of great religious diversity. White settlement began there in the 1840s (the local Aboriginal people were displaced, killed by settlers or died from white settler's diseases) and Catholic and Anglican churches were built soon after. Today the suburb has many churches and all the major Australian denominations are represented: Catholic, Anglican, Uniting, Presbyterian, Baptist, Orthodox, Churches of Christ, and Lutheran, among others. There are other churches too, established more recently, which include the Mormons, Assemblies of God, and other smaller, independent evangelical and Pentecostal congregations. The largest church in the area is Pentecostal and boasts a congregation of about 800.

Beginning shortly after the Second World War, large groups of migrants from non-English-speaking countries settled in Maribyrnong. The first major wave of post-war migrants originated in Greece and Italy and other parts of southern Europe. In the 1970s, the Australian government removed racially based qualifications for those wishing to immigrate, thus clearing the way for large-scale Asian immigration (Economou 1998: 364). Maribyrnong proved to be an extremely popular destination for people from South-East Asia, particularly Viet Nam. The most recent wave of migrants come from the Horn of Africa. Modern Maribyrnong is a genuine cultural 'melting pot'.

As is so often the case, migrant groups brought their religions with them. Some ethnic groups have established their own Christian Churches, such as the Vietnamese and Chinese independent evangelical congregations. Older mainline congregations also welcomed groups of new migrants. The Lutheran, Baptist, Uniting and Anglican churches all conduct services in African languages (e.g. Dinka), and some have African pastors. Migrant Christians are not the only ethnic religious presence. In Maribyrnong there are three major Buddhist temples, Chinese religion temples and a small mosque. Migration, clearly, has been a significant factor in shaping the current religious character of the area.

According to the 2011 Australian government census, 10 percent of the population of Maribyrnong identifies as Buddhist (the proportion in the Australian population as a whole is 2.6 percent) and 3.2 percent identify as Hindu (the proportion in the Australian population is 1.3 percent). The proportion of Hindus living in Maribyrnong increased by 50 percent between 2006–2011. The proportion of Buddhists living in Maribyrnong stayed the same between 2006–2011; this religion was already well settled by the 2000s.

(Continued)

(Continued)

Figures 9.1, 9.2 and 9.3 demonstrate aspects of the Hindu and Buddhist presence in Maribyrnong.

Figure 9.1 The Chua Phat Quang Buddhist Temple, West Footscray, Victoria, Australia

Source: The author

Figure 9.2 Shrine at the Quang Minh Buddhist Temple, Braybrook, Victoria, Australia

Source: The author

Figure 9.3 Statues of Lakshmi, Krishna and Ganesh, 'India at Home' store, West Footscray, Victoria, Australia

Source: The author

Modern religious settlement is rarely a 'once-off' move from country of origin to country of settlement, but is instead characterized by a continuing flow of people and resources between origin and destination. The new religious community is not isolated from established religious communities in the country of origin. The terms **'transnationalism'** and **'transmigrants'** are helpful in making sense of this process. Assisted by cheaper transport and faster modes of communication, modern migrants can maintain closer ties to home. According to Schiller et al. (1992: ix), transnationalism is a 'social process in which migrants establish social fields that cross geographic, cultural, and political borders'. Transmigrants are those who 'develop and *maintain* multiple relations – familial, economic, social, organizational, religious, and political – that span borders' (1992: ix) (my italics). Any consideration of ethnic religious groups must recognize that such communities are not isolated, but maintain ties that span borders (for an in-depth discussion see Ebaugh and Chafetz 2002; Wuthnow and Offutt 2008).

As noted above, religious settlement is a corollary of large-scale migration. The globalization of religion, however, is more than the movement of people. It can also involve the flow of practices and beliefs. We have seen in the previous chapter how American forms of religious practice increasingly have become prevalent worldwide. Concomitantly, it seems that practices and beliefs drawn from Eastern religions have become popular in the West. The next section examines how and why this has happened.

THE WEST BECOMES 'ENCHANTED' BY THE EAST

Every year, millions of Hindus around the world celebrate Diwali – the 'festival of lights'. It is one of the most important festivals on the Hindu calendar. Families light candle lamps, exchange gifts and distribute sweets. I have celebrated Diwali several times in recent years. There is a large Indian community where I live which organizes a public celebration of Diwali for all locals. Direct exposure to the religious culture of other people is one way in which religious knowledge spreads, but it is not the only way. This section explores the transmission of religious ideas from one location to another.

I started this chapter by discussing reincarnation. Reincarnation belief is now widespread in the West. Data from the 2008 International Social Science Survey (ISSP) survey show 31 percent of US adults, 24 percent of British adults, 22 percent of Australian adults and 19 percent of German adults believe in reincarnation (my calculations). This is one of many beliefs drawn from Eastern religions now popularly accepted in traditionally Christian countries. Other beliefs include the notions of 'karma' and 'chakras' (centers of energy in the body).

People can toy with such beliefs or take them seriously in a way that makes a difference to their lives. In my qualitative research among young Australian reincarnation believers, I found that some young people took their belief in past lives seriously (to the extent of undertaking past-life therapy or having past-life readings). However, for the majority it appears to be little more than an idea that helps make sense of what may happen after death (Singleton 2012; see also Mason et al. 2007). While such beliefs originated in Eastern religions, Western variations are usually distilled versions of orthodox religious doctrine, and most reincarnation believers are not followers of Eastern religious traditions, or even know much about such religions (see Singleton 2012; Walter 2001; Waterhouse 1999).

In addition to belief in reincarnation, karma and chakras, various practices that have their origins in Buddhism and Hinduism, such as yoga, mindful meditation and reiki healing, are now popular in the West. One recent national study of Australians aged 13–59 found 13 percent of the population have practiced yoga seriously, while an estimated 9 percent have practiced Eastern meditation (Mason et al. 2007). Hasselle-Newcombe (2005: 305) finds approximately half a million Britons practice some form of yoga, and in many cases such practices have been appropriated for particular ends, such as the promotion of health and wellbeing.

Western yoga is one such example. According to Hasselle-Newcombe (2005: 305), yoga can be traced back to 'a system of Indian soteriological [religious doctrine of salvation] philosophy and mystical technology that dates back to at least 1,500 years'. Despite its religious roots, regular yoga practice may not be construed by most Western practitioners as being primarily a spiritual practice, or even about spirituality at all, mainly because people undertake yoga for improved health and wellbeing. Kimberley Lau (cited in Carrette and King 2005: 117) argues 'As first commodified and subsequently practiced in the United States and many other countries in the world, yoga and tai-chi are removed from their philosophical contexts and largely undertaken as physical exercise regimens, though still presented within the context of body-mind integration and spirituality.' Yoga is offered routinely at gymnasiums, alongside aerobics classes, while many schools offer yoga as an alternative to other after-school sports. As such, it is often presented as part of a broader Western trend towards holistic health and wellbeing, rather than a spiritual activity per se (see Carrette and King 2005).

Research conducted among Western yoga practitioners suggests the main reason most people take up yoga is for overall wellbeing, first of the body, then the mind. In her UK study of Iyengar yoga practitioners, Hasselle-Newcombe (2005: 311) found 60 percent of her respondents 'began their practice as an alternative form of exercise'. This is not to say that participants do not draw some spiritual meaning from yoga or meditation, or have feelings and sensations they may describe as spiritual, but if this happens, it is almost certainly a secondary outcome.

This section has demonstrated the widespread appropriation of traditional Eastern religious beliefs and practices, mobilized to suit Western purposes. People are not, for the most part, accepting all the tenets and doctrines of Hinduism and Buddhism. Rather, specific beliefs and practices are drawn on in a haphazard and syncretic fashion. Nonetheless, the popularity of these practices and beliefs, no matter how protean, suggests people in the West are enchanted with Eastern-like beliefs and practices. How did such beliefs and practices arrive in the West, and why are they so popular today?

While it is tempting to think the popularization of Eastern beliefs and practices is a corollary of the mass movement of Hindus and Buddhists to the West since the 1970s, Western interest in Eastern religions long predates this widespread migration and religious settlement. Scholar Courtney Bender (2007: 590), in her American study of reincarnation, argues 'contemporary reincarnation beliefs and practices owe as much to nineteenth and early twentieth-century interpretations as they do to more contemporary encounters with Asian texts and ideas'.

The late-nineteenth and early-twentieth century was a time when dalliances with non-Christian religious and spiritual views became more widespread. According to Pike (2004: 45), 'Occult beliefs that had gone underground resurfaced and were adopted by an emerging middle class looking for ways to exercise its newfound social power.' Chapter 2 documented the rise of the Spiritualist movement and noted how societal conditions at that time made possible the widespread exploration of alternative spiritual and religious beliefs. This period also saw the emergence of the Theosophical Society, which, like the Spiritualist movement, was a popular alternative to traditional Christianity. Founded in 1875 by Russian medium Helena Petrovna Blavatsky and American lawyer Henry Steele Olcott, the Theosophical Society introduced the world to Theosophy, a syncretic belief system drawing on Eastern religions and other Western esoteric beliefs. (Esoteric means hidden knowledge. In this instance, it refers to various Western occult beliefs.)

The Theosophical Society can be credited, in large part, with introducing and popularizing reincarnation and other Eastern religious beliefs in the late nineteenth and early twentieth centuries (see Bender 2007). For example, in 1892 Annie Besant, a well-known Theosophist published a book, *Reincarnation*, in which she explains the Theosophical view of this belief. She writes:

> It is interesting to note that the mere idea of Reincarnation is no longer regarded in the West – at least by educated people – as absurd. It is gradually assuming the position of a possible hypothesis … Reincarnation and Karma are said … to be the two doctrines of which the West stands most in need. (1892/1963: 8)

Around the same time as Theosophy was becoming popular, Indian swamis (Hindu teachers) began to visit Australia, the United States and Britain, and staged public lectures and published on the topic of Eastern religions. Swami Abhedananda, an Indian-born swami, is one such example. In his book *Life Beyond Death: A Critical Study of Spiritualism* (1944), he rails against various Spiritualist beliefs and reaffirms the correctness of reincarnation doctrine: 'Through this doctrine of reincarnation, the vast majority of people in India, China, and Japan have found consolation in their lives and solved the extremely difficult problems that disturb the minds of scientists and other thinkers of the world' (1944: 84).

Pike (2004: 60) suggests that while the spiritual fervor of the late nineteenth century settled quickly, 'alternative religious practices were institutionalized … the beliefs and practices that would serve as the heart of the New Age movement were now part of [Western] culture'.

Reincarnation belief in the West has persisted since the early twentieth century, but its acceptance and infiltration, along with a whole host of beliefs and practices drawn from Eastern religions, became more widespread in the 1950s and beyond, mainly due to the influence of the Beat, Hippy and the New Age movements, whose followers were keenly interested in Eastern religions. First emerging in the 1930s, the New Age movement reached its apogee in the 1980s (see Sutcliffe 2003) and is an element of the spiritual marketplace discussed in Chapter 7. According to American sociologist William Bainbridge (1997: 365), the New Age movement is

> A strange potpourri of myths and rituals drawn from Asian religion, European legends, and the imaginations of its practitioners. Much of it claims to be science, history, or the arts, rather than religion, but at every turn an explorer of the New Age will confront supernatural forces.

Adam Possamai (2000: 365), a well-known scholar of the New Age, suggests practices and beliefs counted under the umbrella of the New Age include: astrology, automatic writing, Buddhism, channeling, crystals manipulation, feminist spirituality, meditation, naturopathy, numerology, palmistry, reiki, Spiritualism, Tantrism, tarot and urban shamanism. The appropriation and repackaging of various Eastern religious elements is a hallmark of the New Age movement. Many of these practices are offered as 'paid services', of which people partake for individual betterment or improved self-knowledge.

Sutcliffe (2003: 3) notes such practices are usually associated with the contemporary Western desire to achieve unity between 'mind, body and spirit'.

Why do Eastern religious ideas appeal in the West? Scholar Colin Campbell (1999) argues the Western mindset has been 'Easternized'. A large proportion of the Western world no longer thinks in dualistic Western terms (a divide between the human and the divine), but in Eastern terms. This entails 'a conception of divinity as essentially impersonal and immanent in reality' (Hamilton 2002: 244). The putative causes of this paradigm shift are not so much the popularity of Eastern religious practices per se, but the triumph in the West of science and reason, which has critically challenged the traditional dualistic worldview (Campbell 1999: 44–5). In such conditions, alternatives to the Western mindset, such as Eastern religious practices and beliefs, can flourish.

Like other scholars (e.g. Hamilton 2002), I am not persuaded that such a profound shift has occurred. In the first instance, beliefs such as karma and reincarnation are accepted by a smaller proportion of the population than is a traditional belief in God. Moreover, many of the practices taken from Eastern religions, such as yoga and tai-chi, are practiced mainly for health and wellbeing, rather than for expressly spiritual purposes. Nonetheless, the relative popularity of ideas such as karma and reincarnation requires explanation. I suggest social factors identified earlier in this book are responsible, particularly the rise of religious individualism and the emergence of the spiritual marketplace. Chapters 3 and 7 discussed the rise of religious individualism in the West. As Thomas Luckmann (1967) observed in the 1960s, those in the modern West live in societies without a shared 'symbolic universe' (formerly Christianity) and are in a position where they can formulate or decide upon their own 'symbolic universe'.

Where does one look for spiritual inspiration and guidance? It was observed in Chapter 7 that Westerners live in societies with myriad spiritual options, the so-called spiritual marketplace. A range of beliefs is available to Westerners, some of which happen to have their origins in Eastern religions, but are now, as argued above, very much part of the fabric of Western societies. It is equally true that people in the West accept ancient pagan ideas or other esoteric and occult beliefs, along with entirely new beliefs such as alien abduction (see Chapter 13). Eastern religious options are simply some among many. Indeed, as I have discovered in my own research, people will happily blend beliefs, both Eastern and Western (see Mason et al. 2007; Singleton 2012).

Western Buddhism

The previous section examined how Eastern religious practices and beliefs have flowed into Western culture and have been taken up for a variety of purposes, whether those be health and wellbeing or as a way of making sense of what happens after death. While individuals might be committed to particular beliefs and practices that originate from Hinduism and Buddhism, this is not a fully fledged commitment to a religion itself. Nonetheless, some Westerners do convert to these religions.

Conversion, as used here, refers to first *identifying* as a Buddhist or a Hindu, and then also accepting core doctrines and undertaking specific Buddhist or Hindu religious practices. Most Western converts to Eastern religions turn to Buddhism.

Small groups of Westerners began their own, independent investigation of Buddhism in the late nineteenth and early twentieth centuries, coterminous with the development of Spiritualism and Theosophy. Intrigued by what they found, they converted and established their own Western Buddhist communities, largely independent of the small ethnic Buddhist communities which existed at that time. For example, in Australia, the first Buddhist organization was the Little Circle of Dharma, established in 1925 by Buddhist converts (Spuler 2000: 34). Arguably, the Western interest in Buddhism has accelerated in recent years, with interest fueled by regular tours from the Dalai Lama, and endorsements from actors like Richard Gere and rock groups such as the Beastie Boys and the Red Hot Chili Peppers (see Baumann 2001; Wuthnow and Cadge 2004).

Most Buddhist Westerners today practice Western adaptations of the Buddhist tradition, or follow specific traditions such as those of the Zen, Tibetan or Triyana schools. Communities of ethnic Buddhists and Western Buddhists do not mix frequently at services of worship, and ethnic temples operate alongside Western-convert ones. While indebted to various Eastern Buddhist traditions, the practice of Western Buddhism is inevitably an adaptation to local circumstances and values.

Some recent studies have been conducted on the reasons why Westerners convert. Wuthnow and Cadge (2004: 366) note that for many people the appeal of Buddhism lies in the fact 'that in many Buddhist groups the teachings and practices are, if anything, attractive to the people who participate in them because of their flexibility and non-exclusivity'. In their study of Australian Buddhist converts, Phillips and Aarons (2005: 224) found that 'rather than tending towards a short-term attachment to Buddhism as one of multiple religious attachments, respondents were clearly more inclined to favour a more narrowly focused involvement over a more sustained period of time'. For many converts, practice of their new religion is a life-changing endeavor.

CONCLUSION

This chapter is not intended to serve as an exhaustive summary of contemporary Buddhism and Hinduism. The main focus has been on examining developments in these religions in the global age, and how their influence has extended far beyond their regions of origin. Recent, large-scale migration has resulted in the presence of sizeable ethnic Hindu and Buddhist communities in the West (remembering, however, that the overwhelming majority of Buddhists and Hindus live in the Asia-Pacific). The discussion considered different aspects of 'religious settlement', how religious communities and individuals move from country of origin to country of settlement. The second part of the chapter investigated the interest in the West in various Buddhist and Hindu practices and beliefs. While the transmission of these ideas and beliefs predates the current global age, Western interest has increased markedly since the 1960s. Consequently, practices and beliefs with Hindu and Buddhist origins have a place in the contemporary Western spiritual marketplace. There are also some Westerners who convert to Eastern religions, particularly Buddhism. The distance between the religions of Asia and the West has never been closer. The flow of ideas and practices is not all one-way. Some scholars have found Western developments in Hinduism and Buddhism have actually been returned to their countries of origin. Frøystad (2009), for example, reports on how the American spiritual community of Ananda Sangha is teaching meditation techniques in India.

The next chapter continues to investigate the globalization of world religion, focusing on recent developments in Islam.

Points to ponder

Are there Hindu, Sikh, Chinese religion or Buddhist temples near where you live? Try to arrange a visit to one of them. Find out who established these communities, and what role they play for their members. What challenges do you think they faced in establishing these communities? Ask how they assist in settling newly arrived migrants.

Next steps ...

The Pew Forum report, *Faith on the Move: The Religious Affiliation of International Migrants* (2012a) clearly maps the impact religious migration is having worldwide. Edited collections which explore the growth and experiences of Buddhism in the West are Paul Numrich's *North American Buddhists in Social Context* (2008) and Cristina Rocha and Michelle Barker's *Buddhism in Australia: Traditions in Change* (2010). Robert Wuthnow's *America and the Challenges of Religious Diversity* (2005) has chapters on the Hindu and Buddhist communities in America.

Documentaries and film

The British feature films *East is East* (1999), *Bend it Like Beckham* (2002) and *My Beautiful Laundrette* (1985) examine the tensions between expatriate Pakistani Muslim or Punjabi Sikh cultures and Western 'British' values and culture mores. They also show the tight link between religious and ethnic identity.

Web

The Oxford Centre for Hindu Studies has an excellent website with many resources available at http://www.ochs.org.uk. A good website for information and material on Buddhism is: http://buddhanet.net.

10

the rise of the global ummah? recent trends in islam

After reading this chapter you will:

- be aware of the global dimensions of Islam;

- understand why Muslim communities are growing in Muslim-minority countries; and

- be conversant with sociological arguments about religious fundamentalism and religiously motivated violence.

On the banks of the Ohio River in Louisville, Kentucky, USA, is the Muhammad Ali Center. I spent an afternoon there once. The center is a 'living museum' which explores the life and times of Ali, a former heavyweight boxing champion. In the 1960s, at the peak of his career, Ali campaigned vociferously for the civil rights of African-Americans. He also publicly opposed the war in Viet Nam, stating famously, 'I ain't got no quarrel with them Vietcong' (Remnick 1998: 287). He refused to join the army when conscripted, was jailed, stripped of his world boxing titles and banned from the sport. After a boxing exile lasting several years, he returned to the ring in an epic series of fights against reigning champion Joe Frazier.

Visitors to the center walk through exhibits which showcase Ali's considerable boxing achievements, interspersed with an analysis of social events from the 1950s to the present day. There are interactive displays which illustrate the impact of segregation, the work of the civil rights movement and America's role in the Vietnam War. Today, Ali is revered as an American cultural icon – he carried the torch at the 1996 Atlanta

Olympics – and the Ali Center is a testament to his social activism and sporting prowess. He is also, arguably, America's most famous Muslim.

Ali was not always a popular figure in the American cultural landscape. While he had exceptional prowess as a boxer, his outstanding wit, mastery of wordplay and cutting remarks about his opponents often put him offside with sports journalists and the sporting public. Ali's political commitment to advancing African-American rights did not endear him to many whites, particularly in his hometown of Louisville.

Ali refused to fight in the Vietnam War for many reasons. He felt that it was anathema for a black man to fight on behalf of a country where the white majority had done little to address race relations. In his hometown of Louisville, as in much of the American South, there was widespread segregation. Despite being the greatest boxer of his age, a world and Olympic champion, he could not eat or drink in many bars and restaurants throughout the South. His religious convictions were also influential in his refusal to join the war. Ali converted to Islam in the early 1960s and joined a radical Islamic sect called the Nation of Islam (he later converted to a more orthodox style of Islam). He rejected his birth name of Cassius Clay because he regarded it as a 'slave name'. Ali felt his new name represented political and spiritual emancipation. Of his refusal to fight in the Vietnam War he said, 'I either have to follow the laws of the land or the laws of Allah' (Remnick 1998: 290).

This chapter started with a brief description of Muhammad Ali's story to demonstrate that Muslims have long had a religious, social and political presence in America. This dates back centuries, and not just to the last decade, when it seems Americans increasingly viewed Islam as a threat to the 'American way of life'. Ali's story also illustrates the complexity of Islam's relationship with non-Muslim America; how Muslims have often been subject to discrimination and prejudice, and how issues of race and religion are often intertwined.

Now Islam's history in the United States has a new chapter. Fueled by recent immigration, the Muslim population has grown significantly in the past few decades. Similar change has occurred in Europe, Canada and Australia. While Muslims have long been a presence in these countries, an upsurge in migration has resulted in much larger diasporic communities. The West now faces the challenge of accommodating a rapidly growing and often misunderstood religion. Other changes are afoot in the Muslim world. Muslim-majority countries are experiencing a rise in Islamic conservatism, nationalism and religiously motivated violence.

This chapter charts several recent developments in Islam, particularly the growth of Muslim communities in Muslim-minority countries, the consolidation of a global Muslim consciousness (the 'global ummah'), and an apparent rise in violence perpetrated by Islamic 'fundamentalists'. Discussion considers the social and cultural causes of these developments.

THE ISLAMIC RELIGION TODAY: DIVERSE *AND* UNIFIED?

Islam started around 610 CE in Mecca, a city in present-day Saudi Arabia. Islam is the name of the religion, although its followers are commonly referred to as Muslims. Islam began with Muhammad, Islam's most important prophet. According to Islamic sources, Muhammad was a religiously inclined caravan operator (Esposito 1999: 50). He lived in a society in which most of the population followed polytheistic religions. In his early 40s, he began receiving messages – divine revelations from God – from the archangel Gabriel. Muhammad founded a new religion based on the angel's messages. These revelations eventually were collected together to form the Qur'an, Islam's holiest book. Muslims revere the Qur'an as the authentic, unmediated word of God.

The Islamic religion is monotheistic, and followers believe in the one God, called *Allah* (the Arabic word for God). This is effectively the same God worshipped by Christians and Jews (Kheirabadi 2004: 4). Islam, Christianity and Judaism are known as the 'Abrahamic' religions. These faiths share the 'common belief in God, prophets, revelation, a divinely mandated community, and moral responsibility' (Esposito 1999: 49). Modern Jews, Christians and Muslims are inheritors of a religious tradition that goes back to biblical figure Abraham, hence the title of 'Abrahamic' religions.

Islam became the dominant religion of the Arabian area. Muhammad believed he was in possession of a new, divine revelation and urged people to follow the one true God, rather than the polytheistic idol worship common in the Arabian Peninsula. Military struggles between Muslims and other local groups followed, with Muhammad's armies gaining ascendancy.

A Muslim is required to hold several core beliefs, which are called the 'six pillars of faith': belief in the one God; belief in angels; belief in the prophets and messengers of Allah; belief in Holy books (which includes the Qur'an); belief in a day of judgment; and belief in predestination (Allah knows what was and what will be). Muslims are required to fulfill several religious obligations, the 'five pillars of Islam'. These are acceptance of a creed ('There is no God but Allah, and Muhammad is his prophet'), prayer five times daily at set times, fasting (during the month of *Ramadan*), alms (giving to the poor) and pilgrimage (to Mecca, at least once in a Muslim's life, known as the *Hajj*, but only if this is financially viable). The pilgrimage to Mecca is one of the world's largest massed religious rituals, and is the subject of this chapter's case study.

Contemporary Islam has two major branches, Sunni and Shia (the followers are called Sunnis and Shias or Shi'ites). This division stems from the earliest days of Islam, when a schism occurred over the matter of Muhammad's successor. Approximately 87–90 percent of the world's Muslims are followers of the Sunni tradition, with Shi'ites and sects making up the remainder (Pew Forum 2011b: 153). Like all religions Islam has many small sects, some of which diverge considerably from orthodox Islamic teaching.

The Nation of Islam (NOI), of which Muhammad Ali was a member, is a well-known Islamic sect (some Muslims do not see it as true Islam). It grew in the poor suburbs of Detroit, Michigan, where a preacher named Wallace D. Fard Muhammad delivered a message which combined African-American civil rights with Islamic teaching (see Kheirabadi 2004). According to Tinaz (1996: 194) this message 'particularly appealed to the needs of the illiterate and unskilled Southern black migrants who moved to industrial urban areas of Northern America in the early 1930s'.

After Fard's death the leadership was taken over by Elijah Muhammad, who also preached a message of civil rights, African–American separatism and spiritual emancipation from white religion (i.e. Christianity). The movement expanded rapidly under Elijah Muhammad's stewardship, due in large part to the rhetorical skills and charisma of his deputy, Malcolm X (Tinaz 1996: 197–8). Elijah Muhammad taught that the Nation's founder, Fard Muhammad, was a divine messenger. This teaching persisted until shortly after Elijah's death, when the movement turned to more Islamic orthodox teaching. The organization changed its name several times, and there were other divisions and schisms (Tinaz 1996 helpfully maps these changes). In the 1970s, under the leadership of Louis Farrakhan, the NOI movement was revitalized and its leaders again taught that Fard was a prophet. In recent years the NOI has espoused more conventional Islamic doctrine. It is a significant presence in the American Muslim landscape and has many thousands of followers. It continues to promote social justice and black rights (for a description and analysis of present-day community activism, see Akom 2007).

Scholars of Islam note this religion, like other major world religions, is characterized by considerable diversity. There are numerous regional and community differences on matters of religious doctrine, worship style and acceptable rituals and beliefs. The Pew Forum has produced an extensive report, *The World's Muslims: Unity and Diversity* (2012c), which highlights such regional variation. This monumental report, for which researchers surveyed 38,000 Muslims in 39 countries, tracks differences and similarities in the Muslim world. As noted above, daily prayer is one of Islam's five pillars. Pew researchers found:

> Daily prayer features prominently in the lives of Muslims in sub-Saharan Africa, Southeast Asia, South Asia and across the Middle East and North Africa … Muslims in Southern and Eastern Europe and in Central Asia are generally less likely to pray at least once a day. (Pew Forum 2012c: 44)

One of the more conspicuous Islamic practices is the wearing of the *hijab*, a head-scarf worn only by women. (This is not to be confused with the *burqa* which is a full body-covering garment, or the *niqab*, a veil which covers the face.)

The popularity of hijab-wearing has waxed and waned over the past 100 years. Distinguished scholar Leila Ahmed (2011: 45) notes the hijab began disappearing 'gradually and without enforcement' from Arab societies in the first part of the twentieth century. It has made a comeback in recent decades, and is now worn extensively throughout the Muslim world. According to Ahmed (2011), its reappearance is a corollary of a recent Islamic 'resurgence' or 'renewal' (see Esposito 1999;

Sutton and Vertigans 2005; Vertigans 2009; Abbas 2011; Ahmed 2011). According to American scholar John Esposito, this Islamic renewal has personal, political and communal dimensions:

> The indices of an Islamic reawakening in personal life are many: increased attention to religious observances (mosque attendance, prayer, fasting), proliferation of religious programming and publications, more emphasis upon Islamic dress and values [and] the revitalization of Sufism (mysticism). This broader-based renewal has also been accompanied by Islam's reassertion in public life: an increase in Islamically oriented governments, organizations, laws, banks, social welfare services, and educational institutions. (Esposito 1999: 35)

Esposito (1999: 33) nominates places where revival has been 'most forceful' as Egypt, Iran, Lebanon and Tunisia, but other parts of the Muslim world also have been affected. A partial cause (and effect) of this revival has been the rise of Islamism, which, according to Roy (2004: 58)

> is the brand of modern political Islamic fundamentalism that claims to re-create a true Islamic society, not simply by imposing *sharia* [Islamic religious law], but by establishing first an Islamic state through political action. Islamists see Islam not as a mere religion, but a political ideology.

Sutton and Vertigans (2005) offer a sociological explanation of the Muslim resurgence.

Returning to the hijab, there is no one story of veil-wearing and what it means to the women who wear it. Franks (2000: 918) observes: '[the hijab is] neither liberating nor oppressive, and that the power relations with which it is associated are situated … in the circumstances under which it is worn'. Today, in some societies, women are mandated to wear the hijab (e.g. Iran), while in other societies or communities, wearing it is a social expectation that is difficult to transgress. In such cases, women will wear the veil happily or reluctantly. Some women, depending on where they live, have greater freedom, and will adopt it as a sign of their religious devotion, while others will choose not to wear it as an expression of their religious freedom. Many people, particularly non-Muslim Westerners, view the hijab as a sign of 'Islamic patriarchy and oppression of women' (Ahmed 2011: 8), and it has been a flashpoint for debate about religious freedom. In France, Muslim girls are banned from wearing the hijab in public schools, something celebrated by secularists and other opponents of the veil, but this ban is seen by many Muslims, women included, as an impingement on their right to express their religion freely.

The global ummah?

As the foregoing discussion demonstrates, Islam is a diverse religion, and yet it is unified in a unique and important way; the *ummah*. This is the idea that Muslims together constitute a worldwide community of faith that transcends borders, cultures and ethnicities. The ummah is a 'state of mind, a form of social consciousness, or an imagined community' of the faithful (Hassan 2002 in Sutton and Vertigans 2005: 98). While this idea has long been important in Islam, arguably it has grown in significance and meaning in the last few decades and now has an increasingly global dimension.

A recent example of the global ummah in action is the worldwide reaction to the 'Danish cartoon affair'. In 2005 the Danish newspaper, *Jyllands-Posten*, published 12 cartoons of the Prophet Muhammad (see Saunders 2008). Many Danish Muslims were deeply offended by the cartoons. Muslims around the world joined the protest, expressing their displeasure in street protests, through diplomatic channels and in the social media. Saunders (2008: 304) notes that the 'ummah's global response to the "Cartoons Affair" underscores the development of a robust collective identity among the world's Muslims'.

Scholars argue processes associated with globalization, particularly widespread migration, faster and cheaper transport, and far-reaching media networks, have contributed to the rise and development of a truly global ummah (see Esposito 1999; Roy 2004; Casanova 2005; Sutton and Vertigans 2005; Saunders 2008). Casanova (2005: 93) argues: 'The proliferation of transnational Muslim networks of all kinds, transnational migration and the emergence of Muslim diasporas throughout the world, the massive global proportions of the pilgrimage to Mecca [and] the establishment of global Islamic mass media' have all resulted in Islam 'being reconstituted as a transnational religious regime and as a global imagined community.'

It was noted in Chapter 4 that a key element of contemporary globalization is the development and roll out of global forms of communication. The most conspicuous example is the Internet (particularly social media like Facebook, YouTube and Twitter, and Internet radio and TV). Other examples include satellite TV (e.g. Al Jazeera, CNN), and the large-scale piracy of TV shows and movies. The development of mobile phone technology has enabled cheap and efficient access to the Internet to people in economically developing countries. The advent of global forms of information and communications technology (ICT) means that ideas and knowledge can be quickly and widely disseminated. Information now can cross borders – cultural and physical – that could not in the past be so easily broached.

As such, the Internet is described by Saunders (2008: 312) as 'the forge of ummahism'. Muslims make great use of the Internet. Kort (2005: 366) notes the material on Islamic websites includes 'transcribed sermons, translated editions of the Qur'an, hadith (sayings and deeds of the Prophet Muhammad), tafsir (Qur'anic commentary), advice and self-help, fatwas (legal rulings), political news and activism, how to find mosques and halal butchers, matrimonials, chat groups [and] prayer times'. Sermons are also streamed lived across the world.

The Internet is not the only factor contributing to the rise of the global ummah. Cheaper travel has enabled Muslim migrants to nurture transnational religious networks. For example, mosques in England or the United States easily can fly in an imam (cleric) from Egypt to preach. Young men from Indonesia can affordably attend a few weeks of religious training in Saudi Arabia before returning home to share what they have learned with family and friends. Cheaper travel and transnational communication networks have also expanded the global reach and size of the Hajj (see this chapter's case study), and this has also strengthened the sense of a global ummah.

THE HAJJ – A GLOBAL RELIGIOUS RITUAL ...

Religious rituals are deliberate, traditional actions and activities which forge a link between a religious person or religious community and the 'transcendent' (that which is beyond). Examples of rituals found in the world's religions include prayer, silent contemplation, singing, dancing, communion, circumambulism (walking in a circle around a holy object or temple) and meditation. Performing a religious ritual can assist a person to feel some kind of connection, be it intellectual, emotional or physical, to the transcendent. Collectively performed rituals can also unite a religious community. Durkheim (1912/1995) argued 'collective effervescence' is generated in the midst of large religious ceremonies or during religious rituals. The experience of collective effervescence can unite members of the same religion and reinforce group solidarity and collective identity. This is certainly the case with Islam, where 'the annual Hajj ("pilgrimage") has long served as a mechanism for making the global ummah a reality' (Saunders 2008: 309).

One of the five pillars of Islam (see above) is the requirement (if feasible) that 'every Muslim, anywhere in the world, is obliged to perform, at least once in a lifetime, the *Hajj*, or ritual pilgrimage, to Mecca' (Peters 1994: xxi). Mecca is a city in eastern Saudi Arabia and the birthplace of Muhammad, Islam's most important prophet. The Hajj is open to Muslims only. It is undertaken at the same time each year, during the eighth, ninth and tenth days of the last month in the Muslim calendar (Peters 1994: xxi).

Muhammad first performed the pilgrimage in the seventh century and Muslims have been doing it ever since. Sometimes it has been undertaken in the face of grave danger or severe tribulation. In the global era of affordable airfares the number of pilgrims performing the Hajj has increased considerably, and now several million Muslims make the pilgrimage annually. The Saudi government, via its Ministry of Hajj, administers the performance of the Hajj, and places quotas on the number of pilgrims who can visit from any given country. A website, listed below, provides travelers with details and advice about the trip. It is an extraordinary logistical exercise, and requires careful planning and management to ensure the safety and health of the pilgrims. An airport terminal has been specially built in nearby Jedda to accommodate the sheer volume of visitors; it can process 5000 pilgrims per hour (Ruthven 1997). Occasionally, modern pilgrims are killed in the crushing crowds. For most, however, performing the Hajj is a deeply profound religious experience.

Once there, the pilgrim must follow a series of prescribed actions and activities and walk a particular pilgrimage route. According to Peer (2012: 74):

'It begins in Mecca, before moving to the desert of Mina, then to Arafat for a day-long vigil, then to the rocky plain of Muzdalifah, a few miles away, where pilgrims collect pebbles to ritually stone the Devil, and then returns to Mina for three days. Back in Mecca, pilgrims bid farewell to the Kaaba, the cube-shaped granite building that is the holiest site in Islam'

Figure 10.1 Pilgrims walking around the Kaaba during the Hajj
Source: © Ayazad/Fotolia

There is little doubt the modern Hajj has contributed to the development of a burgeoning global Muslim consciousness. Pilgrims come from around the globe to attend (from 100 different countries) and are united by their religious affiliation, rather than by their race or ethnicity. Clingingsmith et al. (2009) conducted a study of 1600 Pakistani Muslims and found that

Hajjis (those who have performed the Hajj) are more likely to undertake universally accepted global Muslim religious practices such as fasting and performing obligatory and supererogatory (optional) prayers. In contrast, the Hajj reduces performance of less universally accepted, more localized practices and beliefs such as using amulets and the necessity of giving dowry. (Clingingsmith et al. 2009: 1135)

(Continued)

(Continued)

They also note: 'Our results support the idea that the Hajj helps to integrate the Muslim world, leading to a strengthening of global Islamic beliefs [and] a weakened attachment to local religious customs' (Clingingsmith et al. 2009:1135). Some commentators suggest the event privileges conservative, Saudi strands of Islam. Overall, however, it appears that massed, international religious events, like the Hajj or the Catholic World Youth Day, do engender a strong sense of transnational unity among participants.

Want to know more?

- The Kingdom of Saudi Arabia's Ministry of Hajj website is a complete guide to the Hajj, with travel advice for prospective pilgrims, information and a historical account of the ritual. It also has videos and a picture gallery. Highly recommended. www.hajinformation.com

Scholars suggest the concept of the ummah has more cachet among some Muslim communities than others (see Kort 2005; Saunders 2008). They argue it is particularly important among marginalized groups in the Western diaspora. According to Saunders (2008: 310) 'Ummahism has found fertile ground in the marginalized Muslim ghettos of European cities.' Via the ummah, marginalized Muslims can experience a sense of community and purpose beyond their immediate circumstances. That said, the growth of the global ummah has not eliminated differences within the faith. Sutton and Vertigans (2005: 111) argue 'international cultural variations have, through contemporary forms of globalization, become more noticeable'. For example, while Muslim men in Indonesia can now easily follow a school of conservative, strict and male-dominated Islamist teaching from Saudi Arabia, feminist Muslims who seek to counter such conservative trends can readily unite via the Internet with other progressive feminist Muslims to promote and disseminate other schools of thought (see Kort 2005 for such examples). Nonetheless, the ummah remains a powerful concept in contemporary Islam, a religion which, as argued below, is now spreading in larger numbers around the globe.

THE GLOBAL DISTRIBUTION OF THE WORLD'S MUSLIMS

Islam, like Christianity, was one of the earliest globalizing forces, moving outward from its starting place in the Arabian peninsula many centuries before transnational capitalism or the mass-media had an impact on the global world order. Within a few centuries of Islam's founding, Muslim communities were spread around the Middle East, Northern Africa, Asia–Minor and parts of Europe. This expansion, aided by military conquests and conversion, continued into the Middle Ages. Muslim communities also grew in Asia (e.g. China, Mongolia, Malaysia, India, and Indonesia). By the end of the nineteenth century small communities of Muslims could be found in Western Europe, Australia and America, peopled by Muslim traders, workers and slaves.

As of 2010, 23.4 percent of people globally – about a quarter of the world's population – are Muslims (Pew Forum 2011b: 13). In the next 20 years, the world's Muslim population is expected to grow at a faster rate than that of non-Muslims, and will make up an estimated 26.3 percent of the world's population by 2030 (Pew Forum 2011b: 13). This continued growth is the consequence of many interrelated social and demographic factors, including higher fertility rates among the Muslim population compared to non-Muslims and improvements in life expectancy and decreasing infant mortality rates in many Muslim-majority countries (Pew Forum 2011b: 15).

In today's world, the majority of Muslims do not live in the Middle East where Islam was founded (although all countries there, apart from Israel, have Muslim-majority populations), but in the Asia-Pacific region. The distribution of the world's Muslims is shown in Figure 10.2.

The world's four most populous Muslim nations are all in the Asia-Pacific region: Indonesia, Pakistan, India and Bangladesh. Apart from India, these are all Muslim-majority countries. Overall, the world's Muslims live mainly in Muslim-majority countries, most of which are economically developing nations in the Global South. Only about 3 percent of the world's Muslims live in the most

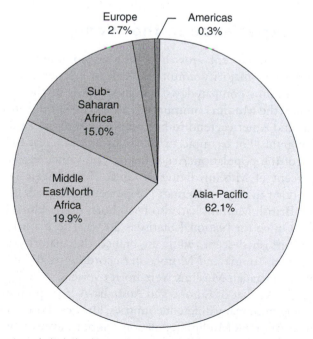

Figure 10.2 Regional distribution of the world's Muslim population

Data Source: Pew Forum (2011b: 14). Percentages may not add up to 100 because of rounding.

developed parts of the world: Europe, North America, Australia, New Zealand and Japan (Pew Forum 2011b: 18).

THE GROWTH OF MUSLIM POPULATIONS IN MUSLIM-MINORITY COUNTRIES

While most of the world's Muslims live in Muslim-majority countries, the proportion who live in Muslim-minority countries, particularly in the West and China, has grown significantly in the past few decades. In America, for example, the proportion of the population identifying as Muslim grew from 0.3 percent in 1990 to 0.6 percent in 2008 (Kosmin and Keysar 2009a). In England and Wales, census data show the proportion of the population identifying as Muslim grew from 3 percent in 2001 to 4.8 percent in 2011 (Office for National Statistics 2012: 1). According to the Australian Bureau of Statistics (2006: 54) the number of Muslims living in Australia tripled between 1986 and 2006.

This growth is projected to continue in the next few decades. The Pew Forum (2011b: 121) notes 'Europe's Muslim population is projected to exceed 58 million by 2030. Muslims today account for about 6 percent of Europe's total population, up from 4.1 percent in 1990. By 2030, Muslims are expected to make up 8 percent of Europe's population'. The Muslim share of the US population (adults and children) is projected to grow to 1.7 percent in 2030 (Pew Forum 2011b: 15).

The Muslim experience in the West

The main drivers of this recent growth of Muslim communities in the West are migration from Muslim-majority countries, and, to a lesser extent, higher fertility rates among Muslims compared with non-Muslims in the country of settlement. Consequently, the Muslim communities within northern and western Europe, Australia, Canada and America, tend to be composed predominantly of migrants or the children of migrants. For example, in 2001 Muslims in Great Britain represented almost 3 percent of the population. According to the Office for National Statistics (2004: 6), 46 percent of Muslims living in Great Britain were born there, while 39 percent were born in Asia – Pakistan (18 percent), Bangladesh (9 percent) and India (3 percent). British Muslims had also been born in the Horn of Africa, Turkey and the Balkans (Office for National Statistics 2004). The majority of Muslims in Germany are of Turkish descent, while in France the majority are of Maghrebi descent (from Algeria, Tunisia and Morocco). According to 2006 Australian census data, 60 percent of Australian Muslims were born overseas.

America's story is like that of Europe and Australia. A large proportion of Muslims are migrants, coming from many different countries. The Pew Forum (2011c) estimates 63 percent of America's adult Muslim population was born overseas, while a further 15 percent was born of migrant parents. Overseas-born Muslims in the United States hail from 77 different countries, but are predominantly from South Asia (Pakistan, India, and Bangladesh), North Africa and the Middle East. It is also important to note 13 percent of US Muslims are African-Americans whose parents were born in the United States (Pew Forum 2011c: 9). As Roy (2007: 100) succinctly puts it: 'The vast majority of the Muslim population in the West consists of recent migrants.'

Religious settlement of Muslims

The previous chapter described at length the concept of religious settlement, a term which encapsulates the processes associated with religions arriving – and growing – in a new country. Religious settlement had four important dimensions, the last of which was the way a rapidly growing migrant religion finds its place in the host country. This involves the reactions of both communities (migrant and host) and the state to the presence of a growing religion (Bouma 1996: 51). The recent growth of Islam has created challenges for host societies, the governments which are required to manage religious diversity, and for Muslim migrants. These various challenges are discussed below.

The growth of religious minorities in the West can be something of a challenge for host societies. How have they reacted to the growth of Muslim communities? Western, Christianized countries have a long history of antipathy to Islam (see Dossa 2008), but sentiment has waxed and waned over the centuries. At present, however, the distrust of Muslims appears to be increasing. Many commentators have noted the rise of 'Islamaphobia' in Western societies, particularly in the decade after the 9/11 terrorist attacks (see, for example, Triandafyllidou 2010; Abbas 2011; Doyle 2011). Barkdull et al. (2011: 140) describe Islamaphobia as 'an intense fear or dislike of Muslims'. According to Bouma (2010: 55) it entails the 'fear that Muslims will do things that will injure the society'.

Many Muslims living in the West have been subjected to discrimination and prejudice. A recent Pew Forum report found a significant proportion of US Muslims (43 percent) had in the past year been treated with suspicion, called offensive names, been singled out by airport security, singled out by police or physically threatened or attacked (Pew Forum 2011c: 46). Other studies in America, Europe and Britain reveal acts of discrimination, prejudice and abuse directed at Muslims (see Dunn et al. 2007; Barkdull et al. 2011). The rise of Islamaphobia is the consequence of many interrelated social factors – long-standing Western suspicion of Muslims, a fear of Muslims fueled by conservative elements in the Western media, anxiety caused by recent acts of terror directed at Western targets and the perception that Muslims dislike secular, Western culture.

Protecting minority religions from discrimination and prejudice is a task largely divested to the state and is one of the many challenges the growth of religious minorities, including Islam, present to national governments. Migrating religions have requirements which may not have a recognized or official place in the host society. Examples of such religious requirements which have needed recognition include special days of celebration (e.g. Eid, the festival which follows the Muslim holy month of Ramadan), dress and dietary obligations (e.g. halal food) and customary practices (e.g. Muslim burial customs). How have Western states managed the requirements of their growing Muslim populations? According to Olivier Roy (2007: x) 'The West has managed its Muslim population by mobilizing two models: multiculturalism, usually associated with English-speaking countries (the United Kingdom, the United States, Canada [and Australia] and northern Europe), and the assimilationist model, specific to France.'

According to Rimmer (1995: 89) the essence of multiculturalism is the promotion of equality and freedom for all regardless of ethnic background, race or religion. Under this policy, Muslims are, in theory, free to practice their religion in ways they see fit. This tolerance, however, does not entail a complete acceptance of all religious beliefs and practices. The limits of religious freedom are dictated by Western standards and in practice moderation and compromise usually are required of minority religions (e.g. polygamy and female circumcision, found in a few Muslim communities, are not permitted). Religious recognition usually does not come easily. Muslims in the West have had to campaign vigorously to have things such as burial practices recognized. Some Muslims have sought to live by sharia law and to allow this to govern their lives. Sharia law, broadly defined, refers to 'Islamically derived rules and norms' (McGoldrick 2009: 606). There is debate in Islamic and legal circles if it can, or should, be legally applied to Muslims living in Western countries (see McGoldrick 2009; Maret 2013). That said, non-legally binding sharia tribunals are already operating in many Western countries.

In contrast to the multicultural model, successive French governments, constitutionally bound to a distinctive form of secular government, the *laïcité* (see Roy 2007 for an extended discussion), have shown an 'intolerance towards public expressions of religious faith' (Doyle 2011: 476). The French government banned the wearing of the hijab in public schools in 2004 and since 2010 has banned the niqab, a cloth which covers the face, from being worn in public.

The process of religious settlement also brings with it challenges for religious settlers, because they must negotiate their new society. As noted above, many Muslims have encountered prejudice and discrimination on the basis of their religion. Also, the migrant Muslim populations in Western countries typically experience higher rates of unemployment, discrimination and poverty than the non-Muslim, non-migrant population. Peach (2006: 637), using British census data, found the 'Muslim population [of Britain], taken as a whole, is poor, badly housed, with low educational qualifications, suffers high levels of male unemployment and has a very low female participation rate in the labour market.'

Certainly, the challenges faced by many Muslims migrants are not the result of their religious affiliation alone, but also stem from the political, social and economic factors related to being migrants (Abbas 2011). These factors might include fewer employment opportunities, language barriers, and problems with access to education. Moreover, Muslims might be discriminated against on the basis of their race. Hopkins (2004: 258–9), for example, focusing on the experiences of young Scottish Muslim men, explores the interconnection between religion and race, noting 'whilst these young men identify as Muslim, they also overwhelmingly belong to a group racialised as South Asian or Pakistani, thus stressing the interconnectivity of race and religion'.

Sometimes Muslims living in the West appear to struggle with aspects of Western culture, for example freedom of speech on religious matters, women's dress styles, or so the media represents their situation. This is taken by critics of Islam as evidence that this religion is incompatible with Western life. The religious requirements of Islam, as spelt out on the Qur'an, are the apparent cause of this tension and place Muslims at odds with some Western values.

An example of this would appear to be the 'Muslim Patrol' who surfaced recently in London. This group came to the public's attention via a series of videos posted on YouTube.com. In these videos, the group, apparently comprised of young Muslim men, can be seen confronting people, and asking them to desist from drinking alcohol or to move away from a mosque. They repeatedly tell people, 'This is a Muslim area', and, in another instance say 'Christianity can go to hell'. Another London group, the 'Shariah Project', hosts a website, www.theshariahproject.com, announcing they have projects to tackle prostitution and gambling in London and to advocate for the legal adoption of sharia law in the West.

The reality, however, of Muslim life in the West is more complex than simply one of abiding tensions between Muslims and the broader, non-Muslim culture (see Roy 2004 for a lucid discussion of these issues). Islam, like all other religions, is theologically diverse, and Muslims adopt a variety of approaches when it comes to dealing with non-Muslims and non-Muslim culture. Some Muslims preach and follow a very strict interpretation of the Qur'an, and are thus reactive to non-Muslim culture and committed to creating a society which reflects Muslim values. (The same is true of some very devout and orthodox followers of other religions, who are opposed to mainstream secular culture.) Many Muslims, however, follow more liberal, progressive and less orthodox doctrine. They are content to live their own religious life without feeling the need to impose their religious values on others. Many Muslims do not see 'Western' and 'Muslim' values as being opposed to one another, and happily create hybrid identities. Muslims, moreover, like followers of other faiths, vary greatly in their individual commitment to their religion (see the next chapter).

That said, for all of the different ways Muslims live out their faith, it does appear that recent dislike of the West from some Muslims has resulted in religiously motivated acts of terror, a topic explored in the final section of this chapter.

UNDERSTANDING SOME 'ISMS' ASSOCIATED WITH CONTEMPORARY ISLAM: FUNDAMENTALISM, EXTREMISM, RADICALISM, TERRORISM

The world was shocked recently by TV images of a young man standing on a southeast London street, holding a machete in his blood-soaked hands. The man and his accomplice had run down a soldier with a car and then proceeded to butcher him as he lay injured on the street. After the deed, the young man sought out a bystander and said: 'The only reason we have killed this man today is because Muslims are dying daily by British soldiers ... By Allah ... we will never stop fighting until you leave us alone' (Snow and Miller 2013). This section focuses on sociological understandings of religiously motivated violence.

Much of the recent scholarly work on Islam centers on Islamic politics, and considers topics such as the relationship between Muslim-majority states and Western governments, tensions in the Middle East, the rise of conservative Islamist regimes (e.g. the Taliban in Afghanistan, or Iran) and the so-called 'Arab Spring' (recent political uprisings in the Middle East and Northern Africa). Scholarship has also been conducted on the radical Muslims who perpetrate acts of terrorism against Western targets, such as the 2001 destruction of the World Trade Center in New York, the 2004 Madrid train bombings and the 2005 London bombings. Many of the scholars who work on these topics are political scientists (whose work focuses largely on politics, statecraft, public policy and political behavior). It is beyond the scope of this book to consider the political dimensions of Islam. Nonetheless, it is important to understand some of the terms which are used in such discussions to characterize Islam, particularly fundamentalism, and to explain also the place, often largely misunderstood, religion has in inspiring acts of violence and terrorism.

Because of the conspicuous acts of terrorism done in the name of Islam, it is bedeviled by perceptions in the West that it is a religion of fanatics, extremism and violence (see Bruce 2008). This is not true of the overwhelming majority of the world's Muslims. It is true, however, that some groups and individuals do perpetrate violent acts 'in the name' of Islam. Such groups are often referred to as 'fundamentalists'. This word has a long and complex history in the study of religions (see Armstrong 2001). At this point, it is worth explaining the term **fundamentalism** as it is used in the sociology of religion, and consider its application to the study of Islam.

The term fundamentalist was first applied to Protestant American Christians who, in the early twentieth century, railed against 'liberal' or 'non-literal' interpretations of the Christian Bible. Two brothers, Milton and Lyman Stewart, published a series of tracts called *Fundamentals: A Testimony of Truth* which 'were aimed at stopping the erosion of what ... [were] considered to be the fundamental beliefs of Protestant Christianity' (Ruthven 2007: 7). Thus, in its first usage, fundamentalism described a tension between traditional, and progressive or modernizing elements within Protestant Christianity. The term was later applied to describe Islamist movements in the Middle East which were opposed to modernization.

These days, when scholars use the term, they usually are referring to theologically strict and conservative religious movements which cultivate a pronounced sense of 'us' (the true followers of the faith) and 'them' (liberals or non-believers). Such movements are not unique to Islam. Every religion encompasses a spectrum of views about matters of doctrine, ranging from the very strict and conservative to the very liberal. Communities which follow a strict doctrinal code typically have rules which govern dress and worship style, gender roles, permissible activities, paid work and social interaction. When living in the PNG highlands I encountered conservatively dressed American missionaries who would not speak to Christians outside their group, let alone other nonreligious expatriates.

Those who adhere to a strict interpretation of their religion appeal to a higher authority – a 'literal' interpretation of religious texts and traditional teachings – in order to justify their doctrinal views. Such groups – whether they be Buddhist, Hindu, Christian, Muslim or Jewish – are often at odds with more liberal followers of their faith and the culture within which they live. Fundamentalism is a term helpfully applied to describe these conservative religious groups, because it encapsulates their strong world-view, their belief in the infallibility of scripture, the commitment to their code, and the tensions between them and more moderate elements in their religion. Some commentators (e.g. Bruce 2008) see the recent rise in fundamentalist groups around the world as a conservative, religious reaction to the social upheaval and uncertainty wrought by modernization (growth of urban poor, political instability, rapid social change).

There are groups and movements in Islam which might be described as fundamentalist in the sense just described. The recently deposed Taliban regime in Afghanistan, for example, professed an extreme version of Sunni Islam. This included strict policies about education, dress, and music and severe restrictions on the roles of women. Not all scholars agree with the use of fundamentalist and see it as 'irrelevant to Islam or, at best, a dubious concept alien to the cultural heritage of Muslims' (Choueiri 2010: 1), preferring to call such movements 'militant', 'radical', 'extremist' or 'Islamist' (see Vertigans 2009; Abbas 2011).

Religious violence

In recent decades extremist Islamic movements have sought to advance their cause using military means or terrorist action. The most infamous of these is the Taliban in Afghanistan. After taking power during the Afghan Civil War, it brutally implemented its theocracy. Some parts of the Muslim world are at present embroiled in sectarian violence. This is particularly the case in Pakistan, Afghanistan and Iraq, and increasingly, in Indonesia and Bangladesh.

Smaller groups of Muslims, such as Osama Bin Laden's Al Qaeda, also have perpetrated acts of terrorism against targets in the West and within the Muslim world. (The perpetrators of such acts are described usually by the media as fundamentalists.) Sometimes such acts of violence are called '*jihad*' (meaning 'struggle', but recast by radicals as 'holy war' against the enemies of Islam). In these different examples religion is implicated, either as the putative inspiration for violence or as the justification for violent acts.

Does religious commitment cause people to take up arms or become terrorists? It is simplistic to argue that religion is the only trigger of violence. The majority of the world's religious people do not perpetrate acts of violence in the name of their religion. Rather, acts of religious violence occur in particular contexts and are perpetrated by particular people, whether those be small terrorist cells active in a British city, Al Qaeda militants in the Pakistan-Afghan border region or Islamic militia in the Horn of Africa.

Social scientists increasingly recognize that violence cannot be explained by one single factor (World Health Organization 2002: 9). Rather, according to the *World Heath Organization* (WHO), violence is 'an extremely complex phenomenon that has its roots in the interaction of many factors – biological, social, cultural, economic and political' (2002: 9). One helpful attempt to explain the multiple factors that give rise to acts of violence is the 'ecological model', proposed in the 2002 WHO report, *World Report on Violence and Health*, and subsequently extended and refined by other scholars.

Proponents of the ecological model argue that violence is a consequence of factors interacting at four levels; the individual, relational, communal and sociocultural. Each of these levels contains factors which influence the way people behave. A helpful description of the model is provided by Krug et al. (2002), which is summarized here. **Individual** factors which influence violent behavior include gender, age and personality characteristics. For example, men are far more likely than women to perpetrate acts of violence, as are those who are susceptible to indoctrination. The next level of influence on behavior is the **relational**, where the likelihood of violence increases if peers and family engage also in such acts, or if a person is socially isolated. The third level is the **communal**, where the likelihood of violence increases if a person's immediate community is transient, poor, vulnerable, does not have strong social networks, or is already mired in conflict or tension between groups (which can be between different religious groups, such as Pakistani Muslims and Christians). The final level is the **societal and cultural**, where the likelihood of violence increases if a person lives in a society in rapid transition, or experiencing political instability. This level also takes into account the *social and cultural norms* which might inspire, justify or legitimize acts of violence. Social and cultural norms can certainly be the product of religious ideology.

If the circumstances of those who perpetrate acts of violence in the name of religion are considered, whether a small terrorist cell operating in Britain or an armed militia in Sudan, it is possible to see all of these factors as instrumental in producing violent action. The more these various trigger factors are present, the greater the likelihood of violence. The spate of terrorism in recent decades is the result of a 'perfect storm' of trigger factors. Thus, while religious ideology is never the *sole* cause of acts of terror, it can play an important part in inspiring or justifying such acts.

CONCLUSION

The past five chapters have examined, among other issues, how globalization – the worldwide flow of people and ideas – has affected the world's religious life. Foremost among these changes is the widespread migration of religious people around the world and the subsequent growth of diasporic religious communities. The concept of 'religious settlement' was introduced to make sense of the many dimensions involved when a religion and religious people move from one location to another. There are now large communities of Muslims, Hindus, Buddhists and Christians who live far from their country of birth.

This chapter also examined the emergence of global religious communities, which is particularly, but not exclusively, a feature of contemporary Islam. Like global Pentecostalism, the transmission of ideas in Islam has been aided by modern communication technologies and faster forms of transport. Without these border-crossing technologies, the global ummah could not have developed in such a fashion. Contemporary religions are now characterized by global patterns of people movement and a greater global consciousness.

Thus far discussion has centered on global and national patterns of religious change. Sociologists are interested also in the meaning of religion to the individual, and how and why some people are religious and others are not. This is the focus of the next chapter.

Points to ponder

Examine recent media reporting about Muslims and Muslim affairs. What evidence of 'Islamaphobia' can you find? How might governments and communities challenge Islamaphobia?

Next steps …

Leila Ahmed's *A Quiet Revolution: The Veil's Resurgence, From the Middle East to America* (2011), examines the recent rise in hijab-wearing around the world, and in doing so discusses recent and important developments in contemporary Islam. French scholar Olivier Roy's (2004, 2007) work on global Islam is extremely lucid, thought-provoking and nuanced. For discussion of Muslims in Britain, see Sophie Gillat-Ray's accessible *Muslims in Britain: An Introduction* (2010); for Europe generally, see Amikam Nachmani's *Europe and its Muslim Minorities* (2009); for Australia, the edited collection *Muslims in Australia: The Dynamics of Exclusion and Inclusion* (Yasmeen 2010); for Hong Kong see Paul O'Connor's (2012) *Islam in Hong Kong: Muslims and Everyday Life in China's World City*; for America, see Jane Smith's *Islam in America* (2010) and Mucahit Bilici's *Finding Mecca in America* (2012).

Documentaries

Britain's Channel Four has produced a very interesting documentary on the hajj, *The Hajj: The Greatest Trip on Earth* www.channel4.com/programmes/the-hajj-the-greatest-trip-on-earth/4od. Equally fascinating is a documentary on the Hajj produced by America's Discovery Channel, *Revealed: The Hajj*.

Web

Baylor University's Institute for Studies of Religion, hosts a podcast series on religion. This is the link for podcasts on Islam: http://www.researchonreligion.org/category/islam.

11

'lived' religion in everyday life

After reading this chapter you will:

- understand the ways in which individuals are religious;
- be familiar with sociological explanations of individual religiosity;
- understand the relationship between religion and gender; and
- have insight into how religiosity changes across the lifecourse.

I interviewed 18-year-old 'Kanisha' (not her real name) for one of my research projects (see Singleton 2012). Kanisha is a science student at a large university. She was born and raised in India and migrated to Australia with her family when she was 11 years old. Kanisha is an Irani, an Indian ethno-religious minority. Iranis are traditionally followers of the Zoroastrian religion, which was founded in ancient Persia in the sixth century BCE. In the nineteenth century large numbers of Zoroastrians migrated from Iran to India, where they became known as Iranis.

Her parents are committed practitioners of the Zoroastrian religion. Kanisha was raised as a Zoroastrian and as a child she followed the faith diligently. At some point in her teens, however, she stopped being religious. She describes herself as an agnostic. Of her former faith she said: 'My parents still do [practice Zoroastrianism] and for them I do sometimes put up a resemblance of following rituals on official days ... but I find my younger brother who I may have influenced a little bit is also moving away from traditional ideas.' (All quotes are from a personal interview conducted by the author.)

Kanisha identified two factors which led her to turn her back on the religious tradition of her family and culture. One is the perceived hypocrisy of other Zoroastrians. Kanisha said:

Amongst my community [people] pray very regularly and do all the rituals and rites [to] ensure they get into a good afterlife but then in this life they are quite hypocritical sometimes. I do think observing a lot of people has made me wary of the original beliefs.

She also felt living in Australia's largely secular culture had caused her to think differently about her religion. She commented:

I'm a very big ideas person and ... then [I] started to challenge traditional Zoroastrians ideas of religion and afterlife and how one must behave and all. I do think coming to a Western country opens up your ideas to more, the word autonomy keeps coming [to mind].

It is possible to identify many factors which have influenced Kanisha's religious outlook. That she was a Zoroastrian, and not a Muslim or Hindu, reflects her cultural background. Her story points to the importance of parents in shaping individual religiosity, particularly in childhood and adolescence. As she got older she began to reflect critically on her religious upbringing and upon reaching adulthood had greater scope to make her own choices. The individualistic, secular culture in which she now lives makes religious commitment more difficult. Clearly, many factors – psychological, developmental, cultural – shape her religiosity.

Stepping back from the broader focus on religious change around the world, this chapter addresses briefly the relationship between culture, society and individual religiosity. It begins with a discussion of the different ways in which individuals are religious and how this is measured by social scientists. Next, it investigates the influence of social and cultural factors on individual religiosity. Finally, it assesses the impact religious faith has on everyday life. The chapter is somewhat Western-centric, if only because such a large volume of work has been done on these topics in English-speaking countries, particularly the United States.

ARE YOU 'RELIGIOUS', 'SPIRITUAL' OR NONRELIGIOUS? AND HOW DO WE KNOW?

Are you religious? Think of the answer to this question. What criteria did you use to determine if you are religious? Belief in God? Frequency of attendance at services of worship? Identification with a religious tradition? A combination of belief, attendance and identification? Social scientists are invested heavily in measuring people's religiosity. Many important sociological arguments are based on such measurements. Protagonists in secularization debates, for example, rely on data about church attendance, religious belief and religious practice in order to substantiate their respective arguments. This section explores how social scientists make judgments about the religiosity of individuals.

Observational techniques for gathering data can be extremely useful in determining accurately behavior such as attendance at services of worship (see Hadaway et al. 1993). However, it is very difficult to determine much about a person's religiosity using observation alone. Scholars can observe a person attending worship but will have little idea of what this means to that person. The example of Kanisha is a case in point. She partakes in certain religious practices for the sake of her parents, yet concedes these are personally empty gestures. The best way to determine what religion means to her is to ask her directly.

To that end, scholars measuring individual religiosity rely typically on people's self-assessment for their data, rather than observation or other techniques. The US National Study of Youth and Religion (NSYR) survey, for example, asked respondents, 'How important is your religious faith in providing guidance in your own day-to-day living?' The survey offered responses ranging from 'Extremely Important' to 'Not Important at all'. It is up to the respondents to determine which answer best describes them. Self-assessment is not entirely reliable. It is an established sociological fact that people routinely overestimate their religious behavior, but it does seem a better way to determine religiosity than simple observation.

Scholars agree that **individual religiosity** has three key dimensions (Pearce and Denton 2011: 13). Sociologists Lisa Pearce and Melinda Denton (2011: 13) note these are:

> The *content* of religious belief, the *conduct* of religious activity, and the *centrality* of religion to life. Understanding what a person believes, how he [sic] practices his religion, and the extent to which religion is an important part of his identity provides a comprehensive sense of a person's religiosity. (italics in original)

As noted in Chapter 5, social scientists often collect data about each of these different areas and bring them together to create a multidimensional measure of religion for each study participant. This can be used to map the religiosity of a given population. It is likely that people's individual religiosity will vary greatly.

Different ways of being religious or nonreligious

One way scholars make sense of the different ways in which people are religious or nonreligious is by using a 'typology' of individual religiosity. A typology is a set of types, or categories, and can be inferred from quantitative or qualitative data, or both. A typology is never perfect or complete, but can be useful nonetheless. Christian Smith and Patricia Snell (2009: 166) note 'empirically formed categories that represent the major differences in groups of people can bring helpful analytical clarity to what would otherwise be a complex mass of data'. Analysis can be conducted to determine the prevalence of different types within a population, to discover why people are one type and not another, and what life outcomes are associated with different types.

A national study of Australian youth spirituality, the *Spirit of Generation Y*, for which I was a co-investigator, took such an approach when mapping the spirituality of Australian youth (see Mason et al. 2007). Using nationally representative survey data and information from in-depth interviews, we created a typology for understanding the range and variety of spiritual types among Australian teens and young adults. We settled on the idea of 'spiritual' types, rather than religious types, to reflect the fact that while some people are not conventionally religious, they do engage in alternative spiritual practices. They might be deeply committed to some aspect of the New Age, such as astrology. The initial classification of spiritual types was derived from theory and previous research, then refined repeatedly in the light of the data so that the final set of types was shaped by both (Mason et al. 2007: 68–9). There were three major spirituality types:

- **Traditional**: grounded in the tradition of a major world-religion;

- **New Age**: non-traditional religions or spiritual paths; and

- **Secular**: based on human experience and human reason, rejecting both traditional religion and New Age spirituality.

Each of these types denotes a person's broader spiritual orientation or worldview. We found variation in the extent to which young people lived out this orientation, so we proposed people were either 'engaged' or 'unengaged' with one of these three major directions. The large majority of young Australians (about 59 percent) were unengaged spiritually, and simply oriented in a particular direction because of what they believed. The engaged minority actively followed one of these paths (i.e. went to church regularly, or used tarot cards regularly and seriously). This is one example of a typology being used to make sense of the different ways people are religious or spiritual. It also proved helpful in subsequent statistical analysis (see below).

Recently, other studies have developed typologies or 'profiles' to describe different religious or spiritual types found among US teens (Clark 2003; Smith and Denton 2005 Pearce and Denton 2011), US young adults (Smith and Snell 2009) and US adults (Roof 1999). Using data from the NSYR, sociologists Lisa Pearce and Melinda Denton (2011) proposed five religious profiles in the population of US teens and young adults: Abiders, Adapters, Assenters, Avoiders and Atheists. Each of these types is used to illuminate the different ways US youth are religious or nonreligious. Abiders, for example, have high levels of religious service attendance, of personal prayer and closeness to God. Atheists completely reject religion, and are consistently nonreligious across all measures (Pearce and Denton 2011: 70–71). Typologies or profiles are particularly helpful in mapping key differences in individual religiosity within a population.

Lived religion

It should be remembered that such classifications are 'ideal types'. Not every person will fit comfortably into a type. Sometimes people are too hard to classify. Nor should it be presumed that people enact religiosity in a consistent, congruent fashion befitting a type. Sociologist Mark Chaves (2010: 2) argues 'people's religious ideas and practices generally are fragmented, compartmentalized, loosely connected, unexamined, and context dependent'. The example of Kanisha from the start of this chapter is a case in point. In some contexts, she behaves in a highly religious fashion, even though the content of her belief does not match her actions. Chaves suggests that religious congruence – belief always matching action – is rare among individuals, rather than the norm.

For such reasons, some social scientists are less interested in mapping the different ways in which people are religious and instead concentrate more on studying how religion is *lived* in everyday life. A leading proponent of this approach is US sociologist Meredith McGuire (2008). She argues the study of individual religiosity should not start with people's responses to questions determined by the researcher, rather it should focus 'first on individuals, the experiences they consider most important and the concrete practices that make up their personal religious experience and expression' (McGuire 2008: 4). Such an approach reveals individual religiosity to be less like an 'ideal type', and more an 'ever-changing, multifaceted, often messy … amalgam of beliefs and practices' (McGuire 2008: 4). An example of this kind of investigation is the subject of this chapter's case study.

A FORENSIC EXAMINATION OF RELIGIOUS BELIEF: AFTERLIFE BELIEF IN 'POST-CHRISTIAN' NATIONS

In 1967 Peter Berger published his influential treatise on the sociology of religion, *The Sacred Canopy* (see Chapter 3). Part of this book discussed increasing secularization in the West. As a consequence of secularization, Berger suggested, rational thinking is steadily replacing superstitious beliefs. On this topic, Berger wrote: 'A sky empty of angels becomes open to intervention of the astronomer, and eventually, of the astronaut' (1967: 112–13).

While religious affiliation, belief and attendance are in decline in 'post-Christian' countries (e.g. Great Britain, Australia and Canada), some spiritual beliefs continue to have fairly widespread acceptance, at least for the present. One of these is belief in the afterlife. Data from the 2008 International Social Survey Programme (ISSP) reveal that 52 percent of British, 46 percent of Australian and 36 percent of German adults 'definitely' or 'probably' believe in life after death (my calculations). A 2001 national poll of Canadians found 57 percent believe in the afterlife. (NB. 75 percent of Americans believe in life after death.)

When people affirm a belief in the afterlife, it prompts the question, in what *kind* of afterlife do they believe? Given the traditional Christian heritage of Britain,

Canada and Australia, it is reasonable to assume that many people's understanding of life after death might be shaped, at least in some part, by Christian teaching on the subject. But the church's influence in late modern societies has waned, and we have seen the emergence of a spiritual marketplace which has popularized other spiritual ideas, such as reincarnation belief (see Chapters 7 and 9). What do people who believe in the afterlife actually believe, and what difference does it make to everyday life?

To explore this question, I conducted a mixed-methods study, *The Afterlife in a Secular Age* (see Singleton 2012, 2013) which examined afterlife belief among Australian teens and adults. Specifically, I explored: the varieties of afterlife belief among people in post-Christian societies; the cultural resources which influence these self-understandings; and the impact belief has on behavior. The qualitative component of the project comprised 52 interviews with a range of people, including clergy, civil celebrants, and the general public (who were variously workers, students, retirees, or unemployed). This sample includes atheists, agnostics, and followers or former followers of the Spiritualist, Islamic, Hindu, Buddhist, Zoroastrian, Jewish and Christian faiths.

There were three *major* strands of afterlife belief: 'survival' after death that includes reincarnation; survival after death but not reincarnation (e.g. the dead go to heaven or another plane), and those who believe that death is the end (rejecting all afterlife possibilities) (see Singleton 2012). Within the first two categories, there were many variations on the broad theme. Approximately two-thirds of my sample believed in life after death, the other third did not. Interestingly, the majority of those who believed in some kind of afterlife were not particularly religious.

The reincarnation believers, apart from those who followed Buddhism and Hinduism, affirmed a Westernized, distilled version of traditional Eastern reincarnation belief, and had formulated their own understanding of how it works. People who believed in some type of heaven, but were not particularly religious, thought the next life will reprise the best parts of this life. For these people, heaven is a place of peace, wholeness and happiness, where one is reunited with family and friends rather than a place to enjoy communion with God (if God is there at all). Only a minority of afterlife believers, people who were highly committed to a religious tradition, expressed orthodox views about the afterlife consistent with the teachings of their tradition.

People's ideas about the afterlife were typically the product of their own thinking and self-reflection, and more were influenced by popular culture than the pulpit. Few believers in reincarnation had studied the teachings of Hinduism or Buddhism. Those who believed in some kind of heaven shared more in common with nineteenth-century Spiritualists (see Chapter 2) than orthodox Christian teaching. Afterlife belief was primarily about *individuals* and what they imagine their future to be.

I investigated the difference, if any, afterlife belief made to everyday life. The answer is 'not that much'. Afterlife belief remained peripheral to everyday experience and was mainly a religious or spiritual opinion. It rarely motivated people to act or behave in ethical ways. That said, for some, personal belief had proved a comfort either at a funeral, or during the grieving process.

The sociology of religious belief is an expanding area of inquiry (see Smith 2008). Paying attention to the content and character of belief provides greater insight in the differences such beliefs make to everyday life.

(Continued)

(Continued)

Want to know more?

Two interesting and readable books that explore afterlife belief:

- McDannell, Colleen and Lang, Bernhard (2001) *Heaven: A History*, 2nd edn. New Haven, CT: Yale University Press.

- Walter, Tony (1996) *The Eclipse of Eternity: A Sociology of the Afterlife*. London: Macmillan Press.

Different approaches are helpful in making sense of individual religiosity. A typology can illuminate people's general religious orientation. It is important to acknowledge also that religion is not practiced consistently in every situation.

EXPLAINING INDIVIDUAL RELIGIOSITY

The NSYR studied a population of several million US teens and young adults. Researchers found many highly religious people, who prayed daily and attended services of worship frequently. Researchers also discovered some teens deeply opposed to organized religion, and a small a group attracted to alternative spiritual paths. While each person's story is unique, there are common reasons why some people are highly religious and others are completely irreligious. This section considers the various social and cultural factors which influence individual religiosity.

At the broadest level, cultural and demographic factors can influence greatly personal religiosity. Data presented in Chapter 7 showed that Filipinos are five times more likely than Australians to attend services of worship 'nearly weekly' or more often. Such differences can be explained through reference to the respective cultures of both countries. In the Philippines, the overwhelming majority of the population identifies as Catholic. Regular attendance at Mass is an expectation of the Catholic faithful the world over. Filipinos live in a culture which supports readily such a practice. While Catholics are the largest denomination in Australia, they only represent about a quarter of the population. Moreover, only a minority of Australian Catholics attend Mass regularly. In this sense, the majority of Catholics behave in a way consistent with the prevailing secular culture of Australia.

Beyond major cultural and geographic differences, demographic factors, such as age, socio-economic status and gender all influence religiosity. Bouma (1992: 117) notes: 'One of the most regularly reported relationships in all of the sociology of religion is that women are more religious than men.' This is not because women are 'naturally' more religious, but because of the socially ascribed 'meanings and role expectations' (Bouma 1992: 117) associated with being female, which in turn lead women to religion (for a summary, see Hood et al. 2009). Later in this chapter, more detailed consideration is given to the issue of gender and religion.

Surveys of religious behavior, attitudes and practices – which usually survey adults and older teens – typically capture a 'moment in time' snapshot of a person. This current snapshot reflects the *sum* of a person's life influences up until that point. Naturally, religious development has to begin somewhere. A person's religious orientation develops, like other aspects of personhood, in childhood and adolescence.

Influences on child, teen and young adult religiosity

Decades of research have provided valuable insights into the different influences on young people's personal religiosity. These findings are summarized briefly below.

Parental influence

It is widely agreed that the most important influence on the religiosity of a young person is family context (Smith and Denton 2005; Mason et al. 2007; Hood et al. 2009). For example, Smith and Denton (2005: 111), reporting on their analysis of NSYR data, find that teens are more likely to be religiously devoted if 'they have highly religious parents'. What is it *about* parents that influences their children's and teen's religiosity? Because individuals are socialized primarily in a family or extended family environment, what parents think and do shapes the practices and attitudes of their children. In their representative study of Australian teens and young adults, Mason et al. (2007: 156) found regular attendance of parents at religious services, along with regular family talk about religion, increased the probability of a teen or young adult being highly religious. If parents are not positive about religion, and do not participate regularly in religious activities, this tends to result in teens who are not themselves religious. Smith and Denton (2005: 91) found that teens with parents who attend religious services less often, and for whom faith is less important, are more likely to be nonreligious than teens whose parents attend more often.

Peer influence

Research confirms that peer support is also an important factor in predicting levels of religious attendance. Regnerus et al. (2004: 34) found that 'when the attendance patterns of one's friends are low, the anticipated probability that a given youth will attend church regularly diminishes'. Similar results among Australian youth are reported by Mason et al. (2007).

Other factors

Research has also discovered that factors such as gender, the kind of religious tradition to which a person belongs, family intactness, place of residence, socio-economic status and race can all influence personal religiosity in childhood and adolescence (see Hood et al. 2009; Pearce and Denton 2011). Smith and Denton (2005: 116), for example, found:

> Certain religious traditions in the United States appear more or less capable of eliciting serious, multifaceted religious devotion in their teenagers. Conservative Protestantism and Mormonism seem especially likely and Catholicism appears particularly unlikely to produce highly religiously devoted teenagers (all compared to mainline Protestantism).

Such factors interact with the effect of parental influence.

How does this relate to conversion? Most people who follow a religion were born into that religion; it is the religion of immediate family, relatives, friends and their local culture. That said, some people 'take up' a religion which is not the religion of their cultural background. This is typically called conversion. A young British woman, for example, may have been raised as a Catholic but chooses to become a Muslim. Barbour (1994: 2) observes that scholars of religion since William James take conversion to mean 'the conscious adherence to new religious convictions'. Social scientific research treating conversion as an 'observable' process abounds (e.g. Snow and Machalek 1984). Scholars have debated whether conversion is a single event – such as Saint Paul's 'road to Damascus' conversion experience – or whether it involves a change over time, a combination of certain events, social situation and life circumstances. Most agree that it is the latter.

Various explanations have been posited as to why people convert, ranging from having 'predisposing personality traits and cognitive orientations' (Snow and Machalek 1984: 178), to social factors, such as social networks, the influence of peers and a person's age (conversion is more common among young people). Social networks – knowing people who follow the prospective faith – appear particularly critical to conversion. Snow and Machalek (1984: 183) argue:

> Since a positive, interpersonal tie to one or more group members can function as an information bridge, increase the credibility of appeals, and intensify the pressure to accept those appeals and corresponding practices, it is not surprising that conversion is unlikely, especially for nonseekers, in the absence of affective [social] ties.

As the foregoing discussion suggests, a complex matrix of factors – socialization in childhood, demographic and broader cultural factors – all influence personal religiosity. Individual psychology and personality traits are also influential. Importantly, the kind of religiosity (or nonreligiosity) that develops in childhood will not necessarily stay the same across the course of a lifetime. This kind of religious change is explored in the next section.

RELIGION AND THE LIFECOURSE

For a long time, explanations of religious change over the lifecourse were dominated by theories of faith development, which in turn reflected the preeminence of theories of cognitive development in the social sciences (Hood et al. 2009: 77). Perhaps the most famous of these theories is James Fowler's (1981) stages of faith development. This theory posits that faith development begins in childhood. From childhood, faith develops in six discrete stages that correspond to different stages in the life cycle. Such a perspective treats faith as something that 'matures' with age, and develops in a linear trajectory. There is little doubt that as people get older, life experiences, relationships and education can cause people to think more deeply about their faith.

However, this model does not say much about other ways religiosity might change as a person ages. A person might be deeply religious as a teenager, and yet, in the space of a few short years, no longer be religious. Recent studies have shed new light first, on religious change between adolescence and young adulthood, and second, on change across a longer time span.

Religious trajectories among teens and young adults

Thanks to some excellent recent data, particularly from US studies, scholars have been able to better map out 'trajectories' of teen and emerging adult religiosity and explain what influences change in one direction or another. These studies include the NSYR (Smith and Snell 2009), the *National Longitudinal Study of Adolescent Health* (called Add Health) (see Regnerus and Uecker 2006) and the *National Longitudinal Survey of Youth* (Petts 2009).

The NSYR study was conducted on the same group of young people over the span of several years. Researchers found 'most youth tend as emerging adults to remain generally the kind of religious people [or nonreligious people] they were as teenagers' (Smith and Snell 2009: 224). That said, they found a tendency for some religious teens to become slightly less religious in emerging adulthood. Analyzing a different US data set, Petts (2009: 567) finds: 'Although some youth are able to maintain a relatively stable level of religious participation, most youth experience a decline – early, late, or gradually throughout adolescence – in religious involvement and attend religious services relatively infrequently by young adulthood.' What social and cultural factors might explain such patterns?

Explaining *declining* religiosity, Smith and Snell (2009: 230) suggest 'lack of strong parental … ties to religious faith combined with holding a religious faith that is not extremely important to one's life', among other factors, puts highly religious youth '"at risk" of becoming low religion emerging adults'. Uecker et al. (2007), using data from the US Add Health study, identify several sources of religious decline in the late teen years. Decreasing religious attendance is associated with an increase in behaviors such as more frequent sexual intercourse, higher levels of alcohol consumption and the onset of marijuana use (Uecker et al. 2007: 1679). In another study using the same data, Regnerus and Uecker (2006: 232) report that large decreases in religiosity are influenced by personality, behavioral, and family factors, but that 'demographic factors do not appear to have much effect at all'. Scholars are recognizing increasingly that college education has a generally deleterious effect on religious faith (see Hill 2011).

Among those *maintaining* high levels of religious commitment and practice through the teen and young adult years, Smith and Snell (2009), drawing on three waves of NSYR data, find several factors are especially important, including relational modeling (i.e. parents, caregivers) and support for religious commitment; internalization of religious significance (which includes having religious experiences), and the personal practice of faith (prayer) (Smith and Snell 2009: 217–19).

What about *substantial increases* in religious practice between the teen and young adult years? This kind of trajectory is less common (see Smith and Snell 2009). Petts (2009) identifies several trajectories of religious participation up to early adulthood, noting that while most youth experience decline, there are exceptions. One group experiencing an increase in participation are those following a 'trajectory of high or moderate religious participation' (Petts 2009: 568), that is, they already had some base of religiousness. These kinds of people might marry a religious spouse and thus experience an increase in religious participation (Petts 2009: 568).

Other factors might cause religious youth to increase their religious practice. Trinitapoli and Vaisey (2009: 125) observe 'religious experiences [broadly defined] … may manifest either as dramatic religious change or the intensification of existing beliefs and practices'. Using NSYR data they considered the impact of short-term mission trips – described as an 'institutionalized religious experience' – on the religiosity of US youth. They found that mission trips predict 'increases in attendance at religious services … and prayer' (Trinitapoli and Vaisey 2009: 132–3). I studied participants at the Catholic World Youth Day, and found that some began attending Mass more frequently once the event was over (Singleton 2011). For the most part, these were already highly committed young people, and a positive experience at the event reinforced their religious commitment.

All of the findings discussed above suggest that maintaining high levels of religious practice, in a highly supportive context, sustains faith through the teen years to young adulthood. Without such factors, religiosity would likely decrease. Nonreligious teens typically become nonreligious adults.

...and in later life

An outstanding study which tracks religious change over the course of a lifetime was conducted by the University of California's Institute for Human Development (IHD). It is the subject of a recent book by scholars Michele Dillon and Paul Wink (2007). The project studied a cohort of people born in the 1920s. The participants were interviewed first as adolescents and re-interviewed every decade until the 1990s. Dillon and Wink (2007: 82) found adolescence to be a peak period of religiosity, followed by a decline in early adulthood and then an upswing in late adulthood. Beyond the people who experienced upswings and downswings, there were people for whom the pattern established early in life was the pattern maintained across the lifecourse. Dillon and Wink (2007: 90) argue 'fine-grained analysis ... indicated that stability was the norm for many others. Some interviewees maintained a stable adulthood pattern of high religiousness, and still others maintained a stable pattern of little or no interest in religion'.

This view concurs with that of Smith and Snell (2009: 256), who suggest 'What people have been in the past is generally the best indicator of ... what they will likely be in the future.' The research suggests highly religious people, with strong social support for their faith, will remain this way across their lifetime. Nonreligious people, living in a social context that does not support faith, are not especially likely to ever become religious.

Having examined the individual dimensions of religiosity, it is valuable to consider more deeply an important aspect of religiosity: gender and religion.

GENDER AND RELIGION

A recent book by Ophelia Benson and Jeremy Stangroom (2009) is provocatively titled *Does God Hate Women?* The book examines the oppression of women in the name of religion. The first chapter provides heinous examples of religiously motivated violence perpetrated against women. In one case, the authors describe how a teenage girl in northern Nigeria was tried by a sharia law court for having pre-marital sex. She had been coerced into having sex with three men in order to settle debts accrued by her father. Found guilty, she was sentenced to 180 lashes. This is just one of many such excoriating examples. The book is unflinching in its criticism of women's treatment in the name of religion. Benson and Stangroom (2009: 10) argue:

> One human institution that has always cast its lot with the stronger side – that has strengthened the arm of the already strong, added weight to the already heavy, given the halo of sanctity to the existing power imbalance – that has for millennia helped the stronger go on dominating the weaker – is religion.

As this chapter has shown, various social and cultural factors influence a person's religious experience. Arguably, the most significant of these is gender. While women are more likely than men to be religious the world over, many religious organizations are deeply patriarchal. Women are systematically excluded from positions of leadership, decision-making, and in some religions, from participating in worship. Religious organizations and groups also regulate women's reproductive rights and dress styles, their right to work and personal relationships, among other things. This section explores the gendered dimensions of religion, why religious discrimination occurs, and how such discrimination is being addressed.

Religion as a source of gendered oppression

Many social factors condition everyday life, include race, social class, age and gender. Gender refers to the social norms, expectations and behaviors associated with either men or women (Buchbinder 1994). In most societies, men are expected to be practical, aggressive and unemotional, while women are expected to be passive, impractical, nurturing and emotional. Boys and girls are socialized from birth to conform to these gendered norms and standards. Gendered norms and standards can change, and are subject to cultural variation. When I was living in Papua New Guinea recently, I spied several men pushing prams or carrying babies strapped to their chests. A local woman told me this was a new phenomenon, and reflects (slowly) changing cultural expectations about a father's role in his children's lives.

All societies have a 'gender order' or 'gender regime', which is the overall structure and pattern of relations between men and women (see Connell 1987). The gender order in most societies is patriarchal. Patriarchy is the systematized, institutionalized domination of men over women, and a patriarchal gender order typically benefits men. An example of this is the gender division of labor in the average Western household. There is a greater social expectation upon women to cook, look after children and maintain an orderly household. Men, in contrast, are expected to act as helpers rather than managers of the household enterprise. Such an arrangement benefits men, as they have someone to look after them and, freed from domestic labor, have more time to pursue leisure activities (McMahon 1999). The ideology of patriarchy is sustained by various assumptions about men and women, including the idea that men are 'biologically' fit for leadership. Such essentialist assumptions are replayed endlessly in the mass media, however, most sociologists and psychologists agree that the purported brain and psychological differences between men and women are greatly exaggerated and grossly misunderstood (see Fausto-Sterling 1997; Fine 2010).

Religion, like all social institutions, is the product of society (see Chapter 3 and the discussion of Peter Berger's work) and consequently reflects *and* reinforces societal norms and standards. Because most societies are traditionally patriarchal, religious organizations are as well. Religious organizations have theologies and expectations about men's and women's roles, and for the most part, these benefit or privilege men. Men assume positions of leadership and authority and regulate women's behaviors and actions. The Catholic Church, for example, does not permit women to be ordained as priests, while some fringe Mormon sects allow polygamous marriages (a man may take several wives).

Gender inequality is found in many religions. Muslim scholar and activist Susan Carland (2004) has studied Muslim women's systematic exclusion from mosques in Australia. Carland (2004: 9) suggests that in Australia, 'It is now commonplace for women to be separated from the men/main mosque area by curtains, barriers and walls, and to have limited or prohibited access to mosque facilities and committees.' She argues this should not be the case: 'At the time of the Prophet Muhammad there were no barriers or partitions in the mosque separating men from women; women prayed in the main space, as did the men, having full visual and auditory access' (Carland 2004: 13; see also Roded 2012). Carland's interviews with ten Muslim women revealed many negative experiences of attending the mosque. Among the factors that made mosque attendance difficult was the lack of child-friendly facilities, and second-class entrances for women.

Men's justification for such treatment usually comes from a patriarchal interpretation of religious teaching or because male leadership and the subjugation of women is a long-standing tradition within that religion, or the local culture where the given religion is practiced. And because most religious texts are the product of patriarchal societies, they are often full of patriarchal assumptions or claims. It should be noted that other transgressions of the established gender order of a religion, such as homosexuality, lead to religious discrimination or exclusion.

Just as social norms and expectations change, the same is true of religious standards and roles. Some notable progress towards gender equality has been made in recent decades, with some religious organizations allowing women to hold religious roles which were once the domain of men. The ordination of women has occurred in many religious traditions, including Protestant Christianity, Buddhism and Judaism. Moreover, feminist theologians in Christianity, Judaism, Islam and Buddhism have produced progressive theologies which reimagine women's place in these religions. Notable examples include biblical scholar Elisabeth Schüssler Fiorenza, who wrote the profoundly influential work, *In Memory of Her: A Feminist Theological Reconstruction of Christian Origins* (1983). In the Islamic world, Amina Wadud (1999) has produced a pro-feminist reading of the Qur'an, *Qur'an and Woman: Rereading the Sacred Text From a Woman's Perspective* (see also Wadud 2004). In such interpretations, these theologians find a theologically justified, equal place for women in religion. For example, Amani Hamdan (2012: 211) writes: '[the] Qur'an and the authentic *Hadith* ... emphasize the importance of every Muslim participating in education and in all aspects of public life'. Such views are gaining greater acceptance in their respective religious communities.

The production of feminist theologies is accompanied also by social activism. In 2005 Amina Wadud famously led Friday prayers at a New York mosque. Roded (2012: 5–6) notes:

Moreover, Muslim women scholars in various parts of the world ... have been negotiating their place in communal prayers using their knowledge of the foundation texts of Islam and Islamic law. These concrete efforts by Muslim women to enhance their position in the communal prayer, as well as their scholarly endeavors to reclaim Islamic learning, have been linked to a movement known as Islamic feminism.

Although drawing strong opposition from many men, such endeavor has also won significant male support.

Religion as a source of liberation

While religious organizations are largely patriarchal, it is not a simple story of oppression, and women both sustain, and benefit greatly, from religion. Journalist Cristina Odone (2009), writing in *The Observer*, argues:

> For millennia, women have found in God their greatest ally and muse – witness the writings of mystics such as Julian of Norwich and the charitable work of peasant Muslim women. For centuries, the most powerful and liberated women were the abbesses, nuns and consecrated virgins who devoted themselves to God.

There are many such examples of religion benefiting women.

The Spiritualist movement of the nineteenth century forged a close alliance with the women's suffrage movement. According to scholar Anne Braude (2001: 3) 'The two movements intertwined continually ... Not all feminists were Spiritualists, but all Spiritualists advocated woman's rights, and women were ... equal to men within Spiritualist practice, polity and ideology.' Spiritualist mediums were mostly women, and as arbiters of the messages coming from the 'other side', they also became the source of religious authority for this large-scale and important spiritual movement.

In the contemporary era, religion sometimes plays an important part in improving women's lives. Women in Papua New Guinea (PNG), for example, struggle for equality and are underrepresented in public life. In their homes, many are subject to domestic violence. Scholar Anne Dickson-Waiko (2003: 99), examining the nascent feminist movement in PNG, finds an important 'catalyst for women's activism right across the Pacific region has been provided by church women's organizations'. Other religions also privilege women's role and status. An excellent example of this are the modern Pagan religions (e.g. Wicca, Druidism) which actively champion equality between men and women, and people with different sexual identities.

Religion, as can be seen, is a source of emancipation and social progress in the cause of gender equality. Religion's capacity to effect other social outcomes is discussed in the next section.

CONSEQUENCES OF RELIGIOSITY

In Chapter 1, I considered briefly some of the effects religious faith can have on everyday life. This is one of the most extensively researched topics in the sociology and psychology of religion. Studies have shown religiosity influences views of morality, produces moral behavior, assists individuals in coping with difficult life circumstances, and promotes wellbeing and social connectedness (see Hood et al.

2009). Rather than reprise these findings, this chapter concludes with a discussion of the relationship between citizenship and religiosity.

Recent studies of teens and young adults in Australia and the United States have considered the association between religiosity and life outcomes in great detail (Smith and Denton 2005; Mason et al. 2007; Smith and Snell 2009). One key area of focus has been whether religious youth are more likely than nonreligious youth to be 'civically minded', that is, people who are involved in volunteering and community service, and who perform acts of generosity and altruism. The Australian *Spirit of Generation Y* study, using robust statistical methods, found religiously active youth are more likely than nonreligious youth to have positive civic attitudes, display high levels of social concern and be actively involved in community service (see Mason et al. 2007). Active Christians, for example, do many more hours of volunteer work per month than secular youth. Similar patterns were found in the NSYR (see Smith and Denton 2005).

These findings make sense if we consider that regular attendees at religious services are reminded regularly to lead altruistic and ethical lives and given ample opportunities to partake in community service. Many religious organizations have dedicated social justice programs and young people are encouraged to participate in these (see Webber et al. 2010). What about the nonreligious? Most secular-minded youth are arguably more 'self-oriented' because there is no obvious, society-wide nonreligious ethical paradigm on which to model their lives, nor the clearly defined support structures and opportunities for community work of the kind found in religious organizations.

Not all the consequences of personal religiosity are positive. Hood et al. (2009: 411), summarizing a large body of research, find 'as a broad generalization, the more religious an individual is, the more prejudiced that person is', particularly around tolerance of other religions, abortion, homosexuality, drug legalization, euthanasia and same-sex marriage. Critics of religion, particularly atheists such as Christopher Hitchens and Richard Dawkins, have drawn attention recently to the profound destructiveness of religiously inspired violence, religious extremism and sectarianism. For these kinds of reasons, more people seem to be concluding that we are better off without religion. These kinds of arguments are explored in the next chapter, which focuses on the New Atheism.

Points to ponder

Why are women more likely than men to be religious? Why are men more likely than women to be nonreligious? What do you believe happens after death? How did you come to hold this belief? What difference does this belief make to your everyday life?

Next steps ...

Lisa Pearce and Melinda Lundquist Denton's book, *A Faith of Their Own: Stability and Change in the Religiosity of America's Adolescents* (2011) offers a lucid explanation of factors influencing individual religiosity, along with an account of how religion changes in later adolescence. Vern Bengtson and colleagues' book, *Families and Faith: How Religion is Passed Down Across Generations* (2013) usefully examines the role of families in faith transmission. The comprehensive *The Psychology of Religion: An Empirical Approach*, 4th edn by Ralph Hood, Peter Hill and Bernard Spilka (2009) covers in detail many of the topics discussed in this chapter. Abby Day's *Believing in Belonging* (2011) is an innovative look at the complex ways in which people hold religious beliefs.

12

the end of religion? the new atheism and secularism

After reading this chapter you will:

- be able to define atheism, secularism and humanism;

- be introduced to new sociological ways of understanding the nonreligious; and

- understand the reasons behind the rise of the 'New Atheist' movement.

In the past decade or so, atheists in the West appear to have mobilized themselves against the forces of religion. Examples of atheist activity include the funding of bus advertising campaigns in Britain and elsewhere promoting reason over religious belief; the establishment of atheist 'churches', called the Sunday Assemblies, in London and other major cities; the staging of international atheist conventions attracting thousands of attendees; and the publication of several best-selling books which take aim at the beliefs of religious people and the apparent 'fence-sitting' of agnostics.

Each of these activities is part of what might be described as the 'New Atheist' social movement. This movement has focused public attention on unbelievers and brought new passion to debates about the role of religion in personal life, politics and education. This chapter examines why atheism is enjoying an apparent surge in popularity, and how this relates to earlier ideas about secularism and religion's place in society. The aim of this discussion is not to reprise earlier arguments about secularization, but to focus on the lives, beliefs and activities of atheists and other nonreligious people. The chapter begins by defining atheism and other related terms. Next, it examines recent social-scientific efforts to understand the nonreligious. From there, consideration is given to the rise of the New Atheism as a social movement. The chapter concludes with a case study of the battle between science and religion in the United States.

WHAT IS ATHEISM? WHO ARE ATHEISTS?

Every person believes something about the supernatural world, even if this is the belief that there is no supernatural world. Atheism is first and foremost a certain kind of (Western) rejection of belief in the supernatural. More specifically, it is a rejection of a belief in God or the gods. According to philosopher Julian Baggini (2003: 3) 'Atheism is in fact extremely simple to define: it is the belief that there is no God or gods.' This is distinct from a **theist**, who believes in the existence of God or gods. An **agnostic** is a person who believes that it is impossible to know if there is a God or gods. Today, agnostics are regarded mainly as people who cannot decide one way or another, so-called 'fence sitters'. In the nineteenth century, however, it commonly meant 'the considered conviction that nothing of ultimate things can be known with certainty' (Vernon 2007: 9).

Such terms are largely centered around Western, dualistic understandings of the spirit world (i.e. there is a 'natural' realm and a 'supernatural' realm), and treat individuals as engaging in rational decision-making about the possibility of the supernatural. Individuals claim either that, 'Yes, I believe there is a God' or, 'No, I don't believe there is a God'. Some societies have a worldview in which there is no clear distinction between the natural and supernatural worlds. In the traditional Melanesian worldview (peoples from Papua New Guinea, Fiji, the Solomon Islands), for example, all things are interconnected – humans, the elements, animals, flora *and* the spirit world (souls of the dead, spirits of nature etc.) (see Zocca 2007; Gibbs 2007). For those inculcated in this worldview, there is no easy division of the world into the supernatural and natural realms. Rather the whole world, and life itself, is suffused with supernatural possibilities. The idea that one can choose to believe or not believe in the gods or God is not universal.

Atheism is a personal conviction. Broader efforts to achieve the removal of religion from public life are an expression of **secularism**, the belief religion should play no part 'in a nation's political realm and public life' (Kosmin 2007: 1). There have been concerted efforts to secularize public life in Britain, America, Australia and Europe since the nineteenth century, mainly in the spheres of education and government. As the case study in this chapter illustrates, such efforts continue in the present day.

Atheists are often characterized as negative people, who do not stand for anything apart from being opposed to religion. However, as Baggini (2003: 3) argues, 'there is nothing to stop atheists believing in a morality, a meaning for life, or human goodness'. Indeed, many atheists and agnostics are committed to the intellectual and philosophical tradition and values of secular **humanism**. Humanism has antecedents going back to ancient Greece, and has become a key component of the Western worldview. Humanism exists in both secular and religious forms. According to philosopher Konstantin Kolenda (1995: 340), humanism, at its core, affirms the primacy of human beings and the skills and knowledge of humanity. Humanism is optimistic, and places great faith in values such as 'endurance, nobility, intelligence, moderation, flexibility, sympathy and love' (Kolenda 1995: 341). From a secular humanistic perspective, one can live a good and ethical life without religion, because humanism provides the ethics and explanations necessary to make life meaningful.

How widespread is atheism?

Table 12.1 shows the proportion of the adult population in the Philippines, America, Ireland, Australia, Great Britain and Germany which matches the definition of atheism; non-believers in God. The data come from the 2008 International Social Survey Program (ISSP) religion module.

This table shows the proportion of the adult population which do not believe in God is very low in the Philippines (3 percent), while in the United States it is 10 percent and in Ireland, 11 percent. As might be expected, the proportion of non-believers is much higher in the 'post-Christian' countries: Great Britain (35 percent), Australia (37 percent) and Germany (38 percent). In these nations, less than half the population believes in God, while a significant proportion 'can't choose'.

Would all of these non-believers describe themselves as atheists? According to our stated definition they are atheists, but almost certainly not all of these non-believers would accept the label of 'atheist'. The evidence for this assertion? There exists a discrepancy between the number of self-identified atheists and the figures shown in Table 12.1. For example, while Table 12.1 shows that 37 percent of Australians do not believe in God, in the 2011 Australian census just 58,899 people – 0.27 percent of the population – described themselves as atheists. Using data from the 2008 American

Table 12.1   Adult population of selected countries: belief in God (percentage of population)

Believes in God	Country					
	Philippines %	USA %	Ireland %	Great Britain %	Australia %	Germany %
Yes	96	87	77	42	43	49
Can't choose	<1	2	12	22	18	12
No	3	10	11	35	37	38
Missing/no answer	<1	<1	<1	2	3	2
Total	100	100	100	100	100	100

Note: Figures have been rounded and columns may not add to 100 percent.

Data source: 2008 International Socal Survey Program (ISSP 2008) survey for various countries. Figures quoted are from analysis done by the author. Those who carried out the original collection of the data bear no responsibility for this analysis.

Religious Identification Survey (ARIS), Kosmin and Keysar (2009a: 5) found just 0.7 percent of Americans identified themselves as atheists, obviously a much lower number than the 10 percent reported in the table above as not believing in God. In the 2011 Census of England and Wales only 29,267 people wrote they were atheists. Quite simply, a very small proportion of the population in America, Australia and Britain use this label when given the opportunity to describe themselves as atheists.

There are many possible reasons for the discrepancy between stated non-belief in God and self-identification as an atheist. One reason, particularly in the United States, is a fear of social stigma. Research suggests atheists largely are held in disdain in the United States. Edgell et al. (2006: 212), reporting on a nationally representative survey of US adults, found: 'From a list of groups that also includes Muslims, recent immigrants, and homosexuals, Americans name atheists as those least likely to share their vision of American society. They are also more likely to disapprove of their children marrying atheists.' It is not surprising so many avoid the label.

Other non-believers might reject the label of atheist as too strident or harsh, or choose another 'nonreligious' way to describe themselves (in the Australian and UK censuses people call themselves rationalists, humanists, secularists, or simply as having 'no religion'). Others may not see the label as applicable because, while not believing in God, they hold other supernatural beliefs. For example, further analysis of the ISSP data reveals *of the 37 percent of Australians who said they do not believe in God*, about 22 percent believe in reincarnation, 27 percent believe in some kind of afterlife and 25 percent believe in a 'higher power'.

The atheist label is unhelpful in a sociological sense because it obscures the many and varied ways in which people are nonreligious or secular in their life orientation, something which becomes apparent when we consider recent social scientific efforts to study those for whom religion and spirituality are not important.

THE SOCIAL SCIENTIFIC STUDY OF ATHEISTS, RELIGIOUS 'NONES' AND SECULARS: WHAT THE STUDIES SHOW ABOUT NONRELIGIOUS PEOPLE

This section explores recent social scientific investigation of atheists and other nonreligious people. Until very recently this has been an under-researched, even neglected, area in the social scientific study of religion. A recent wave of books, reports, journal articles and conference papers is addressing this shortcoming, and offering new insights into the different ways people are nonreligious.

Self-described atheists

In the past decade some social scientists have become particularly interested in the study of *self-described* atheists, humanists and rationalists, moving beyond labels to understand what an atheistic life means. These studies have examined the everyday lives, values and beliefs of atheists, including the pathways to atheism and how atheists raise children (for example, see Hunsberger and Altemeyer 2006; Ecklund and Lee 2011). One notable American study is Bruce Hunsberger and Bob Altemeyer's book *Atheists: A Groundbreaking Study of America's Nonbelievers* (2006). The authors surveyed 253 people who were members of atheist clubs in the San Francisco area. Among a range of findings, they discovered the overwhelming majority were not raised in religious families, had once believed in God, but then had doubts, mainly in their adolescent years. Reflecting the broader American context, few in their sample were particularly zealous in proselytizing the atheist point of view, and 'most of [the] active atheists had paid some sort of price for their disbelief in God, and the more active they were, the more they had been avoided, excluded, or harassed' (Hunsberger and Altemeyer 2006: 167). It is difficult to imagine atheists in Britain or Australian being subject to opprobrium because of their non-belief.

Just as there is variation in ways in which people are religious (discussed fully in Chapter 11), recent research shows there are differences in the ways in which atheists practice their beliefs (in addition to the studies cited above, I am drawing here on my own research projects in which I have interviewed self-described atheists; see Mason et al. 2007; Singleton 2012). For some, being atheist is an important part of their identity and the way they think about themselves. Some participate in anti-religious activities, are members of humanist or atheist societies and campaign against attempts to bring religion into their lives, or public life. This kind of atheism entails a broad and deep opposition to religion. For such people, the path to such strident atheism is usually the result of considerable thought and direct action (leaving a church, for example). Other atheists are less strident. While religion is not a part of their lives, they are not actively opposed to it.

Religious 'nones'

While some social scientists have studied self-described atheists, others have paid attention to so-called religious 'nones'; an American phrase for people, who in surveys and censuses, claim to not identify or affiliate with a religious group. Chapters 6 and 7 revealed this to be a growing constituency in Australia, Canada, Britain and America. Recent American books and reports have produced insights into America's religious nones (Smith and Denton 2005; Jones et al. 2012; Pew Forum 2012d; Kosmin et al. 2009):

- Males are more likely than females to be religious nones;

- The majority of American nones were raised in a religious tradition;

- American nones cluster around the West Coast and New England;

- Younger age groups (i.e. emerging adults) are more likely than older ages groups to be religious nones;

- Some religious nones hold spiritual and other religious beliefs.

Less in-depth research has been conducted on religious nones elsewhere. However, my analysis of Australian census data (2011 census) reveals males are more likely than females to have no religious identification, while those aged under 40 are more likely than those over 40 to have no religion. Analysis of the 2001 Census of England and Wales reveals males are more likely than females to have no religion, while 'among 16 to 34 year olds in Great Britain, almost a quarter (23 per cent) said that they had no religion compared with less than 5 per cent of people aged 65 or over' (Office for National Statistics 2004: 3). Clearly gender and age are associated with having no religion.

The designation religious 'none' is one-dimensional. If we ask, 'What is your religion?', we might find out about a person's religious identification, but we have no idea how important religion is for this person, their opinion about religion, and what role it plays in the person's life. The US research cited above shows some religious nones hold supernatural beliefs, including a belief in God, or a belief in a higher power. Some attend services of worship, while others believe in reincarnation. If this is the case, are such people actually nonreligious or are they something in between being religious or not?

Seculars

Social scientists in recent times have been exploring the *varieties* of ways in which people are secular or nonreligious. One approach has been to develop more complex, multidimensional measures of secularity, which recognize that being nonreligious or secular ought to involve some combination of 'not believing, not practicing and not identifying with a religion' (Voas and Day 2007: 96). This would probably be recorded on a continuum from strident atheism (and all that entails) to religious indifference.

A national study of Australian youth spirituality, the *Spirit of Generation Y*, of which I was a co-investigator, offers a more comprehensive classification scheme of secularity (see Mason et al. 2007). Using nationally representative survey data, several major spiritual/non-spiritual types among Australians aged 13–24 were discovered. One of these was the 'secular' type. These people are those for whom religion and spirituality has little meaning in their daily lives. There were three major ways in which Australian youth were 'secular', and the proportion of the population who fitted into these categories was calculated:

- *Nonreligious*. People who have *never* believed in God, do not engage in religious practices, do not hold an eclectic mix of spiritual beliefs (e.g. belief in reincarnation) and do not affiliate with a religion (10 percent of Australians aged 13–24);

- *Ex-religious*. People who *used* to believe in God but now do not believe, do not identify with a religion or hold an eclectic mix of spiritual beliefs (4 percent of Australians aged 13–24); and

- *Undecided.* People who are unsure if they believe in God, do not now identify with a religious tradition, nor hold an eclectic mix of spiritual beliefs. People in this group have always been equivocal about the existence of God, with the majority having *never* had a definite belief in God, while some once believed and are now unsure (14 percent of Australians aged 13–24).

Such detailed classifications reveal the myriad ways in which people are secular in their outlooks on life. The social scientific study of nonreligious people is a developing enterprise, and represents an exciting and growing branch of inquiry, and one which will continue to reveal new insights into being nonreligious.

Living the nonreligious life

In the previous chapter, discussion focused on 'lived' or everyday religion, and how faith informs people's understanding of life matters. Just as religious people use religious 'symbolic universes' to make sense of their lives, secular people use nonreligious 'symbolic universes' – humanist values, secular philosophies, rationalism – to engage in sense-making about life matters.

One such example is 29-year-old 'Richard', a self-identified atheist who was interviewed as part of the afterlife study discussed in the previous chapter. In this study, I examined how different beliefs about the afterlife, including not believing, condition attitudes towards death and dying. His own view of life after death was straightforward:

> I personally believe that nothing happens [once you die], once it is over, it is over and yeah … I am an atheist and believe, I personally prefer an existence without God, I think it is a bit nicer that there is an end to things and you don't carry on and there's no person in the background pulling strings and playing things out.

He felt religion, rather than comforting people in the face of death, actually created fear and apprehension: 'Because people are more afraid of there being some big consequence or something at the end and I think religion drives more fear around death than anything else and drives confusion.'

How did Richard deal with the fact he would die, if he received no comfort from the idea of an afterlife? Richard chose to place his faith in secular humanism. This meant he was particularly attuned to making the most out of this life, but it also gave him an ethical framework for living:

> I believe in nature and have a respect and a love of nature and that living things should continue regardless of my impact so I would like to live a better life now for the people who are going to come after me and not destroy or ruin everything for the next people who come.

As with many other secular people, Richard's answers to life's existential questions rejected the possibility that there is more to life than that which can be seen, tested or verified, and he organizes his life accordingly.

ATHEISTS ON THE MARCH? THE RISE OF THE NEW ATHEISM

As is the case with those who do not affiliate with a religion, the proportion of the population who are self-identifying atheists, while very small, is on the rise in many countries. Data from the US ARIS surveys show the number of self-identified atheists in the United States increased by 77 percent between 2001 and 2008. Similarly, census data show the number of Australians identifying as atheists increased by 88 percent between 2006 and 2011. In England and Wales, census data show the number of atheists increased by 182 percent between 2001 and 2011.

Thus, it is an opportune time for those who are opposed to religion to speak their minds. As the comments at the start of this chapter suggest, atheists have found renewed voice in the public sphere. Well-known Australian atheist and comedian Catherine Deveny is one such example. She recently wrote a pro-atheist opinion piece in a daily newspaper, *The Age*. Among other things, Deveny noted:

> The number of churchgoers in Australia is about 9% and dwindling, the diversity of spiritual belief is flourishing and atheism is going off like a frog in a sock. In his inauguration speech, President Barack Obama, a man raised by atheists, mentioned non-believers. We exist. Like it or not. (Deveny 2009)

In the West, there is little doubt atheist perspectives have figured prominently in recent public debates about religious education in schools, abortion and euthanasia.

This current wave of public prominence has been described as 'the New Atheism' (see Amarasingam 2010; Geertz and Markússon 2010). The **New Atheism** is a social movement representing an apparently new (or, as will be argued below, a resurgent) wave of anti-religious sentiment and activity. It is not a description of increased unbelief in the West. Literature promulgating the ideas associated with the New Atheism include books such as Richard Dawkins' *The God Delusion* (2006), Sam Harris' *The End of Faith: Religion, Terror, and the Future of Reason* (2004) and *Letter to a Christian Nation* (2007), Christopher Hitchens' *God Is Not Great: How Religion Poisons Everything* (2007) and Daniel Dennett's *Breaking the Spell: Religion as a Natural Phenomenon* (2006). Additionally, according to Geertz and Markússon (2010: 153), 'There are a growing number of blogs, Internet journals and special issues of magazines on the subject of religion, science and atheism.'

Various humanist and atheist groups also have contributed to the rise of New Atheist discourse. They have organized atheist gatherings, such as the 2010 and 2012 Global Atheist Conventions, paid for advertisements on buses which promote the atheist worldview and, in Britain and Australia, staged campaigns to encourage people to select the 'no religion' option in the 2011 census.

While there are several important dimensions to the New Atheist movement, its central aim appears to be the popular revival of scientific and rationalist critiques of religion. This is particularly the case with the books by Dawkins and others (see below). A second aim is to promote efforts to maintain the separation of church and state and prevent the encroachment of religious values into public life.

Caution needs to be exercised in claiming this expression of atheism as 'new'. Non-belief is as old as religion itself. Different forms of unbelief have persisted for millennia (see Thrower 1971; Baggini 2003). Thrower (1971: 28) notes there was widespread empirical and naturalistic ways of explaining events among ancient Greek philosophers, around the fifth century BCE. Beginning with the Enlightenment, and intensifying in the early modern era, the rise of science, rationalism and secular philosophies made the possibility of a 'coherent system' of unbelief – modern atheism – more viable and popular (see Berman 1988).

Throughout the nineteenth and early twentieth century, an increasing number of atheistic works was published, and more strident challenges to religion were offered in the public sphere, many of which emphasized the triumph of reason and science over unbelief and supestition. A famous work is philosopher Bertrand Russell's *Why I Am Not a Christian* (1957). In this book he makes a case for mid-twentieth-century atheism, addressing logical shortcomings in the argument for the existence of God and criticizing aspects of organized religion. He makes his case in strident language: 'I say quite deliberately that the Christian religion, as organized in its Churches, has been and still is the principal enemy of moral progress in the world' (Russell 1957: 15). When reading this book (the original 1957 edition), borrowed from my university library, I was intrigued to see notes scrawled in the margins by those attacking and supporting Russell's arguments. These topics have been raising passionate debate for decades.

Moreover, atheistic and humanist societies are not new, nor is their activism against religion and their work towards the advancement of 'free thinking' and secular forms of society. The British Humanist Association was founded in 1896. Biddington (2004) notes rationalist societies first emerged in Australia in the 1860s. Modern freethinkers like Dawkins are indebted to and share much in common with these earlier atheistic expressions. New Atheism is a continuation of an ongoing anti-religious tradition.

While rationalist, anti-religious forces became increasingly widespread in the nineteenth and early twentieth centuries, there is little doubt that in contemporary society atheistic points of view are being expressed as strongly and publicly as at any other time in recent history. According to Amarasingam (2010: 574):

Although much of the content of the new atheism may have past precedents, what is original is the new-found urgency in the message of atheism, as well as a kind of atheist social revival that their writings, lectures, and conferences have produced. In other words, the 'new' atheism is not entirely about new ideas, but takes the form of a kind of evangelical revival and repackaging of old ideas.

Why has there been an atheist revival? The apparent popularity of strident atheism says a lot about the dynamics of religion worldwide. As noted in earlier chapters, recent decades have witnessed the emergence of new, more fundamentalist forms of religious expression across the globe. Many of the associated groups maintain a high public profile, actively making plays for greater influence in public life.

This has produced strident responses among atheists, a group whose own numbers are growing. According to Geertz and Markússon (2010: 153), atheistic and human-ist responses have

> Arisen in response to extremist, especially conservative Christian organizations that are constantly and systematically attempting to undermine democracy, enlightenment, education, science and public opinion in the United States [and elsewhere] in the name of religious dogma. The creationist debate and attempts to legislate creationist ideology into State school curricula is just one example of the anti-Enlightenment movement.

Hyman (2010: xiv) also suggests the rise of the new atheism is fueled by religiously motivated acts of terror which 'serves to feed the rhetoric of those atheistic apolo-gists who see an indelible link between religion and violent intolerance'. In short, increased activity on the religious front has produced strong resistance from those opposed to organized religion. This criticism of religion is epitomized in the work of Dawkins and other popular atheist authors, whose work is considered briefly below.

'The Four Horsemen of the Anti-Apocalypse'

This phrase, 'The Four Horsemen of the Anti-Apocalypse', appeared in promo-tional literature for an atheism conference, which was to feature the best-selling authors Dawkins, Dennett, Hitchens and Harris (Hitchens died before the confer-ence). The description of the authors is a play on the biblical reference to the Four Horsemen of the Apocalypse, found in the Book of Revelation. The authors have been the leading voices of the New Atheism. In 2006–7 their books combined sold more than a million copies in the United States alone (Geertz and Markússon 2010: 153).

The most well-known proponent of the new atheism is Richard Dawkins, author of the popular *The God Delusion* (2006). Dawkins is a British evolutionary scien-tist and public intellectual. He also has made TV shows. He is particularly active in his advocacy of rationalism, and has founded the Richard Dawkins Foundation for Reason and Science.

The God Delusion is a wide-ranging book that refutes arguments for the existence of God, rails against agnosticism, debunks creationism and intelligent design (see below) and criticizes religion for the hate and harm it brings. The heart of the book is a critique of the so-called 'God Hypothesis', the argument there is a supernatural intelligence responsible for creating the universe (2006: 31). Dawkins proposes instead 'any creative intelligence … comes into existence only as the end product of an extended process of gradual evolution' (2006: 31) and this occurs without supernatural intervention. Dawkins writes directly and unsparingly against religion and religious sensibilities. For example, discussing the burka worn by many Muslim women, he says: 'The burka is … an instrument of oppression of women and claustral repression of their liberty and their beauty' (Dawkins 2006: 362).

American author and public intellectual Sam Harris is another well-known atheist author. His two major books, noted above, also have been bestsellers. The shorter, more concise of the two books is *Letter to a Christian Nation*, and takes the form of a response to those religious people who criticized his earlier book. In *Letter*, he directly addresses religious people, writing in the second person. He begins: 'You believe that the Bible is the word of God, that Jesus is the son of God … you believe these propositions' (Harris 2007: 1). Harris's main concern is with religious people who believe that the Bible is the literal word of God. He points out many of the contradictions he sees with this view: the belief in Jesus as a peacemaker is at odds with Old Testament directives to kill sinners of one kind or another. (Very few modern Christians take those Old Testament directives seriously.) He also rails against liberal or moderate Christians: 'liberal theology must stand revealed for what it is: the sheerest of moral pretenses' (2007: 31).

Overall, Harris sees religion as a source of bigotry, ignorance and hypocrisy and devotes much of his work to exploring examples of these characteristics. Harris also is particularly critical of Islam. He argues: 'Forced marriages, honor killings, punitive gang rapes, and a homicidal loathing of homosexuals are now features of an otherwise secular Europe, courtesy of Islam' (2007: 46). This is strident, provocative material and typifies the approach of New Atheism authors.

There have been many religious responses to Dawkins et al., and these public argument have been dubbed the 'atheism wars', pitting New Atheists against moderate Christian apologists, such as former British PM Tony Blair (see Griffiths 2011; Markham 2010). The most well-known book response to Dawkins is from British theologian Alister McGrath and scholar Joanna Collicutt McGrath in their book *The Dawkins Delusion* (2007). They argue Dawkins' book: 'is often little more than an aggregation of convenient factoids, suitably overstated to achieve maximum impact, and loosely arranged to suggest that they constitute an argument' (McGrath and McGrath 2007: xi). And so the debates roll on.

In all likelihood, there will be no clear winner from these 'atheism' wars. The current global pattern of rising fundamentalism – religious and atheistic – appears likely to continue for some time. Various forms of nonreligion, atheism, agnosticism, secularity, will continue to grow worldwide, and the spokespeople for strident atheism likely will continue to produce works decrying religion. But theirs is a significant challenge. Strong forms of religion will also prosper.

In the public sphere, those committed to secularism will continue to work to ensure religious influence is removed from education, politics, government and health care. Religious groups also will agitate for greater religious freedom – the right to live according to the tenets of their faith. Many religious groups seek more than religious freedom; they also are committed to enacting a religious agenda in public life, such as the teaching of religious doctrine in public schools. On this theme, this chapter concludes with a case study examining the teaching of evolution and creationism in American schools. One can see in this example how the battle between religion and science has been fought in the public arena.

CASE STUDY

SCIENCE VS. RELIGION IN AMERICAN EDUCATION: FROM THE SCOPES MONKEY TRIAL TO THE FLYING SPAGHETTI MONSTER

How was the world – mountains, rivers, oceans, flora and fauna – created? Where did humans come from? These questions seemingly have been asked since time immemorial. Ancient and pre-modern cultures answered these questions through creation myths: stories which explain how the world was made, account for the appearance of humans and describe the cosmological order of things. More often than not such accounts credited creation to the supernatural – the spirits, gods or God.

Today, probably the most well-known creation myth is the Genesis creation story, versions of which are central to the Abrahamic religions and told in the Torah, Bible and Qur'an (it is not called the Genesis myth in the Qur'an but the story shares many of the same elements). In this narrative, God created the universe from nothing, created plants and humans (Adam and Eve) individually and uniquely, and did so in six consecutive days (or six periods of time). This myth first emerged in ancient times and for centuries served as an explanation to people of these faiths as to how the world was made.

In recent centuries, modern science has produced naturalistic explanations for the origins and development of the universe (e.g. the Big Bang theory) and the appearance of humans (evolution). Such explanations came about through deduction, reasoning, and the evaluation of scientific evidence and dispensed with any notion of divine involvement in creation; they are entirely naturalistic and do not posit any supernatural authorship, design or action. These explanations have broad acceptance beyond the scientific community. Many religious people accept scientific explanations about creation – for them, the weight of evidence is irrefutable. Such people do not feel bound to accept a religious myth *in place* of a scientific explanation, but see them as complementary. The religious myth is a metaphor or symbol for a greater truth, namely, God is the author of creation, even if this process took billions of years. For many religious people, the so-called debate between science and religion is not actually a debate at all: science and religion are complementary.

Other religious people, none more so than millions of American Christians, have a more literalist approach to matters of creation – they believe the Bible is the divinely authored, infallible word of God and therefore the scriptural account is historically (and scientifically) accurate. They believe the world was literally created *ex nihilo* (from nothing) in six days. This doctrine is called **Creationism** and those who follow it are **creationists**. It has had – and continues to have – a loyal and surprisingly large following in the United States but less so in Australia, Canada or Great Britain. The Pew Forum (2005) reports 42 percent of US adults believe living things have existed in their present form since the beginning of time (i.e. there is no evolution), only 26 percent think life evolved through natural selection (no divine being involved), while 64 percent think creationism should be taught alongside evolution in US public schools.

Beginning in the 1960s, creationists refined their approach, and increasingly used the language and 'methodology' of the natural sciences to substantiate creationist claims. One version is **creation science**, which dates the six-day period of creation as happening about 6,000–10,000 years ago, believing in a 'young earth'. Creation scientists reject conventional geological dating of rocks and fossils, along with evidence of evolution, and propose alternative dating and interpretations. They argue fossils were all produced during a catastrophic flood that once engulfed the world (the story of Noah contained in the book of Genesis). Talks are presented by creationists who have recognized science degrees, and present explanations of the 'young earth' hypothesis. This leads to vigorous criticisms of the quality and veracity of the 'science' upon which the creationists rely. Critics dub creationism a 'pseudo-science'. Australian geologist Ian Plimer is a long-standing opponent of creationism and his book *Telling Lies for God: Reason vs. Creationism* (1994) is an incandescent riposte to various creationist claims.

Creationist/God-authored accounts of the earth's creation typically are favored by Christian **fundamentalists**. Such views are not kept to themselves. For more than a century Christian conservatives and fundamentalist in the United States have sought to influence aspects of public life, especially education and politics. Although the US constitution enshrines a separation of church and state – meaning, for example, religious education is prohibited in public schools – fundamentalists have not been deterred from efforts to have religious doctrine taught in schools. These have met with strident resistance from those who seek to uphold the constitutional separation between church and state. There are several examples in recent American history where attempts either to allow or limit the teaching of religious doctrine in schools have played out in a very public manner. These battles – in reality, battles between Christian fundamentalists and moderate forces over Christianity's place in public life – typically take the form of a 'contest' between science and religion, reason and faith.

The famous 1925 Scopes Monkey Trial was the first notable battle in the war between evolutionists and creationists (see Larson 1997). It caused a national sensation at the time. A science teacher, John Scopes, was prosecuted in Dayton, Tennessee, for teaching evolution, a practice banned by the state. Scopes was defended by a well-known activist lawyer, Clarence Darrow. The prosecution hired William Jennings Bryan, a former presidential candidate. The trial was something of a media circus, and both attorneys gave rousing speeches. Scopes was found guilty and fined a small amount, a decision later overturned by the Tennessee

(Continued)

(Continued)

Supreme Court because due process had not been followed. While the case provided something of a lightning rod for pro and anti-secular forces, the motives of some associated with it were more pragmatic. The idea of prosecuting originally came because some local businessmen in Dayton were seeking publicity for their small southern town. John Scopes was a willing participant. Since that time, however, a tussle over the teaching of creation and evolution in schools has continued.

A 1987 US Supreme Court case, Edwards vs. Aguillard, dealt again with the teaching of creationism in schools. In the 1980s the US state of Louisiana had passed a law requiring creation science be taught alongside evolution. Creationists lobbied for such legislation on the basis of 'fairness'. The fact that this law was passed shows the political influence wielded by Christians in America. It was overturned by a US District Court, and an appeal was heard in the US Supreme Court. The appellant, Edwards (Governor of Louisiana) lost, with the Supreme Court ruling the law was a state attempt to advance religion, which is unconstitutional in America.

Since that court ruling, efforts to introduce religious dogma into schools have not abated. Related to creationism is the **intelligent design** (ID) movement, promoted in recent years by the American-based Discovery Institute, a think-tank devoted to advocating such views. Less overtly religious than creation science, but religious nonetheless, ID is an attempt to highlight apparent shortcomings with evolutionary theories. Critics see it at as a cynical way of promoting religious dogma in the guise of science. According to its proponents, 'certain aspects of the natural world ... are too complex and too unlikely to have been produced by processes of genetic mutation and natural selection' (Dixon 2008: 81). This missing link is obviously some kind of designer (God). Like creation science, ID is widely criticized as being a pseudo-science misrepresenting scientific facts. Following intense lobbying, including a campaign called 'Teach the Controversy', some school boards in the United States allowed ID to be taught as a valid theory alongside evolution. These decisions later were overturned.

One response to the attempts to introduce ID into US schools has been the development of a spoof religion, Pastafarianism, whose followers worship the Flying Spaghetti Monster. The idea was proposed first by Bobby Henderson, who argued Rastafarian beliefs about creation be taught alongside ID and creationism. The campaign went viral and followers have continued to develop this 'religion'. One can now purchase books, t-shirts and other paraphernalia on the Internet.

Want to know more?

I suggest the following books, which look at different aspects of the battle between science and religion, creationism and evolution:

- Larson, Edward J. (1997) *Summer of the Gods: The Scopes Trial and America's Continuing Debate over Science and Religion*. New York: Basic Books.

- Larson, Edward J. (2007) *The Creation-Evolution Debate*. Athens, GA: University of Georgia Press.

- Barbour, Ian (1997) *Religion and Science: Historical and Contemporary Issues*. San Francisco, CA: Harper.

Points to ponder

Stage a debate, arguing for and against the proposition that 'ID should be taught alongside evolution in American public schools'.

Next steps ...

Bruce Hunsberger and Bob Altemeyer's book *Atheists: A Groundbreaking Study of America's Nonbelievers* (2006) provides an excellent insight into the lives of self-identified atheists. Barry Kosmin and Ariela Keysar's edited book, *Secularism and Secularity: Contemporary International Perspectives* (2007) examines the growth of nonreligion around the world and deals with methodological issues in the study of secularity. It is available as a free PDF from http://prog.trincoll.edu/ISSSC/Book/Access.asp.

Documentaries and films

A famous film, *Inherit the Wind*, made in 1960, is a dramatization of the Scopes Monkey Trial. To this observer the film is very hammy, but it is interesting nonetheless. Richard Dawkins wrote and presented a two-part Channel Four documentary, *Root of all Evil?* Part I is called 'The God Delusion', Part II is 'The Virus of Faith'. These present in documentary form some of his criticisms of religion.

Web

The Institute for the Study of Secularism in Society and Culture (ISSSC) http://www.trincoll.edu/Academics/centers/isssc/Pages/default.aspx is part of the developing social scientific study of secularism and nonreligion.

13

the future of religion? young people, religion and spirituality

After reading this chapter you will:

- be aware of recent developments in the religiosity of young people;

- understand how young people are engaging with alternative faiths and spiritualities;

- understand how religion works on the Internet; and

- be able to make informed conclusions about the future of religion.

At key seasonal times of the year – such as the summer and winter solstices – scores of Wiccans (witches) gather together in parks, forests and other open spaces to enact rituals that celebrate the seasons. Dressed in robes, or even skyclad (naked), one of the rituals involves casting (drawing) a circle on the ground. Different points of the circle honor ritually the elements of earth, air, fire and water.

Wiccans are part of the broader Neo-Pagan religious movement, which includes Druids, shamans, Pagans, Wiccans and other kinds of witches. These are among the fastest growing religions in the West, and young people are those most likely to affiliate with these religions (see Mason et al. 2007, 2010).

Neo-Paganism is not the only religious movement which is proving attractive to young people in the West. Evangelical and Pentecostal megachurches draw young people in huge numbers. Hillsong Church in Australia is one such example. Its main campus is located in the outer suburbs of Sydney. From the outside it looks more like a sports stadium than a traditional church. In the foyer is a coffee shop and a bookstore. The actual church is a huge auditorium seating thousands.

Congregants are shown to their seats by ushers equipped with two-way radios who communicate with one another in order to best organize seating. At the front is an enormous stage, with room enough for a large band and choir. Behind them is a huge video screen.

Once the service begins the congregation feels the full force of the sound system and the music really booms out. The band plays contemporary Christian rock music rather than traditional hymns. In front of the stage a 'mosh pit' is formed by some of the more enthusiastic congregants. Most of the congregation wave their arms in the air or clap. The words to the songs are flashed on the screen, one line at a time. (Hillsong is famous for its music, most of it written in-house. It is also is played in churches throughout the world.)

In Chapters 6 and 7 it was noted that young people in the West are increasingly turning away from Christianity, particularly from the mainline Protestant denominations. Is the growth and popularity of Neo-Paganism and Pentecostalism indicative of a religious and spiritual revival of a style befitting the twenty-first century? Or is the future looking increasingly secular? And how do patterns in the West compare to other parts of the globe?

Fortunately, one of the most productive areas in the recent sociology of religion has been research on youth religion and spirituality. Major national studies of youth religion have been conducted in several countries. This work provides great insight into young people's religion and is the subject of this final chapter. (In this chapter when talking about 'youth' and 'young people', I am referring to people in their teens through to those in their early thirties.) Discussion begins with an overview of recent research.

'BIG PICTURE' RESEARCH ON RELIGION AND SPIRITUALITY AMONG YOUNG PEOPLE: AN OVERVIEW

Starting with scholar Reg Bibby's first national study of Canadian young people in 1984, there have been several important national-level research projects that have examined the religion and spirituality of teenagers and 'emerging' adults in different countries. This section details some of the major national studies and compares the findings.

National Study of Youth Religion

United States

Arguably, the most comprehensive study of youth and religion is the *National Study of Youth and Religion* (NSYR) which began in 2001. The third wave of surveys was completed in 2008. A fourth wave has recently been completed. Full details of this study were discussed in Chapter 5. To recap, both in-depth interviews and national survey data were collected from the study cohort when they were teenagers (13–17) emerging adults (18–24) and young adults (25–29).

Australia

The first national study of youth religion in Australia was the *Spirit of Generation Y* (SGY) study conducted in 2002–6 (see Mason et al. 2007). This project involved more than 100 qualitative interviews, and a nationally representative telephone survey of 1219 people aged 13–24. The survey inquired about religious and spiritual beliefs and practices. Helpfully, many of the survey questions were drawn from the NSYR, so direct comparison between US and Australian teens is possible.

England and Wales

Throughout the 1990s, Leslie Francis and colleagues conducted the *Teenage Religion and Values Survey* (TRVS) (see Francis 2001; Robbins and Francis 2010), which surveyed a total of 33,982 school-attending teens aged 13–15.

Canada

Reg Bibby has long collected national level data on the religious life of Canadian teens. The latest study, *Project Teen Canada*, was conducted in 2008 and surveyed more than 3500 school-attending teens aged 15–19 (see Bibby 2009).

Papua New Guinea

An extremely interesting counterpoint to studies conducted in the West is a national study of youth religion conducted in Papua New Guinea, the *Young Melanesian Project* (YMP) (see Zocca and de Groot 1997). Scholars from the Melanesia Institute in Goroka surveyed 1630 people aged 15–24 in the mid 1990s.

While the research discussed above is primarily large-scale and quantitative, there are many other worthy, smaller quantitative and qualitative studies of teens and young adults conducted in these countries and elsewhere (see Collins-Mayo and Dandelion 2010; Giordan 2010). These larger studies are a helpful starting point for understanding the trends and trajectories of youth religion in contemporary society.

International comparison of teen and young adult religiosity

I start with patterns in the West. Table 13.1 presents some comparable findings from the US, Canadian, Australian and England and Wales surveys. The TRVS in England

Table 13.1   Teenagers in Australia, Britain, Canada, United States: religious beliefs, identification and practices by country (percentage of age group within country)

Selected beliefs and practices	Australia 13–15%	England/Wales 13–15%	Australia 15–19%	Canada 15–19%	Australia 13–17%	US 13–17%
Believe in God – No	16	26	18	16	17	3
– Unsure	34	33	34	48	34	12
– Yes	50	41	47	37	49	84
No religious identification	44	49	51	32	48	18
Believe in life after death	59	45	75	75	56	49
Attend church – weekly	16	13	13	21	15	40
– less than weekly	47	37	45	32	46	42
– never	37	49	42	47	39	18
Pray privately once a week or more	–	–	27	30	27	65

Data sources: Australia: SGY survey (Mason et al. 2007: 84, 90, 96, 101); England and Wales: Values Survey (Francis 2001: 27–44, 96); Canada: Project Teen Canada 2008 (Bibby 2009: 163–87); US: National Study of Youth and Religion (Smith and Denton 2005: 31–43).

and Wales covered only the 13–15 age-group; so the first two columns in the table compare Australian and British data for that age range. Next, Australian 15–19-year-olds are compared with Canadians 15–19, then Australians 13–17 with US teens of the same age. (The Canadian figure on belief in life after death reported here is for those who answered 'Yes' and 'I think so' combined, so Australian responses 'Yes' and 'Maybe' have been added for this comparison.)

The data in this table show that US teens are more religious than their counterparts in Canada, Australian and England and Wales. This is to be expected, and these data reflect the different religious cultures of the respective countries.

These current patterns of youth religion need to be placed in historical context. As discussed in Chapters 6 and 7, research reveals young Westerners today are less religious than the youth of the 1960s (see Mason et al. 2010; Putnam and Campbell 2010; Voas 2010). This is true of Australia, Western Europe, Canada and the United States.

Moreover, compared with earlier generations of youth, a greater proportion of young people today do not affiliate with a religion. Some of these young people were never raised in a religious tradition, while some were raised in a religious tradition as children and have abandoned this affiliation by their teen and early adult years (Mason et al. 2010: 94). This loss of members is particularly acute among the mainline Protestant denominations and the Catholic Church (Mason et al. 2007: 75–76; Smith and Snell 2009: 110). In sum, there is a continuing drift of young people away from Christian affiliation and practice throughout the industrialized world, although the magnitude of this varies from country to country.

A proportion of young people – more in the United States than other Western countries – continue to be committed to Christianity (attending church regularly).

Young people who go to church regularly show a preference for the conservative Protestant denominations, which includes Pentecostal and evangelical churches (Smith and Denton 2005; Mason et al. 2007; Smith and Snell 2009). The evangelical and Pentecostal megachurches have done particularly well in attracting young people. These congregations eschew traditional forms of worship. Services feature loud contemporary music, extensive use of video during worship and topical preaching. This is far different to traditional Catholic Mass or Anglican Eucharist. According to Flory and Miller (2010: 9), traditional churches are 'culturally out of touch, packaging their religion in ways that does not communicate to … the post-boomer generations'.

However, youthful disaffiliation from Christianity is not occurring the world over. Census data from Papua New Guinea show that between the 1960s and 2000 there was an overall increase in the proportion of the population who identify as Christian (Zocca 2004). While data for specific age cohorts are not available, the overall increase in Christian identification suggests there is no major youth drift from Christianity in PNG. The YMP study in Papua New Guinea found an estimated 75 percent of PNG teens and young adults attended church regularly, 10 percent attended sporadically, and about half pray daily (Zocca and de Groot 1997: 101, 105). Young Papua New Guineans are clearly more religious than young people in nearby Australia.

China is officially an atheist nation, yet in this context Christianity and Buddhism are growing quickly. Scholar Fenggang Yang (2010), observes that it is Chinese youth who are at the forefront of this religious expansion. According to Yang (2010: 147): 'Within one hundred years, the Chinese youth have turned around 180 degrees from [being] the driving force for total secularization to the driving force for religious awakening.'

Other trends in youth religion

Another value of well-constructed, large-scale studies is their ability to identify important religious trends, beyond patterns of belief, attendance and practice.

Moralistic Therapeutic Deism

One phenomenon detected among US teens was something NSYR researchers termed 'Moralistic Therapeutic Deism' and is reported extensively in the book *Soul Searching* (Smith and Denton 2005) and revisited in *Souls in Transition* (Smith and Snell 2009). Smith and Denton suggest that a dominant **religious outlook** commonly found among US teens is 'Moralistic Therapeutic Deism' (MTD). Specifically, this is a broad worldview that entails a belief (more or less) in the following:

1. A God exists who created and orders the world and watches over human life on earth.

2. God wants people to be good, nice, and fair to each other, as taught in the Bible and most of the world religions.

3. The central goal of life is to be happy and to feel good about oneself.

4. God does not need to be particularly involved in one's life except when God is needed to resolve a problem.

5. Good people go to heaven when they die (Smith and Denton 2005: 163).

Smith and Denton suggest that this perspective is 'particularly evident among main-line Protestant and Catholic youth, but is also visible among black and conservative Protestants, Jewish teens, other religious types of teenagers, and even many non-religious teens in the United States' (Smith and Denton 2005: 163). In other words, it is a dominant ethos of the age, widely shared among American youth, and indeed, many older people.

The **moralistic** element of this worldview is the idea that life should have some kind of moral center, and that individuals ought to take broad, personal responsibility for one's life, and be 'nice, kind, pleasant, respectful, responsible, at work on self improvement, taking care of one's health, and doing one's best to be successful' (Smith and Denton 2005: 163). The **therapeutic** element is the idea that faith 'is about attaining subjective well-being, being able to resolve problems, and getting along amiably with other people' (Smith and Denton 2005: 164). This places the individual at the center of religious faith. The **deistic** element involves an idea of what God is like: 'one who exists, created the world, and defines our general moral order, but not one who is particularly personally involved in one's affairs' (Smith and Denton 2005: 164). Smith and Denton are careful to suggest that this worldview is tacit rather than explicit, and is an orientation that colors the way many people approach their faith. This particular orientation did not emerge in a vacuum, but is a consequence of broader social forces: the prevalence of individualism in late modern life, consumer capitalism and the rise of a therapeutic culture that emphasizes personal wellbeing.

Religious individualism

As discussed in Chapter 2, Emile Durkheim predicted 100 years ago that individualism would increasingly characterize modern societies. Most scholars agree that Western societies are highly individualistic (see Beck and Beck-Gernsheim 2002; Beck 2010). Scholar Kath Engebretson (2007: 111) argues: 'Individualistic values are typical of prosperous societies, where the freedom and autonomy of the individual are prized and protected ... individualistic cultures emphasize the role and rights of the individual.' The primacy of the individual is reflected in the way in which many people approach religious faith.

The national research on youth religion in Australia and the United States revealed considerable **religious individualism** among young people (Mason et al. 2007; Smith and Denton 2005). Summarizing their findings from Australia, Mason et al. (2007: 324) conclude: 'In matters of religion, "truth" means what it means for *me*;

what is true for someone else may be quite different, and has its own perfect right to exist independently, without being constrained by any standard external to the individual.' Smith and Denton (2005: 147) reached a similar conclusion in their analysis of NSYR data, arguing US teens believe 'each individual is uniquely distinct from all others and deserves a faith that fits his or her singular self; that individuals must freely choose their own religion; that the individual is the authority over religion and not vice versa'. Similar religious individualism is evident in studies of young people in Britain and Canada (Savage et al. 2006; Bibby 2009).

According to Mason et al. (2010: 97) 'the worldview of younger [people] has been shaped by some common influences that make them similarly individualistic'. These common influences arise in part because of the globalization of youth culture. Young people, perhaps more than any other age cohort, participate together in a global web of communication. Ideas, values and culture which originate in one place move readily to another.

Some scholars think the decline of organized religion is conterminous with the rise of alternative religions and spiritualities. Houtman and Aupers (2007: 315), for example, argue: 'What we are witnessing today is not so much a disappearance of religion, but rather a relocation of the sacred.' As Mason et al. (2010: 98) suggest, many of the alternatives to traditional religion are 'well-tailored to suit the individualistic turn in spiritual tastes'.

ALTERNATIVE SPIRITUALITIES

Much has been written about the changing spiritual landscape in late modern societies, especially the emergence of faiths, spiritualities and spiritual practices that are outside the bounds of traditional, organized religion (see Partridge 2004; Heelas and Woodhead 2005). None of these new religious or spiritual movements constitutes anything like a broad-based replacement for traditional religion, but they do represent a proliferation of spiritual choices. This section explores research findings on young people's response to the alternative religions and alternative spiritual beliefs now on offer in the spiritual marketplace.

Alternative religions

As noted in Chapter 7, the West experienced an 'alternative spiritual awakening' in the 1960s and 1970s. Part of this involved the rise of new, alternative religions. Alternative religions are 'the range of faiths outside the remit of traditional [religion]' (Hunt 2003: xv). Well-known alternative religious groups, such as the International Society for Krishna Consciousness (Hare Krishnas), the Unification Church (the Moonies) and Scientology were either founded or gained significantly in popularity in the 1960s. From the late 1970s, nature religions – witchcraft (Wicca), Druidism, Neo-Paganism – have achieved considerable prominence in the West.

Recent census data from Australia, England and Wales, show that among the alternative religions, nature religions have more adherents than other alternatives, such as Satanism, Rastafarianism and Scientology. Young people (those aged under 40) are more likely than older people (40+) to affiliate with a nature religion.

While many new religions and faiths enjoy a high, if sometimes controversial, profile their followers represent only a small percentage of the total population in Western countries (see for example, Kosmin and Keysar 2006; Bouma 2006). According to the 2011 Census, only 8291 Australians aged 10–29 identify with a nature religion (Pagans, Druids, witches and Wiccans). In the United States, Smith and Denton (2005) report that only 0.3 percent of US youth (aged 13–17) are Pagans or Wiccans. Clearly, the profile of, and media interest in, youth witchcraft and Paganism greatly exceeds the number of serious practitioners. That said, as this chapter's case study reveals, young witches take their faith very seriously.

CONTEMPORARY WITCHES: MORE THAN A FAD

Contemporary witchcraft, particularly Wicca, is growing in popularity in countries and regions like Australia, the UK, the United States, New Zealand and Western Europe. Wiccans – those who follow Wicca – celebrate ritually major seasonal and solar changes. They also practice 'magic', which involves spell-casting. Wicca was founded in the twentieth century, mainly due to the efforts of Briton Gerald Gardner, although its origins are the subject of some debate. Some practitioners believe that it is a religious tradition that goes all the way back to pre-Christian times. Others, including most scholars, argue it is a revival of ancient, earth-focused Pagan practices. It is popular with females, with many practitioners seeing it as a religion free from patriarchal authority (see Berger and Ezzy 2007).

Young people are more likely than older people to be attracted to witchcraft. Sociologists Helen Berger and Douglas Ezzy interviewed 90 American, English and Australian teenage witches for their insightful book *Teenage Witches: Magical Youth and the Search for the Self* (2007; see also Berger and Ezzy 2009). The teens they interviewed were serious practitioners of the craft. Many had come to witchcraft as part of a general exploration of different kinds of alternative spirituality, and many admitted that a recent media fascination with witches and witchcraft had caught their attention. Young people are drawn to Wicca because it is a religion which cares for the self and cares for the environment. Most teenagers witches do not feel part of the mainstream and many practiced the craft alone. Cush (2010: 85) notes many teen witches are 'individualistic in seeing the self as authority, but [are] not selfish'.

Representations of witches are increasingly common in the mass media. Berger and Ezzy (2009: 501) find a complex relationship between witchcraft and the media: 'On the one hand, the visual media helps to legitimize their religion, providing a framework or cultural backdrop within which they begin to explore Witchcraft and

(Continued)

(Continued)

develop their religious identities. On the other hand, the young often see the media representations as inaccurate.' They find that many factors influence young people to engage in witchcraft, including family background and individual psychology. Ultimately, the media representations are something against which young witches react: 'By doing this they can present themselves as serious practitioners of the religion and not as "just kids" playing at being Witches' (Berger and Ezzy 2009: 510).

The phenomenon of teenage witchcraft is evidence of the globalization of youth culture. Berger and Ezzy (2009: 511) note: 'We find that country, or local culture, has relatively little effect on the practice of young Witches. This speaks to the globalization of media and its influence on identity formation, including religious identity formation.' Many practitioners enjoy community with one another via the Internet. With its emphasis on female empowerment, care of the environment and religious individualism, modern Witchcraft embodies many of the broader social sentiments of the age.

Berger and Ezzy (2007: 37) argue witchcraft has a 'larger impact than its numbers would suggest, as many more people explore the religion than actually become witches'. Data from recent surveys of youth in Australia and the United States suggest that this exploration is not particularly widespread or serious. Both the SGY and the NSYR surveys asked participants about investigating Paganism or Wicca. About 10 percent of Australian young people have explored either of these two nature religions, though only a minority were serious about this exploration, to the extent of reading Pagan writings or attending some kind of ceremony. Among US teens, about 3 percent try to 'include in their own spirituality' some kind of practice from witchcraft or Paganism (this figure does not include those who already identify as Pagan or Wiccan) (Smith and Denton 2005: 78). It would seem that for the very large majority of young people in Australia and the United States, witchcraft, like other alternative religions, is a distant curiosity at best.

Belief in the supernatural

Belief in the paranormal, occult and supernatural has long been part of Western societies, co-existing alongside traditional religious beliefs. These beliefs might include belief in ghosts, clairvoyance, astrology, evil spirits, premonitions, and a little more recently, belief in UFOs (see Bader et al. 2010). Is it possible the turn from organized religion and the rise of religious individualism has led to an increase in the acceptance of supernatural beliefs, especially among young people?

Tables 13.2 and 13.3 show levels of teenage belief in astrology and contact with the dead in Australia, the United States, Canada and England and Wales. These data show that belief in the supernatural is reasonably strong in these countries. Qualitative data, however, reveal that for most young people, these beliefs are idly held superstitions, rather than strong beliefs that influence action (see Mason et al. 2007; Singleton 2012).

Table 13.2   Teenagers in Australia, Britain, Canada, United States: belief in astrology (percentage of age group within country)

Question asked	Country, date of survey	Age range	Yes	Maybe
Do you believe in astrology (that stars and planets affect people's fates)?	Australia 2005	13–17	24%	19%
Do you believe in astrology (that stars and planets affect people's fates)?	USA 2003	13–17	9%	31%
Do you believe in astrology?	Canada 2008	15–19	47% (% 'definitely' + 'I think I do')	
I believe in my horoscope	UK late 1990s	13–15	35%	33% ('unsure')

Data sources: Australia: SGY survey; England and Wales: Values Survey (Francis 2001: 195); Canada: Project Teen Canada 2008 (Bibby 2009:175); United States: National Study of Youth and Religion (Smith and Denton 2005: 43).

Table 13.2 shows that 24 percent of teens (13–17) in Australia definitely believe in astrology, compared to 9 percent in the United States. A higher proportion of teens in the UK definitely believe in astrology. The published data for Canada combines responses, so that 47 percent of teens aged 15–19 are certain about or open to belief in astrology. Notwithstanding these figures, it is reasonable to assume that few young people are really serious about it. Bibby (2009) finds that among Canadian teens aged 15–19, only 24 percent 'check their horoscopes at least once a week'. Far fewer would have the resources or inclination to pay for a professional casting (see Mason et al. 2007).

Another popular supernatural belief is the idea that people can contact those who have 'passed over' to the afterlife. Table 13.3 shows teen belief in the idea that it is possible to contact the dead.

Table 13.3   Teenagers in Australia, Britain, Canada, United States: belief in 'contact with the dead' (percentage of age group within country)

Question asked	Country, date of survey	Age range	Yes	Maybe
Do you believe in the possibility of communicating with the dead directly or through séances?	Australia 2005	13–17	23%	19%
Do you believe in the possibility of communicating with the dead directly or through séances?	USA 2003	13–17	9%	30%
We can have contact with the spirit world	Canada 2008	15–19	46% (% 'definitely' + 'I think I do')	
I believe it is possible to contact the spirits of the dead	UK late 1990s	13–15	31%	33% ('unsure')

Data sources: Australia: SGY survey; England and Wales: Values Survey (Francis 2001: 195); Canada: Project Teen Canada 2008 (Bibby 2009: 175); US: National Study of Youth and Religion (Smith and Denton 2005: 43).

Like belief in astrology, almost a quarter of Australian teens, and more in the UK, definitely believe that contact with the dead is possible. Far fewer in the United States are definite about this belief. Again, we might question the salience of this belief. It is one thing to believe in the possibility of communicating with the dead, another to actually act on it: by regularly consulting a medium, or participating in a séance. Most young people probably believe merely that contact is *possible*.

Is belief in the supernatural on the rise?

There is a tendency among some scholars to think that belief in the supernatural and the paranormal is increasing in contemporary Western societies. Media studies scholar Annette Hill (2011), for example, argues, '[paranormal] beliefs are on the rise in contemporary Western societies'. She then cites statistics about *present-day* levels of belief in an effort to substantiate this claim. Few scholars doubt that a substantial proportion of the population in the West hold various alternative beliefs, but the incidence of such beliefs is hardly rising.

The truth is that large numbers of Westerners have always believed in ghosts, spirits, clairvoyance, and other related phenomena. The Spiritualist movement of the nineteenth century found ready acceptance because belief in ghosts and the like was remarkably commonplace. Historian Barbara Weisberg (2004: 24), writing about America in the 1840s observes, 'whatever their religion or social class [Americans] were no strangers to spirits, both the spooky sort and the beatific … a wealth of beliefs about the supernatural, derived from Christian and non-Christian traditions, permeated … popular culture'. Such beliefs have always been part of the fabric of society.

A replacement for religion?

Scholars have questioned whether contemporary belief in the supernatural is a 'functional alternative to mainstream religion' (Emmons and Sobal 1981). Both the SGY and NSYR projects examined the extent of 'spiritual seeking' among teens and young adults. Both studies also concluded that very few young people are genuine 'spiritual seekers' – engaged in a serious quest beyond the mainstream traditions to discover a meaningful spirituality.

But another important trend among young people is also evident, and this is the popularization of individualized, 'mix and match' belief systems, that are not accompanied by any regular religious or spiritual practice. According to Sjödin (2002: 76) 'the process of individualization in society means that individuals can take their choice from among different offerings and build their own individual view of life, often characterized by fragments of different ideologies, which are combined into a personal blend'. For many Australian young people, traditional religious beliefs are not held exclusively, but in combination with supernatural beliefs (for a full description, see Mason et al. 2007). This trend is also evident in the United States, but less so; strong religious practice and religious exclusivism are more prevalent there than in Australia.

What is clear is that alternative religions and supernatural beliefs are not *taking the place* of religion in a widespread fashion. For young people, alternative religions – witchcraft included – remain for most little more than a curiosity. Many young people believe in the supernatural but these beliefs are 'low-cost' and do not reflect a strong commitment to either spiritual practices or a strongly defined or clearly articulated alternative spiritual worldview. There is no large-scale turn towards alternative kinds of spiritualities. That said, there does appear to be a boom in TV shows and movies that have supernatural themes, which may be indicative of a general interest in supernatural themes.

The supernatural in popular culture

The pilot episode of the recent US TV series, *The Secret Circle*, has a stunning sequence in which a young woman comes to believe that witchcraft (of the mythical kind) is real. The sequence begins when the main protagonist, Cassie, new in town, is confronted by other five teens in a deserted house near a forest. They tell her they are all witches, and that they need her to join them to make their coven complete. Upon hearing this news, she flees through the forest until one of the teens, Adam, catches up with her. She declares, 'There's no such thing as witches and magic. I don't believe it. I can't.' Adam responds: 'Let me show you.' He takes a leaf with water on it, places it in her hand and tells her to close her eyes. Using magic, he makes thousands of drops of water rise from the forest floor. The scene is wonderfully filmed, with the light sparkling off the raindrops. This is media that makes magic seem real.

At present there is a monumental popular appetite for teen and young adult-oriented TV shows and movies which feature the paranormal, occult, mystical and magical. Examples include *Medium*, *Buffy: The Vampire Slayer*, *Charmed*, *Ghost Whisperer*, *Sabrina: The Teenage Witch*, *Supernatural*, *Angel*, *Crossing Over*, *Moonlight*, *True Blood*, *Poltergeist*, *The Amityville Horror*, *Paranormal Activity*, *The Sixth Sense* and the *Harry Potter* series among many other shows and movies (see Clark 2003; Hill 2011). Does the widespread popularity of these shows influence the beliefs of contemporary teens and young adults?

US sociologist Lynn Schofield Clark's (2003) book *From Angels to Aliens: Teenagers, the Media and the Supernatural* is arguably the best work examining the relationship between beliefs and the media. Clark conducted more than 100 face-to-face interviews with a range of teens and found:

> While it might seem that some young people find the images and stories of the entertainment media persuasive, the fact that such depictions belong to the realm

of entertainment signal to most that such things should not be taken seriously at all. This theme ... emerged among the teens I talked with. (Clark 2003: 225)

The SGY researchers found Australian young people expressed similar sentiments: 'supernatural' shows are about entertainment and are not taken seriously. That said, such media do create a cultural backdrop that quite likely validates the idea of the supernatural. Some commentators, however, believe the current popularity of supernatural shows and movies is evidence of young people's yearning for spiritual meaning in their lives, making up for the loss of organized religion (e.g. Tacey 2003).

The prevalence of religious and magical themes in the media sets the scene for the final section of this book: the rise of digital religion.

DIGITAL RELIGION

Given that young people have only ever known a world suffused with global digital realities, it is apposite in a chapter about youth religion to conclude with discussion of how digital communication technologies are influencing the world's religious life. To that end, 'digital religion' (also known as 'e-religion' or 'cyber religion') is the focus of this final section (for a discussion of the terms see Campbell 2013a).

The impact of the Internet on everyday life

The invention and popularization of the Internet has transformed radically the ways in which people obtain, disseminate and communicate information, points explained briefly below. In the course of writing this book, I have often needed to provide a statistic or obtain an article on a particular topic. Rather than trudging off to my campus library, armed with a notebook and credit for a photocopier, I have simply clicked my way to my university library catalogue, Google Scholar or another trusted website to get the information I needed. Once protracted tasks, requiring some advanced skills, are now quicker and easier to perform. The Internet is the world's most used and powerful information clearinghouse.

The Internet has also made the dissemination of information far more democratic and open than in earlier times. When the Spiritualist movement rose in popularity in the mid-nineteenth century (see Chapter 2), people heard about it via word of mouth, public mediumistic performances or by reading a newspaper. Public debate about the movement was largely in the hands of those who controlled the main channels of communication of the age, namely the pulpit and the newspapers. In order for ordinary folk to have their opinions of Spiritualism heard publicly, they had to pass the gatekeeping of newspaper editors (some of whom were sympathetic to Spiritualism) or produce, at some considerable expense, their own Spiritualist newspapers or pamphlets on the topic (see Weisberg 2004). How could the average woman follower of the movement have her opinion heard and counted?

Modern-day mediums still use word of mouth and public performances (often TV) to promote their wares. The Internet is yet another channel for making one-self known. As for public opinion? Type 'John Edward medium' into Google and see what comes up. One can find sites which support this well-known TV psychic, others which decry him as a 'hustler of the bereaved'. Expressing oneself in the digital age is easy, cheap and unregulated. Because of the Internet, the individual is less constrained by traditional forms of authority and traditional modes of cultural communication.

The other great achievement of the Internet is that it has allowed the creation of new, global networks of communication, belonging and sociality. Theorist Manuel Castells (2004: 3) calls this the 'network society':

A network society is a society whose social structure is made of networks pow-ered by microelectronics-based information and communication technologies. By social structure, I understand the organizational arrangements of humans in relations of production, consumption, reproduction, experience, and power ex-pressed in meaningful communication coded by culture.

Blogs, chat rooms, Facebook, Twitter, Skype and YouTube are all Internet tools which facilitate the network society, linking together people on the basis of hob-bies, interests, values, ethnicity or religion. As will be seen in the next section, such changes wrought by the Internet affect religion.

Religion online, online religion

Scholars agree that religion on the Internet typically takes one of two forms: 'reli-gion online' and 'online religion' (see Campbell 2013a: 2). These two kinds of engagement will be discussed briefly, beginning with religion online. Most of the world's religious life occurs in the real, rather than the virtual, world. Most religions are comprised of communities of people who gather together to physically enact rituals and most religions have a material dimension, such as sacred people, spaces, objects and places of worship. That said, many religious people and organizations take aspects of their religion online. The various tools of the Internet are deployed as a means of proselytizing, sharing information or maintaining community.

An example of religion online is the Catholic World Youth Day. World Youth Day (WYD), a youth-focused Catholic celebration, is the largest recurring youth event in the world and is held at intervals of approximately three years. As part of the event, the Pope presides over a Mass and up to several million young people attend. In recent years, the WYD experience has incorporated online elements (see worldyouthday.com). Pilgrims register for the event online, receive information via websites and email, and then use social networking tools to link with other pilgrims and upload videos and blogs. In this example, the Internet is an *extension* of offline religious practice, rather than the primary space in which religious practice or rituals occur. This is the main way religions engage with digital technologies. As noted in the chapter on Islam, and the example of the global Ummah, the Internet has the unique capacity to create globalized religious communities.

Online religion is a rarer form of digital religious engagement (Campbell 2013a). In this kind of religious expression, a movement or group's religious rituals, practices and gatherings occur *primarily* in the online environment. According to Campbell (2013a: 3), 'online religion [demonstrates] how the Internet [offers] a new social landscape for imaging the spiritual contemporary society'. Ally Ostrowski (2006: 94), writing about American Buddhism, describes the existence of 'Cybersanghas that have no physical home and exist solely in an online environment' (a Sangha is a religious community).

The online environment also offers a space for new religious or spiritual movements to begin. An intriguing example is the Otherkin movement (see Kirby 2012, 2013). According to Danielle Kirby (2012: 130), Otherkin followers are united by the 'shared belief is that some people are, either partially or completely, non-human'. Otherkin could be: 'dragons, elves, vampires, lycanthropes, fairies … and angels, as well as a plethora of specific creatures sourced from ancient myth through to popular culture media creations' (Kirby 2012: 130). This is a spiritual movement which began online and conducts almost all its business in the online environment. Otherkin social networks unite people from Australia, Europe and North America (Kirby 2013). (See Otherkin.net.)

The online environment is also a potential space for *religious experiences* to occur, not just for communities to form. For example, Scheifinger (2008: 234), finds that Hindu websites 'allow pujas (a puja is an act of worship in Hinduism which involves the presentation of 'honor offerings' to the deity) to be ordered and performed … festivals to be broadcast and cremations witnessed'. Many churches broadcast their worship services online. While forging online-only religious communities is straightforward, having a genuine religious experience or performing a ritual in front of a screen is altogether more difficult. Can watching a streamed video of a Hindu cremation or worship at the Abyssinian Baptist Church in Harlem, New York City, compare to the visceral experience of being physically present? And does the cyber experience *replace* the material encounter or merely complement it?

Some scholars have considered also whether digital popular culture (i.e. movies, games) can serve as a source of *inspiration* (not just the platform) for the development of new religious movements (see, for example, Possamai 2005, 2012). Recent censuses in England and Wales, New Zealand and Australia saw thousands of people nominate their religion as 'Jedi', an homage to the Jedi religion depicted in the *Star Wars* films. A few sociologists contend that beyond those who jokingly put down Jedi in the census there are real followers of Jediism, a religious form invented in the cinema, and apparently made real in cyberspace (Possamai and Lee 2011; McCormick 2012). Certainly, there is plenty of online activity devoted to the 'religion' of Jediism, but in the absence of any face-to-face, in-depth interviews with serious practitioners, it is difficult to determine properly how online religious activity is enacted in a lived, everyday way. Further research is required to better understand what role digital elements play in the entirety of a person's religious experience.

There is little doubt, however, that the Internet is transforming religion. It enables religious people, communities and organizations to overcome great distances or physical barriers. Perhaps, however, the most radical and far-reaching consequence of digital religion is the challenge it brings to traditional religious authority, placing 'control of religious interpretation and ritual performance increasingly in the hands of individuals' (Wagner 2013: 199). Anyone with access to a computer, tablet or smartphone can express a religious opinion and find supporters for that opinion online.

CONCLUSION: WHAT IS THE FUTURE OF RELIGION?

Clearly, religion in the future will be something done in both the material and the virtual worlds. What other trends might we see in the future of religion? Will secularization continue in Western Europe, Canada and Australia? Will the United States experience secularization as the growing population of nonreligious youth age and have nonreligious children? Is religious revival destined to continue in other parts of the world? Can atheism grow even stronger? The findings from the various studies of youth religion, along with other arguments presented in this book, can be used to make reasonable predictions about the future of religion in the remainder of the twenty-first century.

A handful of scholars see little future for religion in some societies. A recent paper by Abrams et al. (2011), for example, uses mathematical modeling to predict future religious trends in secular, Western societies. Their model suggests 'in these societies the perceived utility of religious non-affiliation is greater than that of adhering to a religion and [the model] therefore predicts continued growth of non-affiliation, tending toward the disappearance of religion' (Abrams et al. 2011: 4).

While the numbers of people who have no religious affiliation is growing in Great Britain, Australia, Canada and Western Europe, particularly among young people, it does not seem plausible that Christianity will 'disappear' from these countries anytime soon. Current patterns of youth affiliation and attendance indicate that while mainline churches might struggle to attract members, there will be enduring pockets of Christian vitality, particularly within evangelical and Pentecostal churches. Waves of recent migrants have also filled the pews of some congregations. For these reasons, the churches have some future. While New Age and other spiritual and religious alternatives are attractive to some people, the evidence does not point to a wholesale 're-enchantment of the West' in the next few decades. Rather, these stand as one option among many possible spiritual choices.

Significantly, the Muslim, Sikh, Buddhist and Hindu populations living in the West will continue to grow in size. According to Pew Forum (2011b: 121) estimates, Muslims are expected to make up 8 percent of Europe's population by 2030. All of this suggests religion will continue to be an important factor in Western Europe,

Canada and Australia. These societies will continue to face the challenge of successfully managing religious diversity.

It will be interesting to see what happens with religion in the United States in the next few decades. A recent, small decline in affiliation and attendance is discernible, due in large part to youth disaffiliation from the churches. But this is just one pattern. The NSYR research shows there are many highly religious US teens and young adults, who, in all likelihood, will remain religious as they grow older. Moreover, the United States is the world's number one destination for Christian migrants (Pew Forum 2012a). Already, the migrant influence on churches is evident, and this will only continue. As is the case with other Western countries, faiths apart from Christianity will also continue to grow, due mainly to immigration. It is also true that an increasing proportion of Americans see themselves as nonreligious. New Age and other spiritual alternatives continue to find favour in the United States. Religious pluralism, it seems, is the reality for Western countries.

Prominent American philosopher Charles Taylor published recently a monumental and highly influential work, *A Secular Age* (2007), which considers the religious situation of the West. His concern is with tracing the emergence of contemporary 'conditions of belief', a 'move from a society where belief in God is unchallenged and indeed, unproblematic, to one in which it is understood to be one option among others, and frequently not the easiest to embrace' (Taylor 2007: 3). For Taylor, a 'secular age' is not devoid entirely of religious participation, symbols and meaning, but rather, one in which 'Belief in God is no longer axiomatic. There are alternatives ... This has been a recognizable experience in our societies, at least since the mid-nineteenth century' (Taylor 2007: 3). All the signs indicate that greater pluralism, choice and diversity will characterize religious life in the West.

Even the most ardent proponents of secularization concede this paradigm is not applicable to countries outside the West. Many religious trends are evident. This book has documented the Islamic resurgence in majority Islamic countries, the development of a global Muslim consciousness, the emergence of Hindu and Buddhist nationalism and the rise of Pentecostal Christianity in Africa, Latin America and Asia.

I have demonstrated in previous chapters that these developments, while specific to various regions, have had global implications. Islamist schools of thought nurtured in the Middle East have exerted considerable influence on Muslim communities elsewhere. Churches in the Global South are sending missionaries to post-industrial nations. The Dalai Lama has toured the world for several decades, promoting the Tibetan Buddhist tradition. Wiccans in Britain and Australia create community on the Internet. These developments are just the beginning of what will be a truly global age of religion.

Points to ponder

What do you think the future of religion will look like, both in your country and around the globe? Why?

Next steps ...

There are many good books available on the topic of youth religion. For the United States, I suggest the five books based on NSYR data: *Soul Searching: The Religious and Spiritual Lives of Teenagers* (Smith and Denton 2005); *Forbidden Fruit: Sex and Religion in the Lives of American Teenagers* (Regnerus 2007); *Souls in Transition: The Religious and Spiritual Lives of Emerging Adults* (Smith and Snell 2009); *A Faith of Their Own: Stability and Change in the Religiosity of American's Adolescents* (Pearce and Denton 2011); and *Lost in Translation: The Dark Side of Emerging Adulthood* (Smith et al. 2011). For Great Britain, see: *Making Sense of Generation Y: The World View of 15–25-Year-olds* (Savage et al. 2006); *The Faith of Generation Y* (Collins-Mayo et al. 2010); and *The Values Debate* (Francis 2001). For Canada, see *The Emerging Millennials* (Bibby 2009). For Australia, see: *The Spirit of Generation Y: Young People's Spirituality in a Changing Australia* (Mason et al. 2007). Two edited collections contain many excellent essays about youth religion in a number of countries: *Religion and youth* (Collins-Mayo and Dandelion 2010) and *Annual Review of the Sociology of Religion, vol 1: Youth and Religion* (Giordan 2010). The best recent work I have seen on digital religion is the edited collection, *Digital Religion: Understanding Religious Practice in New Media Worlds* (Campbell 2013b). An excellent, applied study of online spiritual movements is Danielle Kirby's *Fantasy and Belief: Alternative Religions, Popular Narratives and Digital Cultures* (2013). For those seeking a thought-provoking, challenging meditation of the religious situation of the West, I suggest Charles Taylor's *A Secular Age* (2007).

Documentaries

Y God (2008) Examines the ways in which young Australians are religious, spiritual, and secular. Available online at http://www.sbs.com.au/documentary/video/11669571756/mY-generation-Ep-1-Y-God.

A film about the NSYR project, *Soul Searching* (2008) is also highly recommended. It is available through Amazon.com.

references

Abbas, Tahir (2011) *Islamic Radicalism and Multicultural Politics: The British Experience.* London: Routledge.

Abhedananda, Swami (1944) *Life Beyond Death: A Critical Study of Spiritualism.* Kolkata: Ramakrishna Vedanta Math.

Abrams, Daniel M., Yaple, Haley A. and Wiener, Richard J. (2011) 'Dynamics of social group competition: modeling the decline of religious affiliation', *Physical Review Letters*, 107 (8): np, (paper no. 088701).

Ahmed, Leila (2011) *A Quiet Revolution: The Veil's Resurgence, from the Middle East to America.* New Haven, CT: Yale University Press.

Akom, Antwi A. (2007) 'Cities as battlefields: understanding how the Nation of Islam impacts civic engagement, environmental racism, and community development in a low income neighborhood', *International Journal of Qualitative Studies in Education*, 20 (6): 711–30.

Amarasingam, Amarnath (2010) 'To err in their ways: the attribution biases of the New Atheists', *Studies in Religion/Sciences Religieuses*, 39 (4): 573–88.

Anderson, Allan (2000) 'Pentecostalism in East Asia: indigenous oriental Christianity', *Pneuma*, 22 (1): 115–32.

Anderson, Allan (2004) *An Introduction to Pentecostalism: Global Charismatic Christianity.* Cambridge: Cambridge University Press.

Anderson, Allan (2010) 'Varieties, taxonomies, and definitions', in Alan Anderson (ed.), *Studying Global Pentecostalism: Theories and Methods.* Berkeley, CA: University of California Press, pp. 23–42.

Armstrong, Karen (2001) *The Battle for God: A History of Fundamentalism.* New York: Random House.

Asad, Talal (1993) *Genealogies of Religion: Discipline and Reasons of Power in Christianity and Islam.* Baltimore, MD: Johns Hopkins University Press.

Australian Bureau of Statistics (2006) *A Picture of the Nation.* Canberra: ABS, cat no. 2070.0.

Bader, Christopher, Mencken, Frederick and Baker, Joe (2010) *Paranormal America: Ghost Encounters, UFO Sightings, Bigfoot Hunts, and Other Curiosities in Religion and Culture.* New York: New York University Press.

Baggini, Julian (2003) *Atheism: A Very Short Introduction.* Oxford: Oxford University Press.

Bainbridge, William Sims (1997) *The Sociology of Religious Movements.* New York: Routledge.

Bankston, Carl L. and Hidalgo, Danielle (2008) 'Temple and society in the New World: Theravada Buddhism and social order in North America', in Paul Numrich (ed.), *North American Buddhists in Social Context.* Leiden: Brill, pp. 51–86.

Barbour, Ian (1997) *Religion and Science: Historical and Contemporary Issues*. San Francisco, CA: Harper.

Barbour, John D. (1994) *Versions of Deconversion*. Charlottesville, VA: University of Virginia Press.

Barkdull, Carenlee, Khaja, Khadija, Queiro-Tajalli, Irene, Swart, Amy, Cunningham, Dianne and Dennis, Sheila (2011) 'Experiences of Muslims in four western countries post-9/11', *Affilia*, 26 (2): 139–53.

Barker, Eileen (1984) *The Making of a Moonie: Choice or Brainwashing?* Oxford: Blackwell Publishers.

Barker, Eileen, Beckford, James A. and Dobbelaere, Karel (eds.) (1993) *Secularization, Rationalism, and Sectarianism: Essays in Honour of Bryan R. Wilson*. Oxford: Clarendon Press.

Bartholomeusz, Tessa J. and De Silva, Chandra R. (eds.) (1998) *Buddhist Fundamentalism and Minority Identities in Sri Lanka*. Albany, NY: State University of New York Press.

Baumann, Martin (2001) 'Global Buddhism: developmental periods, regional histories, and a new analytical perspective', *Journal of Global Buddhism*, 2: 1–43.

Bauzon, Stephane (2008) 'Catholic reflections for an updated Donum Vitae Instruction: a new Catholic challenge in a post-Christian Europe', *Christian Bioethics*, 14 (1): 42–57.

Beck, Ulrich (2010) *A God of One's Own*. Cambridge: Polity.

Beck, Ulrich and Beck-Gernsheim, Elisabeth (2002) *Individualization: Institutionalized Individualism and its Social and Political Consequences*. London: SAGE.

Beckford, James A. (2003) *Social Theory and Religion*. Cambridge: Cambridge University Press.

Bellah, Robert (1967) 'Civil religion in America', *Daedalus*, 96 (1): 1–21.

Bender, Courtney (2007) 'American reincarnations: what the many lives of past lives tell us about contemporary spiritual practice', *Journal of the American Academy of Religion*, 75 (3): 589–614.

Bender, Courtney (2010) *The New Metaphysicals: Spirituality and the American Religious Imagination*. Chicago, IL: University of Chicago Press.

Bengtson, Vern, Putney, Norella and Harris, Susan (2013) *Families and Faith: How Religion is Passed Down Across Generations*. Oxford: Oxford University Press.

Benson, Ophelia and Stangroom, Jeremy (2009) *Does God Hate Women?* London: Continuum.

Berger, Helen and Ezzy, Douglas (2007) *Teenage Witches: Magical Youth and the Search for the Self*. New Brunswick, NJ: Rutgers University Press.

Berger, Helen and Ezzy, Douglas (2009) 'Mass media and religious identity: a case study of young witches', *Journal for the Scientific Study of Religion*, 48 (3): 501–14.

Berger, Peter (1967) *The Sacred Canopy: Elements of a Sociological Theory of Religion*. New York: Anchor Books.

Berger, Peter (1969) *A Rumor of Angels: Modern Society and the Rediscovery of the Supernatural*. New York: Anchor Books.

Berger, Peter (2006) 'Postscript', in Linda Woodhead, Paul Heelas and David Martin (eds.), *Peter Berger and the Study of Religions*. London: Routledge, pp. 189–98.

Berger, Peter, Davie, Grace and Fokkas, Effie (2008) *Religious America, Secular Europe? A Theme and Its Variations*. Farnham: Ashgate.

Berger, Peter and Luckmann, Thomas (1966) *The Social Construction of Reality*. New York: Anchor Books.

Berman, David (1988) *History of Atheism in Britain: From Hobbes to Russell*. London: Croom Helm.

Besant, Annie (1892/1963) *Reincarnation*. Adyar: The Theosophical Publishing House.

Beyer, Peter (2006) *Religions in Global Society*. London: Routledge.

Beyerlein, Kraig (2003) 'Educational elites and the movement to secularize public education: the case of the National Education Association', in Christian Smith (ed.), *The Secular Revolution: Power, Interests, and Conflict in the Secularization of American Public Life*, Berkeley, CA: University of California Press, pp. 160–97.

Bhatt, Chetan (2000) '*Dharmo rakshati rakshitah* [religion protects its protectors]: Hindutva movements in the UK', *Ethnic and Racial Studies*, 23 (3): 559–93.

Bibby, Reginald (2009) *The Emerging Millennials*. Lethbridge: Project Canada Books.

Biddington, Ralph (2004) 'Eclectic association: Victoria's first rationalists, 1866–1894', *Australian Rationalist*, 66: 35–45.

Bilici, Mucahit (2012) *Finding Mecca in America: How Islam is Becoming an American Religion*. Chicago, IL: University of Chicago Press.

Black, Alan (1991) 'Australian Pentecostalism in comparative perspective', in Alan Black (ed.), *Religion in Australia: Sociological Perspectives*. Sydney: Allen and Unwin, pp. 106–20.

Blum, Deborah (2006) *Ghost Hunters: William James and the Search for Scientific Proof of Life After Death*. New York: Penguin.

Bouma, Gary D. (1992) *Religion: Meaning, Transcendence and Community in Australia*. Melbourne: Longman.

Bouma, Gary D. (1996) 'Religious settlement: religion and the migration process', in Gary Bouma (ed.), *Many Religions, All Australian: Religious Settlement, Identity and Cultural Diversity*. Kew: Christian Research Association, pp. 45–65.

Bouma, Gary D. (2006) *Australian Soul: Religion and Spirituality in the 21st Century*. Melbourne: Cambridge University Press.

Bouma, Gary D. (2010) *Being Faithful in Diversity: Religions and Social Policy in Multi-faith Societies*. Adelaide: ATF Press.

Bowman, Matthew (2012) *The Mormon People: The Making of an American Faith*. New York: Random House.

Braude, Ann (2001) *Radical Spirits: Spiritualism and Women's Rights in Nineteenth-Century America*, 2nd edn. Bloomington, IN: University of Indiana Press.

Brouwer, Steve, Gifford, Paul and Rose, Susan (1996) *Exporting the American Gospel: Global Christian Fundamentalism*. New York: Routledge.

Brown, Callum (2003) 'The secularisation decade: what the 1960s have done to the study of religious history', in Hugh McLeod and Werner Ustorf (eds.), *The Decline of Christendom in Western Europe*. Cambridge: Cambridge University Press, pp. 29–46.

Brown, Callum (2006) *Religion and Society in Twentieth-Century Britain*. Harlow: Pearson Education.

Brown, Callum (2009) *The Death of Christian Britain*, 2nd edn. London: Routledge.

Bruce, Steve (2001) 'Christianity in Britain, R. I. P.', *Sociology of Religion*, 62 (2): 191–203.

Bruce, Steve (2002) *God is Dead: Secularization in the West*. Oxford: Blackwell.

Bruce, Steve (2006) 'The curious case of the unnecessary recantation: Berger and secularization', in Linda Woodhead, Paul Heelas and David Martin (eds.), *Peter Berger and the Study of Religions*. London: Routledge, pp. 87–100.

Bruce, Steve (2008) *Fundamentalism*, 2nd edn. Cambridge: Polity Press.

Bruce, Steve (2011) *Secularization: In Defence of an Unfashionable Theory*. Oxford: Oxford University Press.

Bruce, Steve and Glendinning, Tony (2010) 'When was secularization? Dating the decline of the British churches and locating its cause', *The British Journal of Sociology*, 61 (1): 107–26.

Buchbinder, David (1994) *Masculinities and Identities*. Melbourne: Melbourne University Press.

Campbell, Colin (1999) 'The Easternization of the West', in Bryan Wilson and Jamie Cresswell (eds.), *New Religious Movements: Challenge and Response*. London: Routledge, pp. 35–48.

Campbell, Heidi (2013a) 'Introduction: the rise of the study of digital religion', in Heidi Campbell (ed.), *Digital Religion: Understanding Religious Practice in New Media Worlds*. Oxford: Routledge, pp. 1–22.

Campbell, Heidi (ed.) (2013b) *Digital Religion: Understanding Religious Practice in New Media Worlds*. Oxford: Routledge.

Carland, Susan (2004) *The Women's Space: A Study of Muslim Women's Access to the Mosque*. Honors dissertation, Monash University, Melbourne.

Carman, John B. (1996) 'Handing down and reaching across: stability and movement in Indian religious traditions', in Raymond B. Williams (ed.), *A Sacred Thread: Modern Transmission of Hindu Traditions in India and Abroad*. New York: Columbia University Press, pp. 7–22.

Carrette, Jeremy and King, Richard (2005) *Selling Spirituality: The Silent Takeover of Religion*. Routledge: London.

Carroll, Anthony (2007) *Protestant Modernity: Weber, Secularisation, and Protestantism*. Scranton, NJ: University of Scranton Press.

Casanova, Jose (2005) 'Catholic and Muslim politics in comparative perspective', *Taiwan Journal of Democracy*, 1 (2): 89–108.

Castells, Manuel (2004) 'Informationalism, networks, and the Network Society: a theoretical blueprint' in Manuel Castells (ed.), *The Network Society: A Cross-cultural Perspective*. Cheltenham: Edward Elgar Publishing, pp. 3–48.

Chadwick, Owen (1975) *The Secularization of the European Mind in the Nineteenth Century*. Cambridge: Cambridge University Press.

Chaves, Mark (1994) 'Secularization as declining religious authority', *Social Forces*, 72 (3): 749–74.

Chaves, Mark (1995) 'On the rational choice approach to religion', *Journal for the Scientific Study of Religion*, 34 (1): 98–104.

Chaves, Mark (2010) 'Rain dances in the dry season: overcoming the religious congruence fallacy', *Journal for the Scientific Study of Religion*, 49 (1): 1–14.

Cheng, M. M. and Wong, S. L. (1997) 'Religious convictions and sentiments', in Lau Siu-kai, Lee Ming-kwan and Wan Po-san (eds.), *Indicators of Social Development: Hong Kong 1995*. Hong Kong: Hong Kong Institute of Asia Pacific Studies, Chinese University of Hong Kong, pp. 299–329

Choquette, Robert (2004) *Canada's Religions: An Historical Introduction*. Ottawa: University of Ottawa Press.

Choueiri, Youssef M. (2010) *Islamic Fundamentalism: The Story of Islamist Movements*, 3rd edn. London: Continuum.

Christian Science (nd) 'What is Christian Science?' http://christianscience.com/what-is-christian-science/a-closer-look-at-health/press-room-blog/three-questions-you-may-have-about-christian-science, accessed 9 September 2013.

Clark, Lynne S. (2003) *From Angels to Aliens: Teenagers, the Media, and the Supernatural*. New York: Oxford University Press.

Clingingsmith, David, Khwaja, Asim Ijaz and Kremer, Michael (2009) 'Estimating the impact of the Hajj: religion and tolerance in Islam's global gathering', *The Quarterly Journal of Economics*, 124 (3): 1133–70.

Coleman, Simon (2000) *The Globalisation of Charismatic Christianity*. Cambridge: Cambridge University Press.

Collins, Randall (2007) 'The classical tradition in the sociology of religion', in James A. Beckford and N. Jay Demerath III (eds.), *The SAGE Handbook of the Sociology of Religion*. London: SAGE, pp. 19–38.

Collins-Mayo, Sylvia and Dandelion, Pink (eds.) (2010) *Religion and Youth*. Farnham: Ashgate.

Collins-Mayo, Sylvia, Mayo, Bob, Nash, Sally and Cocksworth, Christopher (2010) *The Faith of Generation Y*. London: Church House Publishing.

Connell, R. W. (1987) *Gender and Power: Society, The Person and Sexual Politics*. Palo Alto, CA: Stanford University Press.

Cox, Harvey (1965) *The Secular City*. New York: The Macmillan Company.

Cox, Harvey (1995) *Fire from Heaven: The Rise of Pentecostal Spirituality and the Reshaping of Religion in the Twenty-First Century*. Reading, MA: Perseus Books.

Crockett, Alasdair and Voas, David (2006) 'Generations of decline: religious change in 20th-century Britain', *Journal for the Scientific Study of Religion*, 45 (4): 567–84.

Cush, Denise (2010) 'Teenage witchcraft in Britain', in Sylvia Collins-Mayo and Pink Dandelion (eds.), *Religion and Youth*. Farnham: Ashgate, pp. 74–88.

Davie, Grace (1990) 'Believing without belonging: is this the future of religion in Britain?', *Social Compass*, 37 (4): 455–69.

Davie, Grace (1994) *Religion in Britain Since 1945: Believing Without Belonging*. Oxford: Blackwell.

Davie, Grace (2002) *Europe: The Exceptional Case: Parameters of Faith in the Modern World*. London: Darton, Longman and Todd.

Dawkins, Richard (2006) *The God Delusion*. London: Bantam Press.

Day, Abby (2011) *Believing in Belonging: Belief and Social Identity in the Modern World*. Oxford: Oxford University Press.

Dennett, Daniel (2006) *Breaking the Spell: Religion as a Natural Phenomenon*. New York: Penguin Group.

Deveny, Catherine (2009) 'Fear of God, or fear of a difference of opinion?', *The Age*, February 18, 2009 (http://www.theage.com.au/opinion/fear-of-god-or-fear-of-a-difference-of-opinion-20090217-8a83.html, accessed 28 January 2011).

Devotta, Neil (2001) 'The utilisation of religio-linguistic identities by the Sinhalese and Bengalis: toward a general explanation', *Commonwealth and Comparative Politics*, 39 (1): 66–95.

Diamond, Jared (1997) *Guns, Germs and Steel: The Fates of Human Societies*. London: Jonathan Cape.

Dickson-Waiko, Anne (2003) 'The missing rib: mobilizing church women for change in Papua New Guinea', *Oceania*, 74 (1/2): 98–119.

Dillon, Michele and Wink, Paul (2007) *In the Course of a Lifetime: Tracing Religious Belief, Practice, and Change*. Berkeley, CA: University of California Press.

Dixon, Robert, Bond, Sharon, Engebretson, Kath, Rymarz, Richard, Cussen, Bryan and Wright, Katherine (2007) *Catholics Who Have Stopped Attending Mass*. Melbourne: Pastoral Projects Office, Australian Catholic Bishops Conference.

Dixon, Thomas (2008) *Science and Religion: A Very Short Introduction*. Oxford: Oxford University Press.

Dobbelaere, Karel (1984) 'Secularization theories and sociological paradigms: convergences and divergences', *Social Compass*, 31 (2–3): 199–219.

Dobbs, Joy, Green, Hazel and Zealey, Linda (eds.) (2006) *National Statistics: Focus on Ethnicity and Religion*. Basingstoke: Macmillan.

Dossa, Shiraz (2008) 'Lethal Muslims: white-trashing Islam and the Arabs', *Journal of Muslim Minority Affairs*, 28 (2): 225–36.

Doyle, Natalie J. (2011) 'Lessons from France: popularist anxiety and veiled fears of Islam', *Islam and Christian–Muslim Relations*, 22 (4): 475–89.

Draulans, V. and Halman, L. (2005). 'Mapping contemporary Europe's moral and religious pluralist landscape: an analysis based on the most recent European values study data', *Journal of Contemporary Religion*, 20 (2): 179–93.

Dunn, Kevin M., Klocker, Natascha and Salabay, Tanya (2007) 'Contemporary racism and Islamaphobia in Australia: racializing religion', *Ethnicities*, 7: 564–89.

Durkheim, Emile (1912/1995) *The Elementary Forms of Religious Life*. Translated by Karen E. Fields. New York: The Free Press.

Durkheim, Emile (1957) *Professional Ethics and Civic Morals*. Translated by C. Brookfield. London: Routledge and Kegan Paul.

Eagle, David (2011) 'Changing patterns of attendance at religious services in Canada, 1986–2008', *Journal for the Scientific Study of Religion*, 50 (1): 187–200.

Ebaugh, Helen R. and Chafetz, Janet S. (eds.) (2002) *Religion Across Borders: Transnational Religious Networks*. Lanham, MD: AltaMira Press.

Eck, Diana L (2001) *A New Religious America: How a 'Christian Country' Has Become the World's Most Religiously Diverse Nation*. New York: HarperCollins.

Ecklund, Elaine H. and Lee, Kirsten S. (2011) 'Atheists and agnostics negotiate religion and family', *Journal for the Scientific Study of Religion*, 50 (4): 728–43.

Economou, Nick (1998) 'The politics of citizenship: identity, ethnicity and race', in Anthony Fenna (ed.), *Introduction to Australian Public Policy*, Melbourne: Longman, pp. 358–84.

Edgell, Penny, Gerteis, Joseph and Hartmann, Douglas (2006) 'Atheists as "other": moral boundaries and cultural membership in American society', *American Sociological Review*, 71: 211–34.

Einstein, Mara (2008) *Brands of Faith: Marketing Religion in a Commercial Age*. New York: Routledge.

Elson, John T. (1966) 'Is God dead?', *Time*, April 8: 40–45.

Emmons, Charles F. and Sobal, Jeff (1981) 'Paranormal beliefs: functional alternatives to mainstream religion?', *Review of Religious Research*, 22: 301–12.

Engebretson, Kath (2007) *Connecting: Teenage Boys, Spirituality and Religious Education*. Sydney: St Pauls Publications.

Ernst, Manfred (2006) 'Factors for growth and change', in Manfred Ernst (ed.), *Globalization and the Re-Shaping of Christianity in the Pacific Islands*. Suva: The Pacific Theological College, pp. 705–38.

Esposito, John (1999) *The Islamic Threat: Myth or Reality?*, 3rd edn. Oxford: Oxford University Press.

Evangelical Fellowship of Zambia (nd) 'About us', http://www.efzsecretariat.org/index. php?option=com_content&view=category&layout=blog&id=1&Itemid=27, accessed 5 September 2013.

Evans, Estella E. (1992) 'Liberation theology, empowerment theory and social work practice with the oppressed', *International Social Work*, 35: 135–47.

Evans, Mariah, D. R. and Jonathan Kelley (2004) *Australian Economy and Society 2002: Religion, Morality and Public Policy in International Perspective 1984–2002*. Leichhardt, NSW: Federation Press.

Falsani, Cathleen (2013) 'In Africa, evangelicals join war against AIDS', *Orange County Register*, 31 May, http://www.ocregister.com/articles/aids-510875-zambia-hiv.html, accessed 10 June 2013.

Faure, Bernard (2009) *Unmasking Buddhism*. Oxford: Wiley-Blackwell.

Fausto-Sterling, Anne (1997) 'Beyond difference: a biologist's perspective', *Journal of Social Issues*, 53 (2): 233–58.

Fenn, Richard K. (1969) 'The secularization of values: an analytical framework for the study of secularization', *Journal for the Scientific Study of Religion*, 8 (1): 112–24.

Fields, Rick (1986) *How the Swans Came to the Lake: A Narrative History of Buddhism in America*. Boston, MA: Shambhala Books.

Fine, Cordelia (2010) *Delusions of Gender*. Sydney: Allen and Unwin.

Finke, Roger and Iannaccone, Laurence R. (1993) 'Supply-side explanations for religious change', *Annals of the American Academy of Political and Social Science*, 527: 27–39.

Finke, Roger and Stark, Rodney (2005) *The Churching of America 1776–2005: Winners and Losers in Our Religious Economy.* New Brunswick, NJ: Rutgers University Press.

Fish, Jonathan (2005) *Defending the Durkheimian Tradition: Religion, Emotion, and Morality.* Aldershot: Ashgate.

Fitzgerald, Timothy (1990) 'Hinduism and the "world religion" fallacy', *Religion*, 20 (2): 101–18.

Flanagan, Kieran and Jupp, Peter (eds.) (2007) *A Sociology of Spirituality.* Aldershot: Ashgate.

Flood, Gavin (1996) *An Introduction to Hinduism.* Cambridge: Cambridge University Press.

Flory, Richard and Miller, Donald E. (2010) 'The expressive communalism of post-boomer religion in the USA' , in Sylvia Collins-Mayo and Pink Dandelion (eds.), *Religion and Youth.* Farnham: Ashgate, pp. 9–16.

Fowler, James (1981) *Stages of Faith: The Psychology of Human Development.* San Francisco, CA: Harper.

Francis, Leslie (2001) *The Values Debate: A Voice from the Pupils.* London: Woburn Press.

Franks, Myfanwy (2000) 'Crossing the borders of whiteness? White Muslim women who wear the hijab in Britain today', *Ethnic and Racial Studies*, 23 (5): 917–29.

Friedan, Betty (1963) *The Feminine Mystique.* New York: W.W. Norton and Co.

Frøystad, Kathinka (2009) 'The return path: anthropology of a Western yogi', in Thomas Csordas (ed.), *Transnational Transcendence: Essays on Religion and Globalization.* Berkeley, CA: University of California Press, pp. 278–304.

Fuller, Robert (2001) *Spiritual But Not Religious: Understanding Unchurched America.* New York: Oxford University Press.

Furseth, Inger and Repstad, Pal (2006) *Introduction to the Sociology of Religion.* Aldershot: Ashgate.

Gabay, Alan (2001) *Messages from the Dead: Spiritualism and Spiritualists in Melbourne's Golden Age.* Melbourne: Melbourne University Press.

Gaustad, Edwin S. and Schmidt, Leigh E. (2002) *Religious History of America.* San Francisco, CA: HarperCollins.

Gautier, Mary L., Perl, Paul M. and Fichter, Stephen J. (2011) *Same Call, Different Men: The Evolution of the Priesthood since Vatican II.* Collegeville, MN: Liturgical Press, St John's Abbey.

Geertz, Armin W. and Markússon, Guðmundur Ingi (2010) 'Religion is natural, atheism is not: on why everybody is both right and wrong', *Religion*, 40: 152–65.

Geertz, Clifford (1966) 'Religion as a cultural system', in Michael Banton (ed.), *Anthropological Approaches to the Study of Religion.* London: Tavistock, pp. 1–46.

Gibbs, Philip (2007) *Bountiful Harvest: The Churches in Papua New Guinea.* Occasional Paper of the Melanesian Institute, no. 13. Goroka, EHP: Melanesian Institute.

Gifford, Paul (2008) 'Trajectories in African Christianity', *International Journal for the Study of the Christian Church*, 8 (4): 275–89.

Gillat-Ray, Sophie (2010) *Muslims in Britain: An Introduction.* Cambridge: Cambridge University Press.

Giordan, Giuseppe (ed.) (2010) *Annual Review of the Sociology of Religion, vol. 1: Youth and Religion*. Leiden: Brill.

Goldstein, Warren (2009) 'Secularization patterns in the old paradigm', *Sociology of Religion*, 70 (2): 157–78.

Graebner, Norman A. (1976) 'Christianity and democracy: Tocqueville's views of religion in America', *The Journal of Religion*, 56 (3): 263–73.

Greeley, Andrew (2003) *Religion in Europe at the End of the Second Millennium*. New Brunswick, NJ: Transaction Publishers.

Griffiths, Rudyard (ed.) (2011) *Hitchens vs. Blair: Be it Resolved Religion is a Force for Good in the World: The Munk Debate on Religion*. Toronto: Anansi.

Grundy, David (1972) *Secular, Compulsory and Free: The Education Act of 1872*. Melbourne: Melbourne University Press.

Gutierrez, Cathy (2009) *Plato's Ghost: Spiritualism in the American Renaissance*. New York: Oxford University Press.

Hadaway, C. Kirk, Marler, Penny Long and Chaves, Mark (1993) 'What the polls don't show: a closer look at U.S. church attendance', *American Sociological Review*, 58 (6): 741–52.

Halafoff, Anna, Fitzpatrick, Ruth and Lam, Kim (2012) 'Buddhism in Australia: an emerging field of study', *Journal of Global Buddhism*, 13: 9–25.

Hall, Irene (2007) 'Mary Baker Eddy and Christian Science', *Feminist Theology*, 16 (1): 79–88.

Halman, Loek and Draulans, Veerle (2006) 'How secular is Europe?', *The British Journal of Sociology*, 57 (2): 263–88.

Hamdan, Amani (2012) 'The role of authentic Islam: the way forward for women in Saudi Arabia', *Hawwa*, 10: 200–220.

Hamilton, Malcolm (2002) 'The Easternisation thesis: critical reflections', *Religion*, 32 (3): 243–58.

Harris, Sam (2004) *The End of Faith: Religion, Terror, and the Future of Reason*. New York: W.W. Horton.

Harris, Sam (2007) *Letter to a Christian Nation*. London: Transworld Publishers.

Hasselle-Newcombe, S. (2005) 'Spirituality and "mystical religion" in contemporary society: a case study of British practitioners of the Iyengar method of yoga', *Journal of Contemporary Religion*, 20 (3): 305–21.

Heelas, Paul and Woodhead, Linda (2005) *The Spiritual Revolution: Why Religion is Giving Way to Spirituality*. Oxford: Blackwell.

Herberg, Will (1960) *Protestant-Catholic-Jew: An Essay in American Religious Sociology*, 2nd edn. New York: Garden Books.

Hervieu-Léger, Danièle (2000) *Religion as a Chain of Memory*. New Brunswick, NJ: Rutgers University Press.

Hill, Annette (2011) *Paranormal Media: Audiences, Spirits and Magic in Population Culture*. London: Routledge.

Hill, Jonathan (2011) 'Faith and understanding: specifying the impact of higher education on religious belief', *Journal for the Scientific Study of Religion*, 50 (3): 533–51.

Hill, Peter C. and Hood, Ralph W. (1999) *Measures of Religiosity*. Birmingham, AL: Religious Education Press.

Hilliard, David (1997) 'The religious crisis of the 1960s: the experience of the Australian church', *Journal of Religious History*, 21 (2): 209–27.

Hitchens, Christopher (2007) *God is Not Great: How Religion Poisons Everything*. New York: Twelve.

Hood, Ralph W., Hill, Peter C. and Spilka, Bernard (2009) *The Psychology of Religion: An Empirical Approach*, 4th edn. New York: The Guilford Press.

Hood, Ralph W. and Williamson, W. Paul (2008) *Them That Believe: The Power and Meaning of the Christian Serpent-Handling Tradition*. Berkeley, CA: University of California Press.

Hopkins, Peter (2004) 'Young Muslim men in Scotland: inclusions and exclusions', *Children's Geographies*, 2 (2): 257–72.

Houtman, Dick and Aupers, Stef (2007) 'The spiritual turn and the decline of tradition: the spread of post-Christian spirituality in 14 Western countries, 1981–2000', *Journal for the Scientific Study of Religion*, 46 (3): 305–20.

Human Rights Watch (2013) *"All You Can Do is Pray": Crimes Against Humanity and Ethnic Cleansing of Rohingya Muslims in Burma's Arakan State*. New York: Human Rights Watch.

Hunsberger, Bruce E. and Altemeyer, Bob (2006) *Atheists: A Groundbreaking Study of America's Nonbelievers*. Amherst, NY: Prometheus Books.

Hunt, Stephen (2003) *Alternative Religions*. Aldershot: Ashgate.

Hunt, Stephen (2004) *The Alpha Enterprise: Evangelism in a Post-Christian Era*. Aldershot: Ashgate.

Hunt, Stephen (2005) *Religion and Everyday Life*. London: Routledge.

Hunter, James and Ainlay, Steven (eds.) (1986) *Making Sense of Modern Times: Peter L. Berger and the Vision of Interpretive Sociology*. New York: Routledge.

Hyman, Gavin (2010) *A Short History of Atheism*. London: I.B. Tauris.

ISSP Research Group (2008) *International Social Survey Programme 2008: Religion III (ISSP 2008)*. GESIS Cologne, Germany ZA4950 Data file Vers. 2.0.0, doi:10.4232/1.10206. Data downloaded from http://zacat.gesis.org/webview/index.jsp.

Jacobsen, Douglas (2011) *The World's Christians: Who They Are, Where They Are, and How They Got There*. Oxford: Wiley-Blackwell.

James, William (1902/1985). *The Varieties of Religious Experience*. Cambridge, MA: Harvard University Press.

Jenkins, Philip (2002) *The Next Christendom: The Coming of Global Christianity*. Oxford: New York, Oxford University Press.

Jenkins, Philip (2007) *God's Continent: Christianity, Islam, and Europe's Religious Crisis*. New York: Oxford University Press.

Johnson, Todd M. (ed.) (2007) *World Christian Database*. Leiden: Brill. www.worldchristiandatabase.org. Accessed 4 September 2013.

Johnson, Todd M. and Grim, Brian J. (2013) *The World's Religions in Figures: An Introduction to International Religious Demography*. Oxford: Wiley-Blackwell.

Johnson, Todd M. and Ross, Kenneth R. (eds.) (2009) *Atlas of Global Christianity 1910–2010*. Edinburgh: Edinburgh University Press.

Jones, Robert P., Cox, Daniel, Navarro-Rivera, Juhem, Dionne, E. J. and Galston, William A. (2012) *The 2012 American Values Survey: How Catholics and the Religiously Unaffiliated Will Shape the 2012 Election and Beyond*. Washington, DC: Public Religion Research Institute.

Kaldor, Peter, Bellamy, John, Powell, Ruth, Castle, Keith and Hughes, Bronwyn (1999a) *Build My Church: Trends and Possibilities for Australian Churches*. Adelaide: Openbook.

Kaldor, Peter, Dixon, Robert and Powell, Ruth (1999b) *Taking Stock: A Profile of Australian Church Attenders*. Adelaide: Openbook

Kalu, Ogbu (2003) 'Pentecostal and charismatic reshaping of the African religious landscape in the 1990s', *Mission Studies*, 20: 84–110.

Kalu, Ogbu (2007) 'Pentecostalism and mission in Africa, 1970–2000', *Mission Studies*, 24: 9–45.

Kalu, Ogbu (2008) *African Pentecostalism: An Introduction*. Oxford: Oxford University Press.

Kheirabadi, Masoud (2004) *Islam*. Philadelphia, PA: Chelsea House.

King, Russell, Black, Richard, Collyer, Michael, Fielding, Anthony J. and Skeldon, Ronald (2010) *The Human Atlas of Migration*. Brighton: Earthscan.

Kinnvall, Catarina (2004) 'Globalization and religious nationalism: self, identity, and the search for ontological security', *Political Psychology*, 25 (5): 741–6.

Kirby, Danielle (2012) 'Alternative worlds: metaphysical questing and virtual community amongst the Otherkin', in Adam Possamai (ed.), *Handbook of Hyper-real Religions*. Leiden: Brill. pp. 129–140.

Kirby, Danielle (2013) *Fantasy and Belief: Alternative Religions, Popular Narratives and Digital Cultures*. Sheffield: Equinox.

Kolenda, Konstantin (1995) 'Humanism', in Robert Audi (ed.), *The Cambridge Dictionary of Philosophy*. Cambridge: Cambridge University Press, pp. 340–1.

Kort, Alexis (2005) 'Dar al-Cyber Islam: women, domestic violence, and the Islamic reformation on the World Wide Web', *Journal of Muslim Minority Affairs*, 25 (3): 363–83.

Kosmin, Barry A. (2007) 'Introduction: contemporary secularity and secularism', in Barry A. Kosmin and Ariela Keysar (eds.), *Secularism and Secularity: Contemporary International Perspectives*. Hartford, CT: Institute for the Study of Secularism in Society and Culture. pp. 1–16.

Kosmin, Barry A. and Keysar, Ariela (2006) *Religion in a Free Market: Religious and Non-Religious Americans: Who, What, Why, Where*. Ithaca, NY: Paramount Market Publishing.

Kosmin, Barry A. and Keysar, Ariela (eds.) (2007) *Secularism and Secularity: Contemporary International Perspectives*. Hartford, CT: Institute for the Study of Secularism in Society and Culture.

Kosmin, Barry A. and Keysar, Ariela (2009a) *American Religious Identification Survey (ARIS 2008), Summary Report*. Hartford, CT: Institute for the Study of Secularism in Society and Culture.

Kosmin, Barry A, and Keysar, Ariela (2009b) 'Catholics on the Move, Non-religious on the Rise' http://www.americanreligionsurvey-aris.org/2009/03/catholics_on_the_move_non-religious_on_the_rise.html, accessed January 8, 2011.

Kosmin, Barry A., Keysar, Ariela, Cragun, Ryanand Navarro-Rivera, Juhem (2009) *American Nones: The Profile of the No Religion Population.* Hartford, CT: Institute for the Study of Secularism in Society and Culture.

Krug, Etienne G, Mercy, James A., Dahlberg, Linda L., and Zwi, Anthony B. (2002) 'The world report on violence and health', *Lancet*, 360: 1083–8.

Landes, David (1972) *The Unbound Prometheus: Technological Change and Industrial Development in Western Europe from 1750 to the Present.* Cambridge: Cambridge University Press.

Larson, Edward J. (1997) *Summer of the Gods: The Scopes Trial and America's Continuing Debate Over Science and Religion.* New York: Basic Books.

Larson, Edward J. (2007) *The Creation-Evolution Debate.* Athens, GA: University of Georgia Press.

Lechner, Frank J. (1991) 'The case against secularization: a rebuttal', *Social Forces*, 69 (4): 1103–19.

Lechner, Frank J. (2007) 'Rational choice and religious economies', in James A. Beckford and N. Jay Demerath III (eds.), *The SAGE Handbook of the Sociology of Religion.* London: SAGE, pp. 81–97.

Lemert, Charles C. (1975) 'Social structure and the absent center: an alternative to new sociologies of religion', *Sociological Analysis*, 36 (2): 95–107.

Linden, Ian (2009) *Global Catholicism: Diversity and Change since Vatican II.* London: Hurst.

Lindsey, D. Michael (2007) *Faith in the Halls of Power: How Evangelicals Joined the American Elite.* New York: Oxford University Press.

Lipka, Michael (2013) 'What surveys say about worship attendance – and why some stay home', *Pew Research Center: Fact Tank*, 13 September, 2013 (http://pewrsr.ch/1bdvBWw, accessed 20 September 2013).

Lloyd Parry, Richard (2013) '"Man of peace" approves of violence to Rohingyas', *The Australian*, June 1–2.

Loveland, Richard (2003) 'Religious switching: preference development, maintenance, and change', *Journal for the Scientific Study of Religion*, 42 (1): 147–57.

Luckmann, Thomas (1967) *The Invisible Religion.* New York: Macmillan.

Maret, Rebecca E. (2013) 'Mind the gap: the equality bill and sharia arbitration in the United Kingdom', *Boston College International and Comparative Law Review*, 36 (1): 255–83.

Markham, Ian (2010) *Against Atheism: Why Dawkins, Hitchens, and Harris are Fundamentally Wrong.* Oxford: Wiley-Blackwell.

Marler, Penny and Hadaway, C. Kirk (2002) 'Being religious or being spiritual in America, a zero-sum proposition?', *Journal for the Scientific Study of Religion*, 41 (2): 289–300.

Martin, David (1965) 'Towards eliminating the concept of secularization', in J. Gould (ed.), *Penguin Survey of the Social Sciences.* Harmondsworth: Penguin Books, pp. 169–82.

Martin, David (1978) *A General Theory of Secularization*. New York: Harper & Row.

Marx, Karl (1970) *Critique of Hegel's 'Philosophy of Right'*. Translated by Joseph O'Malley and Annette Jolin with an introduction by Joseph O'Malley. Cambridge: Cambridge University Press.

Mason, Michael, Singleton, Andrew and Webber, Ruth (2007) *The Spirit of Generation Y: Young People's Spirituality in a Changing Australia*. Melbourne: John Garratt Publishing.

Mason, Michael, Singleton, Andrew and Webber, Ruth (2010) 'Developments in spirituality among youth in Australia and other western societies', in Giuseppe Giordan (ed.), *Annual Review of the Sociology of Religion, vol. 1: Youth and Religion*. Leiden: Brill, pp. 89–114.

Matovina, Timothy (2012) *Latino Catholicism: Transformation in America's Largest Church*. Princeton, NJ: Princeton University Press.

McAra, Sally (2010) 'Buddhifying Australia: multicultural capital and Buddhist material culture in rural Victoria', in Christina Rocha and Michelle Barker (eds.), *Buddhism in Australia: Traditions in Change*. Hoboken, NJ: Taylor and Francis, pp. 63–73.

McClain-Jacobson, Colleen, Rosenfeld, Barry, Kosinski, Anne, Pessin, Hayley, Cimino, James E. and Breitbart, William (2004) 'Belief in an afterlife, spiritual well-being and end-of-life despair in patients with advanced cancer', *General Hospital Psychiatry*, 26: 484–6.

McClenon, James (1994) *Wondrous Events: Foundations of Religious Beliefs*. Philadelphia, PA: University of Pennsylvania Press.

McCormick, Debbie (2012) 'The sanctification of Star Wars: from fans to followers', in Adam Possamai (ed.), *Handbook of Hyper-real Religions*. Leiden: Brill, pp. 165–84.

McDannell, Colleen and Lang, Bernhard (2001) *Heaven: A History*, 2nd edn. New Haven, CT: Yale University Press.

McGarry, Molly (2008) *Ghosts of Futures Past: Spiritualism and the Cultural Politics of Nineteenth-Century America*. Berkeley, CA: University of California Press.

McGoldrick, Dominic (2009) 'Accommodating Muslims in Europe: from adopting Sharia law to religiously based opt outs from generally applicable laws', *Human Rights Law Review*, 9 (4): 603–45.

McGrath, Alister and Collicutt McGrath, Joanna (2007) *The Dawkins Delusion?: Atheist Fundamentalism and the Denial of the Divine*. Downers Grove, IL: InterVarsity Press.

McGuire, Meredith (2008) *Lived Religion: Faith and Practice in Everyday Life*. New York: Oxford University Press.

McLeod, Hugh (2000) *Secularisation in Western Europe 1848–1914*. New York: St. Martin's Press.

McLeod, Hugh (2003) 'Introduction', in Hugh McLeod and Werner Ustorf (eds.), *The Decline of Christendom in Western Europe, 1750–2000*. Cambridge: Cambridge University Press, pp. 1–28.

McLeod, Hugh (2007) *The Religious Crisis of the 1960s*. Oxford: Oxford University Press.

McLeod, Hugh and Ustorf, Werner (eds.) (2003) *The Decline of Christendom in Western Europe, 1750–2000*. Cambridge: Cambridge University Press.

McMahon, Anthony G. (1999) *Taking Care of Men: Sexual Politics in the Public Mind*. Melbourne: Cambridge University Press.

Meyer, Birgit (2004) 'Christianity in Africa: from African independent to pentecostal-charismatic churches', *Annual Review of Anthropology*, 33: 447–74.

Meyer, Birgit (2010) 'Pentecostalism and globalization', in Alan Anderson (ed.), *Studying Global Pentecostalism: Theories and Methods*. Berkeley, CA: University of California Press, pp. 144–66.

Meyer, Katherine, Barker, Eileen, Ebaugh, Helen Rose, Juergensmeyer, Mark (2011) 'Religion in global perspective: SSSR presidential panel', *Journal for the Scientific Study of Religion*, 50 (2): 240–51.

Miller, Donald and Yamamori, Tetsunao (2007) *Global Pentecostalism: The New Face of Christian Social Engagement*. Berkeley, CA: University of California Press.

Mitchell, George (1977) *The Hindu Temple: An Introduction to its Meanings and Form*. London: Paul Elek.

Mol, Hans (1971) *Religion in Australia: A Sociological Investigation*. Melbourne: Thomas Nelson Australia.

Moore, R. Laurence (1994) *Selling God: American Religion in the Marketplace of Culture*. New York: Oxford University Press.

Nachmani, Amikam (2009) *Europe and its Muslim Minorities*. Brighton: Sussex Academic Press.

Nardi, Peter M. (2006) *Interpreting Data: A Guide to Understanding Research*. Boston, MA: Pearson.

Nartonis, David K. (2010) 'The rise of 19th-century American spiritualism 1854–1873', *Journal for the Scientific Study of Religion*, 49 (2): 361–73.

Noll, Mark A. (1992) *A History of Christianity in the United States and Canada*. Grand Rapids, MI: William B. Eardmans.

Noll, Mark A. (2009) *The New Shape of World Christianity: How American Experience Reflects Global Faith*. Downers Green, IL: Intervarsity Press.

Norris, Pippa and Inglehart, Ronald (2011) *Sacred and Secular: Religion and Politics Worldwide*, 2nd edn. Cambridge: Cambridge University Press.

Numrich, Paul (ed.) (2008) *North American Buddhists in Social Context*. Leiden: Brill.

O'Connor, Paul (2012) *Islam in Hong Kong: Muslims and Everyday Life in China's World City*. Hong Kong: Hong Kong University Press.

Odone, Cristina (2009) 'Review: *Does God Hate Women?* by Ophelia Benson and Jeremy Stangroom', *The Observer*, July 12. http://www.guardian.co.uk/books/2009/jul/12/god-hate-women-benson-stangroom, accessed 11 October 2012.

Office for National Statistics (2004) *National Statistics: Focus on Religion*. London: Office for National Statistics.

Office for National Statistics (2012) *Religion in England and Wales 2011*. London: Office for National Statistics.

Offutt, Stephen (2010) 'The transnational location of two leading evangelical churches in the Global South', *Pneuma*, 32 (3): 390–411.

Olsen, Daniel (2008) 'Quantitative evidence favoring and opposing the religious economies model', in Detlef Pollack and Daniel Olsen (eds.), *The Role of Religion in Modern Societies*. New York: Routledge, pp. 95–114.

O'Malley, John (2008) *What Happened at Vatican II*. Cambridge, MA: Belknap Press of Harvard University Press.

Ostrowski, Ally (2006) 'Buddha browsing: American Buddhism and the Internet', *Contemporary Buddhism*, 7 (1): 91–103.

O'Toole, Roger (2006) 'Religion in Canada: its development and contemporary situation', in Lori Beaman (ed.), *Religion and Canadian Society: Traditions, Transitions, and Innovations*. Toronto: Canadian Scholars' Press, pp. 7–21.

Pallant, Julie (2010) *SPSS Survival Manual*, 4th edn. Sydney: Allen and Unwin.

Parsons, Talcott (1966) 'Religion in a modern pluralistic society', *Review of Religious Research*, 7 (3): 125–46.

Partridge, Christopher (2004) *The Re-enchantment of the West*, vol. 1. London: T. and T. Clark.

Peach, Ceri (2006) 'Muslims in the 2001 census of England and Wales: gender and economic disadvantage', *Ethnic and Racial Studies*, 29 (4): 629–55.

Pearce, Lisa D. and Denton, Melinda L. (2011) *A Faith of Their Own: Stability and Change in the Religiosity of America's Adolescents*. New York: Oxford University Press.

Peer, Basharat (2012) 'Modern Mecca', *The New Yorker*, 88 (9): 74–80.

Peters, Francis E. (1994) *The Hajj: The Muslim Pilgrimage to Mecca and the Holy Places*. Princeton, NJ: Princeton University Press.

Petts, Richard J (2009) 'Trajectories of religious participation from adolescence to young adulthood', *Journal for the Scientific Study of Religion*, 48 (4): 552–71.

Pew Forum (Pew Research Center's Forum on Religion and Public Life) (2005) *Public Divided on Origins of Life*. Washington, DC: Pew Research Center.

Pew Forum (Pew Research Center's Forum on Religion and Public Life) (2006) *Spirit and Power: A 10-Country Survey of Pentecostals*. Washington, DC: Pew Research Center.

Pew Forum (Pew Research Center's Forum on Religion and Public Life) (2008) *U.S. Religious Landscape Survey Religious Affiliation: Diverse and Dynamic*. Washington, DC: Pew Research Center.

Pew Forum (Pew Research Center's Forum on Religion and Public Life) (2010) *Tolerance and Tension: Islam and Christianity in Sub-Saharan Africa*. Washington, DC: Pew Research Center.

Pew Forum (Pew Research Center's Forum on Religion and Public Life) (2011a) *Global Christianity: A Report on the Size and Distribution of the World's Christian Population*. Washington, DC: Pew Research Center.

Pew Forum (Pew Research Center's Forum on Religion and Public Life) (2011b) *The Future of the Global Muslim Population: Projections for 2010–2030*. Washington, DC: Pew Research Center.

Pew Forum (Pew Research Center's Forum on Religion and Public Life) (2011c) *Muslim Americans: No Signs of Growth in Alienation or Support for Extremism*. Washington, DC: Pew Research Center.

Pew Forum (Pew Research Center's Forum on Religion and Public Life) (2012a) *Faith on the Move: The Religious Affiliation of International Migrants.* Washington, DC: Pew Research Center.

Pew Forum (Pew Research Center's Forum on Religion and Public Life) (2012b) *The Global Religious Landscape: A Report on the Size and Distribution of the World's Major Religious Groups as of 2010.* Washington, DC: Pew Research Center.

Pew Forum (Pew Research Center's Forum on Religion and Public Life) (2012c) *The World's Muslims: Unity and Diversity.* Washington, DC: Pew Research Center.

Pew Forum (Pew Research Center's Forum on Religion and Public Life) (2012d) *Nones on the Rise.* Washington, DC: Pew Research Center.

Phillips, Tim and Aarons, Haydn (2005) 'Choosing Buddhism in Australia: towards a traditional style of reflexive spiritual engagement', *The British Journal of Sociology*, 56 (2): 215–32.

Pickering, W. S. F. (1984) *Durkheim's Sociology of Religion.* Cambridge: James Clarke and Co.

Pike, Sarah (2004) *New Age and Neopagan Religions in America.* New York: Columbia University Press.

Pinn, Anthony (2005) *The African American Religious Experience in America.* Westport, CT: Greenwood Press.

Plante, Thomas G. and McChesney, Kathleen L. (eds.) (2011) *Sexual Abuse in the Catholic Church: A Decade of Crisis, 2002–2012.* Santa Barbara, CA: Praeger.

Plimer, Ian (1994) *Telling Lies for God: Reason vs. Creationism.* Sydney: Random House.

Pollack, Detlef (2008) 'Introduction', in Detlef Pollack and Daniel Olsen (eds.), *The Role of Religion in Modern Societies.* New York: Routledge, pp. 1–22.

Pollack, Detlef and Olsen, Daniel (eds.) (2008) *The Role of Religion in Modern Societies.* New York: Routledge.

Porter, Roy (1997) *The Greatest Benefit to Mankind.* Hammersmith: Fontana.

Possamai, Adam (2000) 'A profile of New Agers: social and spiritual aspects', *Journal of Sociology*, 36: 364–77.

Possamai, Adam (2005) *Religion and Popular Culture: A Hyper-real Testament.* New York: Peter Lang.

Possamai, Adam (ed.) (2012) *Handbook of Hyper-real Religions.* Leiden: Brill.

Possamai, Adam and Lee, Murray (2011) 'Hyper-real religions: fear, anxiety and late-modern religious innovation', *Journal of Sociology*, 47 (3): 227–42.

Presser, Stanley and Chaves, Mark (2007) 'Is religious service attendance declining?', *Journal for the Scientific Study of Religion*, 46 (3): 417–23.

Prothero, Stephen (2010) *God is Not One: The Eight Rival Religions that Run the World and Why Their Differences Matter.* New York: HarperCollins.

Pryor, Lisa (2012) 'Thinking outside the box', *Good Weekend*, December 15: 29–32.

Putnam, Robert and Campbell, David (2010) *American Grace: How Religion Divides and Unites Us.* New York: Simon & Schuster.

Queen, Christopher (1996) 'Introduction: the shapes and sources of engaged Buddhism', in Christopher Queen and Sallie King (eds.), *Engaged Buddhism: Buddhist Liberation Movements in Asia.* New York: Albany State University Press, pp. 1–44.

Queen, Christopher and King, Sallie (1996) 'Preface', in Christopher Queen and Sallie King (eds.), *Engaged Buddhism: Buddhist Liberation Movements in Asia*. New York: Albany State University Press, pp. ix–xii.

Regnerus, Mark (2007) *Forbidden Fruit: Sex and Religion in the Lives of American Teenagers*. New York: Oxford University Press.

Regnerus, Mark, Smith, Christian and Smith, Brad (2004) 'Social context in the development of adolescent religiosity', *Applied Developmental Science*, 8 (1): 27–38.

Regnerus, Mark and Uecker, Jeremy (2006) 'Finding faith, losing faith: the prevalence and context of religious transformations during adolescence', *Review of Religious Research*, 47 (3): 217–37.

Remnick, David (1998) *King of the World: Muhammad Ali and the Rise of an American Hero*. New York: Random House.

Rimmer, S. (1995) 'The politics of multiculturalism', in E. French (ed.), *Multicultural Australia: Ethnic Claims and Religious Values: Proceedings of the Galatians Group Conference*. Melbourne: Galatians Group, pp. 89–110.

Robbins, Joel (2004) 'The globalization of Pentecostal and charismatic Christianity', *Annual Review of Anthropology*, 33: 117–43.

Robbins, Mandy and Francis, Leslie (2010) 'The teenage religion and values survey in England and Wales', in Sylvia Collins-Mayo and Pink Dandelion (eds.), *Religion and Youth*. Farnham: Ashgate, pp. 47–54.

Robbins, R.G. (2010) *Pentecostalism in America*. Santa Barbara, CA: Praeger.

Robert, Dana L. (2000) 'Shifting southward: global Christianity since 1945', *International Bulletin of Missionary Research*, 24 (2): 50–58.

Robertson, Robbie (2003) *The Three Waves of Globalization: A History of a Developing Global Consciousness*. London: Zed Books.

Rocha, Cristina and Barker, Michelle (eds.) (2010) *Buddhism in Australia: Traditions in Change*. Hoboken, NJ: Taylor & Francis.

Roded, Ruth (2012) 'Middle Eastern women in gendered space: religious legitimacy and social reality', *Hawwa*, 10: 1–17.

Rogers, Alex (2013) 'Where are the most religious states in America in 2013?', *Time Newsfeed*, 13 February, 2013 (http://newsfeed.time.com/2013/02/13/where-are-the-most-religious-states-in-america-in-2013, accessed 9 September 2013).

Roof, Wade C. (1999) *Spiritual Marketplace: Baby Boomers and the Remaking of American Religion*. Princeton, NJ: Princeton University Press.

Roy, Olivier (2004) *Globalized Islam: The Search for a New Ummah*. New York: Columbia University Press.

Roy, Olivier (2007) *Secularism Confronts Islam*. New York: Columbia University Press.

Rubenstein, Mary-Jane (2004) 'An Anglican crisis of comparison: intersections of race, gender, and religious authority, with particular reference to the church of Nigeria', *Journal of the American Academy of Religion*, 72 (2): 341–65.

Russell, H. Bernard (2012) *Social Research Methods: Qualitative and Quantitative Approaches*, 2nd edn. Los Angeles, CA: SAGE.

Russell, Bertrand (1957) *Why I Am Not A Christian*. London: George Allen and Unwin.

Ruthven, Malise (1997) *Islam: A Very Short Introduction*. Oxford: Oxford University Press.

Ruthven, Malise (2007) *Fundamentalism: A Very Short Introduction*. Oxford: Oxford University Press.

Samarin, William (1972) *Tongues of Men and Angels*. New York: Macmillan.

Saunders, Robert (2008) 'The ummah as nation: a reappraisal in the wake of the "Cartoons Affair"', *Nations and Nationalism*, 14 (2): 303–21.

Savage, Sara, Collins-Mayo, Sylvia, Mayo, Bob and Cray, Graham (2006) *Making Sense of Generation Y: The World View of 15–25 year-olds*. London: Church House Publishing.

Scheifinger, Heinz (2008) 'Hinduism and cyberspace', *Religion*, 38 (3): 233–49.

Schiller, N. G., Basch, L. and Blanc-Szanton, C. (1992) 'Towards a definition of transnationalism', *Annals of the New York Academy of Sciences*, 645: ix–xiv.

Schüssler Fiorenza, Elisabeth (1983) *In Memory of Her: A Feminist Theological Reconstruction of Christian Origins*. New York: Crossroad Publishing.

Scott, Jamie S. (ed.) (2012) *The Religions of Canadians*. Toronto: University of Toronto Press.

Seligman, Adam B. (1998) 'Introduction to the Transaction edition: Tawney's world and scholarship', in Richard H. Tawney *Religion and the Rise of Capitalism*. New Brunswick, NJ: Transaction, pp. xi–xliv.

Sherkat, Darren E. and Wilson, John (1995) 'Preferences, constraints, and choices in religious markets: an examination of religious switching and apostasy', *Social Forces*, 73 (3): 993–1026.

Sieber, Joan E. and Tolich, Martin B. (2012) *Planning Ethically Responsible Research*, 2nd edn. London: SAGE.

Sigalow, Emily, Shain, Michelle and Bergey, Meredith (2012) 'Religion and decisions about marriage, residence, occupation and children', *Journal for the Scientific Study of Religion*, 51 (2): 304–23.

Singleton, Andrew (2001a) 'No sympathy for the devil: narratives about evil', *Journal of Contemporary Religion*, 16 (2): 177–91.

Singleton, Andrew (2001b) 'Your faith has made you well: the role of storytelling in the experience of miraculous healing', *Review of Religious Research*, 43 (2): 121–38.

Singleton, Andrew (2002) 'The importance of narrative in negotiating otherworldly experiences: the case of speaking in tongues', *Narrative Inquiry*, 12 (2): 353–75.

Singleton, Andrew (2011) 'The impact of World Youth Day on religious practice', *Journal of Beliefs and Values*, 32 (1): 57–68.

Singleton, Andrew (2012) 'Beyond heaven: young people and the afterlife', *Journal of Contemporary Religion*, 27 (3): 453–68.

Singleton, Andrew (2013) 'Echoes of the past: the influence of Spiritualism on contemporary belief', in Christopher Moreman (ed.), *The Spiritualist Movement: Speaking with the Dead in America and around the World*, vol. 2. Santa Barbara, CA: Praeger, pp. 35–50.

Singleton, Andrew, Mason, Michael and Webber, Ruth (2004) 'Spirituality in adolescence and young adulthood: a method for a qualitative study', *International Journal of Children's Spirituality*, 9 (3): 247–61.

Sjödin, Ulf (2002) 'The Swedes and the paranormal', *Journal of Contemporary Religion*, 17 (1): 75–85.

Smart, Ninian (1996) *Dimensions of the Sacred: An Anatomy of the World's Beliefs*. Berkeley, CA: University of California Press.

Smith, Christian (ed.) (2003a) *The Secular Revolution: Power, Interests, and Conflict in the Secularization of American Public Life*. Berkeley, CA: University of California Press.

Smith, Christian (2003b) 'Preface and introduction: rethinking the secularization of American public life', in Christian Smith (ed.), *The Secular Revolution: Power, Interests, and Conflict in the Secularization of American Public Life*. Berkeley, CA: University of California Press, pp. vii–96.

Smith, Christian (2008) 'Future directions in the sociology of religion', *Social Forces*, 86 (4): 1561–89.

Smith, Christian with Christoffersen, Kari, Davidson, Hillary and Snell, Patricia (2011) *Lost in Translation: The Dark Side of Emerging Adulthood*. New York: Oxford University Press.

Smith, Christian and Denton, Melinda L. (2005) *Soul Searching: The Religious and Spiritual Lives of Teenagers*. New York: Oxford University Press.

Smith, Christian with Emerson, Michael, Gallagher, Sally, Kennedy, Paul and Sikkink, David (1998) *American Evangelicalism: Embattled and Thriving*. Chicago, IL: University of Chicago Press.

Smith, Christian and Snell, Patricia (2009) *Souls in Transition: The Religious and Spiritual Lives of Emerging Adults*. New York: Oxford University Press.

Smith, Jane (2010) *Islam in America*, 2nd edn. New York: Columbia University Press.

Smith, Tom W. and Kim, Seokho (2005) 'The vanishing Protestant majority', *Journal for the Scientific Study of Religion*, 44 (2): 211–23.

Snow, David A. and Machalek, Richard (1984) 'The sociology of conversion', *Annual Review of Sociology*, 10: 167–90.

Snow, Deborah and Miller, Nick (2013) 'DIY terror', *The Age*, May 25.

Spuler, Michelle (2000) 'Characteristics of Buddhism in Australia', *Journal of Contemporary Religion*, 15 (1): 29–44.

Stark, Rodney (1963) 'On the incompatibility of religion and science: a survey of American graduate students', *Journal for the Scientific Study of Religion*, 3 (1): 3–20.

Stark, Rodney (1996) *The Rise of Christianity: A Sociologist Reconsiders History*. Princeton, NJ: Princeton University Press.

Stark, Rodney (1999) 'Secularization, R.I.P.', *Sociology of Religion*, 60 (3): 249–73.

Stark, Rodney and Finke, Roger (2000) *Acts of Faith: Explaining the Human Side of Religion*. Berkeley, CA: University of California Press.

Stark Rodney, Finke, Roger and Iannaccone, Laurence R. (1995) 'Pluralism and piety: England and Wales, 1851', *Journal for the Scientific Study of Religion*, 36 (4):431–44.

Stark, Rodney and Iannaccone, Laurence R. (1994), 'A supply-side reinterpretation of the "secularization" of Europe', *Journal for the Scientific Study of Religion*, 33 (3): 230–52.

Statistics Canada (2003) *2001 Census: Analysis Series: Religions in Canada*. Ottawa: Statistics Canada.

Steger, Manfred (2009) *Globalization: A Very Short Introduction*. Oxford: Oxford University Press.

Stevick, Richard (2007) *Growing up Amish*. Baltimore, MD: Johns Hopkins University Press.

Sutcliffe, Steven (2003) *Children of the New Age: A History of Spiritual Practices*. London: Routledge.

Sutton, Philip and Vertigans, Stephen (2005) *Resurgent Islam: A Sociological Approach*. Cambridge: Polity Press.

Tacey, David (2003) *The Spirituality Revolution: The Emergence of Contemporary Spirituality*. Sydney: Harper.

Tawney, Richard H. (1926/1998) *Religion and the Rise of Capitalism*. New Brunswick, NJ: Transaction.

Taylor, Charles (2007) *A Secular Age*. Cambridge, MA: The Belknap Press of Harvard University Press.

Thrower, James (1971) *A Short History of Western Atheism*. New York: Pemberton Books.

Thumma, Scott and Travis, Dave (2007) *Beyond Megachurch Myths: What We Can Learn from America's Largest Churches*. San Francisco, CA: Jossey Bass.

Tinaz, Nuri (1996) 'The Nation of Islam: historical evolution and transformation of the movement', *Journal of Muslim Minority Affairs*, 16 (2):193–209.

Tombs, David (2002) *Latin American Liberation Theology*. Boston, MA: Brill.

Tomkins, Stephen (2004) 'Matches made in heaven' http://news.bbc.co.uk/2/hi/uk_news/magazine/3828767.stm, accessed 8 August 2011.

Triandafyllidou, Anna (ed.) (2010) *Muslims in 21st Century Europe: Structural and Cultural Perspectives*. London: Routledge.

Trinitapoli, Jenny and Vaisey, Stephen (2009) 'The transformative role of religious experience: the case of short-term missions', *Social Forces*, 88 (1): 121–46.

Troeltsch, Ernest (1931) *The Social Teachings of the Christian Churches*, vol. 1. Translated by Olive Wyon. New York: Macmillan.

Tschannen, Olivier (1991) 'The secularization paradigm: a systematization', *Journal for the Scientific Study of Religion*, 30 (4): 395–415.

Turner, Bryan (1991) *Religion and Social Theory*, 2nd edn. London: SAGE.

Turner, Bryan (2011) *Religion and Modern Society*. Cambridge: Cambridge University Press.

Uecker, Jeremy, Regnerus, Mark and Vaaler, Margaret (2007) 'Losing my religion: the social sources of religious decline in early adulthood', *Social Forces*, 85 (4): 1667–92.

Urban, Hugh (2011) *The Church of Scientology: A History of a New Religion*. Princeton, NJ: Princeton University Press.

Vahanian, Gabriel (1961) *The Death of God: The Culture of Our Post-Christian Era*. New York: George Braziller.

van der Veer, Peter (2009) 'Global breathing: religious utopias in Indian and China', in Thomas Csordas (ed.), *Transnational Transcendence: Essays on Religion and Globalization*. Berkeley, CA: University of California Press, pp. 263–78.

Vasquez, Manuel and Marie Marquardt (2003) *Globalizing the Sacred: Religion Across the Americas*. New Brunswick, NJ: Rutgers University Press.

Vernon, Mark (2007) *After Atheism: Science, Religion, and the Meaning of Life*. Basingstoke: Palgrave Macmillan.

Vertigans, Stephen (2009) *Militant Islam: A Sociology of Characteristics, Causes and Consequences*. London: Routledge.

Voas, David (2008) 'The continuing secular transition', in Detlef Pollack and Daniel Olsen (eds.), *The Role of Religion in Modern Societies*. New York: Routledge, pp. 25–48.

Voas, David (2009) 'The rise and fall of fuzzy fidelity in Europe', *European Sociological Review*, 25 (2): 155–68.

Voas, David (2010) 'Explaining change over time in religious involvement', in Sylvia Collins-Mayo and Pink Dandelion (eds.), *Religion and Youth*. Farnham: Ashgate, pp. 47–54.

Voas, David and Crockett, Alasdair (2005) 'Religion in Britain: neither believing nor belonging', *Sociology*, 39 (1): 11–28.

Voas, David, Crockett, Alasdair and Olson, Daniel (2002) 'Religious pluralism and participation: why previous research is wrong', *American Sociological Review*, 67 (2): 212–30.

Voas, David and Day, Abby (2007) 'Secularity in Great Britain', in Barry Kosmin and Ariela Keyser (eds.), *Secularism and Secularity: Contemporary International Perspectives*. Hartford, CT: Institute for the Study of Secularism in Society and Culture, pp. 95–110.

Wadud, Amina (1999) *Qur'an and Woman: Rereading the Sacred Text from a Woman's Perspective*. Oxford: Oxford University Press.

Wadud, Amina (2004) 'Qur'an, gender and interpretive possibilities', *Hawwa*, 2 (3): 316–36.

Wagner, Rachel (2013) 'You are what you install: religious authenticity and identity in mobile apps', in Heidi Campbell (ed.), *Digital Religion: Understanding Religious Practice in New Media Worlds*. Abingdon: Routledge, pp. 199–206.

Walter, Tony (1996) *The Eclipse of Eternity: A Sociology of the Afterlife*. London: Macmillan.

Walter, Tony (2001) 'Reincarnation, modernity and identity', *Sociology*, 35 (1): 21–38.

Warf, Barney (2006) 'Religious diversity across the North American urban system', *Urban Geography*, 27 (6): 549–66.

Warner, Rob (2010) *Secularization and its Discontents*. London: Continuum.

Warner, Stephen (1993) 'Work in progress toward a new paradigm for the sociological study of religion in the United States', *The American Journal of Sociology*, 98 (5): 1044–93.

Warner, Stephen (2005) *A Church of Our Own: Disestablishment and Diversity in American Religion*. New Brunswick, NJ: Rutgers University Press.

Waterhouse, Helen (1999) 'Reincarnation belief in Britain: New Age orientation or mainstream option?', *Journal of Contemporary Religion*, 14 (1): 97–109.

Webber, Ruth, Singleton, Andrew, Joyce, Marie R. and Dorissa, Arrigo (2010) 'Models of youth ministry in action: the dynamics of Christian Youth Ministry in an Australian City', *Religious Education*, 105 (2): 204–15.

Weber, Max (1930/2001) *The Protestant Ethic and the Spirit of Capitalism*. Translated by Talcott Parsons with an introduction by Anthony Giddens. London: Routledge.

Weber, Max (1958) *The Religion of India: The Sociology of Hinduism and Buddhism.* Glencoe, IL: Free Press.

Weber, Max (1963) *The Sociology of Religion.* Translated by Ephraim Fischoff. Boston, MA: Beacon Press.

Weber, Max (2005) 'The meaning and value of science', in Stephen Kalberg (ed.), *Max Weber: Readings and Commentary on Modernity.* Oxford: Blackwell, pp. 321–7.

Weisberg, Barbara (2004) *Talking to the Dead: Kate and Maggie Fox and the Rise of Spiritualism.* New York: Harper One.

Wicker, Christine (2003) *Lily Dale: The Town That Talks to the Dead.* San Francisco, CA: HarperCollins.

Williams, Emyr, Francis, Leslie J. and Village, Andrew (2009) 'Changing patterns of religious affiliation, church attendance and marriage across five areas of Europe since the early 1980s: trends and associations', *Journal of Beliefs and Values,* 30 (2): 173–82.

Williams, Raymond B. (1996) 'Sacred threads of several textures: strategies of adaptation in the United States', in Raymond B. Williams (ed.), *A Sacred Thread: Modern Transmission of Hindu Traditions in India and Abroad.* New York: Columbia University Press, pp. 228–57.

Wilson, Bryan R. (1966) *Religion in Secular Society.* London: C. A. Watts and Co.

Wilson, Bryan R. (1979) 'The return of the sacred', *Journal for the Scientific Study of Religion,* 18 (3): 268–80.

Wilson, Bryan R. (1982) *Religion in Sociological Perspective.* Oxford: Oxford University Press.

Wilson, Bryan R. (1985) 'Secularization: the inherited model', in P. Hammond (ed.), *The Sacred in a Secular Age.* Berkeley, CA: University of California Press, pp. 9–20.

Wilson, Bryan R. (1992) *The Social Dimensions of Sectarianism: Sects and New Religious Movements in Contemporary Society.* Oxford: Clarendon Press.

Wolfe, Alan (2003) *The Transformation of American Religion: How We Actually Live Our Faith.* New York: Free Press.

Woodhead, Linda, Heelas, Paul and Martin, David (eds.) (2006) *Peter Berger and the Study of Religions.* London: Routledge.

World Health Organization (2002) *World Report on Violence and Health: Summary.* Geneva: World Health Organization.

Wuthnow, Robert (1986) 'Religion as sacred canopy', in James D. Hunter and Stephen Ainlay (eds.), *Making Sense of Modern Times: Peter L. Berger and the Vision of Interpretive Sociology.* London: Routledge and Kegan Paul, pp. 121–43.

Wuthnow, Robert (1996) 'Restructuring of American religion: further evidence', *Sociological Inquiry,* 66 (3): 303–29.

Wuthnow, Robert (1998) *After Heaven: Spirituality in America Since the 1950s.* Berkeley, CA: University of California Press.

Wuthnow, Robert (2001) 'Spirituality and spiritual practice', in Richard Fenn (ed.), *The Blackwell Companion to the Sociology of Religion.* Oxford: Blackwell, pp. 306–20.

Wuthnow, Robert (2005) *America and the Challenges of Religious Diversity.* Princeton, NJ: Princeton University Press.

Wuthnow, Robert (2007) *After the Baby Boomers: How Twenty- and Thirty-Somethings Are Shaping the Future of American Religion*. Princeton NJ: Princeton University Press.

Wuthnow, Robert (2009) *Boundless Faith: The Global Outreach of American Churches*. Berkeley, CA: University of California Press.

Wuthnow, Robert and Cadge, Wendy (2004) 'Buddhists and Buddhism in the United States: the scope of influence', *Journal for the Scientific Study of Religion*, 43 (3): 363–80.

Wuthnow, Robert and Offutt, Stephen (2008) 'Transnational religious connections', *Sociology of Religion*, 69 (2): 209–32.

Yamane, David (1997) 'Secularization on trial: in defense of a neo-secularization paradigm', *Journal for the Scientific Study of Religion*, 36 (1): 109–22.

Yamane, David and Polzer, Megan (1994) 'Ways of seeing ecstasy in modern society: experiential-expressive and cultural-linguistic views', *Sociology of Religion*, 55 (1): 1–25.

Yang, Fenggang (2005) 'Lost in the market, saved at McDonald's: conversion to Christianity in urban China', *Journal for the Scientific Study of Religion*, 44 (4): 423–41.

Yang, Fenggang (2010) 'Youth and religion in modern China', in Giuseppe Giordan (ed.), *Annual Review of the Sociology of Religion, vol 1: Youth and Religion*. Leiden: Brill. pp. 147–61.

Yang, Fenggang (2011) *Religion in China: Survival and Revival Under Communist Rule*. New York: Oxford University Press.

Yasmeen, Samina (ed.) (2010) *Muslims in Australia: The Dynamics of Exclusion and Inclusion*. Melbourne: Melbourne University Publishing.

Yong, Amos (2010) *In The Days of Caesar: Pentecostalism And Political Theology*. Grand Rapids, MI: William B. Eerdmans.

Young, Lawrence A. (1998) 'Assessing and updating the Schoenherr-Young projections of clergy decline in the United States Roman Catholic Church', *Sociology of Religion*, 59 (1): 7–24.

Zavos, John (2010) *The Emergence of Hindu Nationalism in India*. New Delhi: Oxford University Press.

Zocca, Franco (2004) 'Religious affiliation in Papua New Guinea according to the 2000 Census', *Catalyst: Social Pastoral Journal for Melanesia*, 34 (1): 40–56.

Zocca, Franco (2007) *Melanesia and its Churches: Past and Present*. Goroka, PNG: Melanesian Institute.

Zocca, Franco and Nicholas de Groot (1997) *Young Melanesian Project: Data Analysis* (Point Series no. 21). Goroka: Melanesian Institute.

Zwartz, Barney (2013) 'Pell makes admissions', *The Age*, 28 May 2013 (http://www.theage.com.au/national/pell-makes-admissions-20130527-2n7l5.html, accessed 4 September 2013).

index